The Literature of Catastrophe

The Literature of Catastrophe

Nature, Disaster and Revolution in Latin America

Carlos Fonseca

BLOOMSBURY ACADEMIC
NEW YORK · LONDON · OXFORD · NEW DELHI · SYDNEY

BLOOMSBURY ACADEMIC
Bloomsbury Publishing Inc
1385 Broadway, New York, NY 10018, USA
50 Bedford Square, London, WC1B 3DP, UK
29 Earlsfort Terrace, Dublin 2, Ireland

BLOOMSBURY, BLOOMSBURY ACADEMIC and the Diana logo
are trademarks of Bloomsbury Publishing Plc

First published in the United States of America 2020
This paperback edition published in 2021

For legal purposes the Acknowledgements on p. vi constitute
an extension of this copyright page.

Cover design by Eleanor Rose | Cover image: Arena y Pinitos
by Manuel Álvarez Bravo © University of Michigan Museum of Art,
Gift of Frederick J. Meyerson, 1983/1.101.1

All rights reserved. No part of this publication may be reproduced or transmitted
in any form or by any means, electronic or mechanical, including photocopying,
recording, or any information storage or retrieval system, without
prior permission in writing from the publishers.

Bloomsbury Publishing Inc does not have any control over, or responsibility for,
any third-party websites referred to or in this book. All internet addresses given
in this book were correct at the time of going to press. The author and publisher
regret any inconvenience caused if addresses have changed or sites have
ceased to exist, but can accept no responsibility for any such changes.

Library of Congress Cataloging-in-Publication Data
Names: Fonseca, Carlos, 1987- author.
Title: The literature of catastrophe : nature, disaster and revolution in
Latin America / Carlos Fonseca.
Description: New York : Bloomsbury Academic, 2020. | Includes
bibliographical references and index. | Summary: "Through a study of
literary representations of catastrophic figures, this book examines how
nature and history intertwined during the violent aftermath of the
Spanish American Wars of Independence"– Provided by publisher.
Identifiers: LCCN 2019047827 | ISBN 9781501350634 (hardback) | ISBN
9781501350658 (pdf) | ISBN 9781501350641 (epub)
Subjects: LCSH: Latin American fiction–19th century–History and
criticism. | Catastrophical, The, in literature. | Natural disasters in
literature. | Environmental disasters in literature. | Epidemics in
literature. | Diseases in literature. | War in literature. | Political
violence in literature. | Literature and society–Latin
America–History–19th century. | Modernism (Literature)–Latin America.
Classification: LCC PQ7082.N7 F57 2020 | DDC 860.9/3588–dc23
LC record available at https://lccn.loc.gov/2019047827

ISBN:	HB:	978-1-5013-5063-4
	PB:	978-1-5013-7070-0
	ePDF:	978-1-5013-5065-8
	eBook:	978-1-5013-5064-1

Typeset by Integra Software Services Pvt. Ltd.

To find out more about our authors and books visit www.bloomsbury.com
and sign up for our newsletters.

Contents

Acknowledgements — vi

1. Introduction: Radical landscapes — 1
2. Earthquakes: The shaky grounds of Latin American history — 23
   Aftershock: Cesar Aira's *Rugendas*: Photographing the earthquake — 48
3. Volcanoes: Emergencies of an archaeological modernity — 57
   Aftershock: Malcolm Lowry's *Under the Volcano*: On clouds, telegraphs and volcanoes — 96
4. Epidemics: Virality, immunity and the outbreak of modern sovereignty — 113
   Aftershock: Reinaldo Arenas's *El color del verano*: AIDS and the end(s) of the immunological state — 149
5. Conclusion: *One Final Gust:* Macondo and the aftermaths of modernity — 159

Notes — 171
Index — 192

Acknowledgements

Like all, this book stems from a long dialogue. It is a product of conversations, disagreements, agreements and lots of coffee. It is, above all, the product of illuminating friendships. I have a long-outstanding debt with Mark Anderson, Marta Aponte, Chloe Aridjis, Diego Azurdia, María del Pilar Blanco, Bruno Bosteels, Carolina Sá Carvalho, Diamela Eltit, Lucy Foster, Rubén Gallo, Laura Gandolfi, Javier Guerrero, Hans Ulrich Gumbrecht, Alejandra Josiowicz, Geoffrey Kantaris, Florian Klinger, John Kraniauskas, Germán Labrador, Jeff Lawrence, Pedro Meira Montero, Gabriela Nouzeilles, Joanna Page, Alan Pauls, Ricardo Piglia, Mara Polgovsky, Rachel Price, Rory O'Bryen, Julio Ramos, Luis Othoniel Rosa, Ana Sabau, Humberto Schwarzbeck, James Tennant, Juan Villoro, Hayden White and Enea Zaramella. I hope they will be able to find traces of our discussions throughout this book.

I would like to particularly thank Gabriela Nouzeilles for teaching me that thinking stems from a combination of passion and precision, of intuition and accuracy, and for believing in the project from the very beginning. I would also like to thank Katherine De Chant at Bloomsbury for helping me edit and finalize the book.

Finally, this book is dedicated to my family, for trusting and believing in my passions, and in particular to Atalya, who was there throughout making sure I kept a smile whilst writing about catastrophe.

1

Introduction
Radical landscapes

Psychology knows that he who imagines disasters in some way desires them. But why do they come so eagerly to greet him?

– Theodor Adorno, Minima Moralia

In one of the opening passages of Ricardo Piglia's 1980 novel *Respiración artificial*, while contemplating the river and thinking about the recurrence of floods in the border town where he lives, the narrator remembers an idea of a friend: 'Tardewski says that nature does not exist except in dreams. Nature only makes itself manifest, he says, in catastrophes and in lyric poetry. Everything that surrounds us, he says, is artificial, bearing the mark of human life.'[1] Today, almost four decades later, when the discussions regarding the end of nature and the arrival of the era of the Anthropocene seem omnipresent, Piglia's words gain a prophetic tone. Incapable of finding solace in lyric poetry, expelled from the natural garden that comforted the romantics, it would seem that our society can only experience the return of nature under the sign of catastrophe. Today, we witness nature return with the force of the repressed as the catastrophic occurrence that interrupts the passage of empty time, bursting the continuity of homogenous chronology, imposing upon it the time of eventuality. Confronted with the image of its eradication, it would seem that the fear of an end has finally woken nature up from its slumber, forcing it to show its radical face.

No longer the ahistorical and apolitical garden of yesteryear, nature thus proves capable of unearthing the political memory of that which was buried under the landscape of history. The travellers who today visit the state of Bahía, in Brazil, can experience directly this conflation of nature and history. During the summer months, when the droughts that assault the region become pronounced and the *Cocorobó Dam* begins to dry up, the visitor witnesses the re-emergence of a ruinous landscape that recalls the history of an event the Brazilian State wished had been by now forgotten. Built in 1968 under the pretence of supplying water to the often drought-stricken region, the dam was also meant to finally submerge the memory of an infamous episode in Brazilian modern history: the Canudos War, which, from the late months of 1896 till October 1897, the still-burgeoning republican government waged against the more than 8,000 followers of millenarian lay prophet Antonio Vicente Mendes Maciel, better known as Antônio Conselheiro.[2] Unknowingly realizing one of his most famous prophecies – 'The backlands will become the sea and the sea will become the backlands' – the state's construction of the dam was meant to erase the memory of a War that hypostatized the violent foundations upon which the progressivist rails of Brazilian history were built.[3] Little did the government know that the prophecy, like nature, was indeed circular and that the sea was also meant to become once again the backlands. And so, today, as catastrophe periodically strikes the region in the form of prolonged droughts, the waters of the dam subside and the sea becomes once again a desert, allowing the traveller to witness the re-emergence of the ruins of the Conselheiro's church as a long-lost echo of a history that refuses to be silenced.

Watching the ruins of Canudos emerging from the waters of the *Cocorobó Dam* I remember thinking that the image instantiated an intuition that had guided my writing project all along: the belief that what we experience today as the conflation between nature and culture – that which nowadays gains the name of Anthropocene, Capitalocene or even Chthulucene – was in fact the echo of a longer history that in the Latin American case remitted all the way back to the foundational moment of our catastrophic modernity: the nineteenth century, which saw the collapse of empires throughout the continent, alongside the violent emergence of the modern nation-states. The image of Canudos's ruins emerging from beneath the waters concretized the intuition that the relevant answers to our present-day concerns regarding the end of nature, the end of history and the fate of politics were to be found not only in the myopic inspection of the present, but rather by performing an archaeology that uncovered the ways nature and culture overlapped in that seminal century that, under the enlightened pretence of progress, marked Latin America's problematic entrance into the modern landscape.

Seeing that ghostlike landscape, witnessing how the spectres of history had been there conjured by the power of nature, I remember recalling that the phenomenon of Canudos had in fact been constructed upon a myth of return.

It had been around the myth of the return of legendary King Sebastian of Portugal that Antônio Conselheiro was able to weave the millenarian message that recruited the improvised army of more than 8,000 outlaw bandits, *jagunços*, landless farmers, former slaves and indigenous people who bravely defeated three expeditionary army forces sent by the Brazilian government before falling victim to the unmerciful bombardment of the state forces led by General Arthur Oscar de Andrade Guimarães. The Conselheiro's anti-Statist message, in its prophetic annunciation of the return of monarchic rule, had echoed with the multitude composed of all those who felt excluded from the representative apparatus that had emerged in 1889 alongside the republic and its uneven project of modernization. Like the ruins of the church, emerging from within the waters that threatened to condemn its history to oblivion, Canudos was indeed a symptom that marked the return of the repressed: the violence of history inscribed within a political landscape that refused to be tamed or domesticated by the progressivist logic of the state.

To begin then to think of nature's return, today, implies thinking of nature against the social contract, which, since the beginning of modernity, has forced us to conceive of it as an entity beyond culture and outside history. Confronted with the ruins of Canudos and with the catastrophic logic of covering and uncovering that is there disclosed, the question remains: how to think of this radical landscape that refuses to be incorporated into that which Jens Anderman has called 'the optic of the state'?[4] And if, as W.J.T. Mitchell has suggested, 'landscape is an instrument of cultural power', a *dispositif* through which first imperial powers and later state powers legitimized and naturalized their existence, what would it mean to speak of such a radical landscape?[5] These questions point towards the heart of many of the concerns which will echo throughout this book. They suggest that Latin American nature, rather than being the peaceful site of sublime contemplation, has been for centuries the site of power contestations and that as such it bears, inscribed within it, a history of political struggles that it is our task today to decipher, as a geologist would interpret a fossil or a rock. In fact, it is precisely under such geological terms that the figure of Antônio Conselheiro is first brought up in Euclides da Cunha's 1902 classic *Os sertões*, the seminal account of the Canudos War, as well as its most complex and fascinating historical analysis:

> It was not surprising that our deep ethnic strata pushed up the extraordinary figure of Antonio Conselheiro, 'the counsellor'. He is like a fossil. Just as the geologist can reconstruct the inclination and orientation of very old formations

from truncated strata and build models of ancient mountains, so can the historian deduce something about the society that produced this man, who himself was of little worth.⁶

Euclides da Cunha, by then a young civil engineer and an avid supporter of republicanism, originally became interested in the Canudos Rebellion in 1897, after the central government's initial failure to subdue what he took to be a simple barbarous uprising. Afraid that the events in the Northeast would turn into a Brazilian version of the bloody War in the Vendée, where Vendean royalists nearly overthrew the emerging French Republic, da Cunha first wrote an article entitled 'A Nossa Vendeia' and later decided to join the fourth military expedition as an army correspondent for the newspaper *Estado de São Paulo*. It would be there that he would experience first-hand the atrocities of a war that would transcend the dichotomies of civilization and barbarism, progress and regression, positivism and fanaticism, forcing him in turn to rethink his faith in the modernity of the republican model. *Os sertões: campanha de Canudos*, his complex sociological account of the War, was published in 1902, five years later, and remains a fascinating literary rendition of how nature and culture intercepted in the complex process of production of Brazilian history. As the figure of the counsellor as a sociological fossil showcases, his account of the conflict, as well as his exploration of Brazilian character, is profoundly marked by geohistorical considerations. As Mark Anderson has noted, Hippolyte Taine's formulation of environmental determinism had deeply influenced da Cunha in his study of the ungovernable, fanatical and barbaric *sertanejo*, or backlander, whose character he took to be a reflection of the torturous landscape that enveloped him.⁷ The book's own structure – with its three subdivisions entitled 'The Land', 'Man' and 'The Struggle' – suggests the profound knot tying nature, culture and history within a study that, like da Cunha's own perspective on the war, ends up undoing many of its initial presuppositions. Just as the book's famous final line – 'It is regrettable that in these times we do not have a Maudsley, who knew the difference between good sense and insanity, to prevent nations from committing acts of madness and crimes against humanity' – seem to counteract his original commitment to the republican enterprise, the book is marked by subterraneous argumentative currents that suggest that *Os sertões* must be read against the grain as a text that discloses the historical violence inherent to the project of Brazilian modernity, allowing us in turn to sketch the contours of a critique of the progressivist logic that marked the violent emergence of the modern nation-state.⁸

Not surprisingly, it is in da Cunha's portrayal of the landscape of the backlands where we begin to see the dialectic between nature and history that will guide our reading of his account as a veiled critique of progressive modernity. The environment described in the opening pages of the book is one that defies the taming powers of the domesticating eye, refusing to be framed and naturalized. It is, instead, a radical landscape that finds in the trope of natural catastrophe the language for expressing its profound historicity. That is to say, it is a landscape where nature is seen as an agent of change:

> It is an impressive landscape. The structural makeup of the land has been coupled with a great upheaval of external agents in the design of stupendous reliefs [...] The forces that work on the land attack it, in its deepest parts and on its surface, with no letup in their destructive action, each taking over in an inevitable inter cadence during the only seasons that the region has. They break it down during the scorching summers and they break it down during the torrential winters. They go from a gently working molecular imbalance to the wonderful dynamic of storms.[9]

Breaking free from the symbolic chains that tried to imprison it within the realm of the ahistorical, refusing to become mere background, the catastrophic nature of the backlands becomes a historical agent itself. Like George Cuvier's contemporary reflections, where history is seen as a successive series of geological catastrophes aptly called revolutions, da Cunha's nature becomes a revolutionary agent in itself, a realm of competing forces whose complexity ends up being instantiated in that political fossil which is the figure of Antônio Conselheiro. Like the fossil, the historical figure of the counsellor condensed the history of unredeemed struggles that had led to Canudos and which remained inscribed in that landscape as latent potentiality. If we then speak of a radical landscape in relationship to the nature of the backlands, this is because nature opens up there as a space of eventuality. As natural catastrophe, the landscape defies the frames that wish to imprison it and instead becomes the preferred modality for figuring that which following Alain Badiou we could call the political event: the emergence of the new within the coordinates of the political situation or status quo.[10]

Catastrophe then serves to designate that instant in which nature, behaving unnaturally, discloses its historicity.[11] This was one of the great discoveries of geohistory in the eighteenth and nineteenth centuries, as Martin Rudwick has shown, and it is what first comes to light in the *Cocorobó Dam* when, every summer, the droughts that assault the region help bring back the memory of this long-buried seminal event.¹² Interestingly, it is precisely through the dialectic between floods and droughts that Euclides da Cunha decides to illustrate the catastrophic historicity of such a landscape: 'The strong storms that quench the dull fire of the drought, in spite of the rebirth they bring along with them, set up the region for greater troubles. The harshly denude it, leaving it more and more unprotected from summers to come. The region goes through a deplorable interlude that resembles a vicious circle of catastrophes.'¹³ The series of droughts and floods that periodically strike the region are presented by da Cunha as imposing a circular temporality that defied the linear progressivism of the First Brazilian Republic, on whose flag one finds a statement of modernity: 'Ordem e Progresso.'

Neither ordered nor progressive, the circular historicity disclosed by this vicious circle of catastrophes should not, however, be read as signalling towards an archaic conservatism, just as the figure of Conselheiro should not be viewed as being merely a conservative monarchist. Rather, what this dialectic between drought and flood already expressed was a dialectic between lack and excess that should be understood as defying what Badiou has elsewhere called 'the state of the situation' and what we, in the context at hand, could rephrase as the First Republic's failed attempt to posit itself as the representative of the totality of its citizens.¹⁴ Either by transforming the *sertão* into a desert, as droughts do, or by turning it into a sea, as floods do, catastrophic nature signals towards a political site which exceeds the representative apparatus of the modern state. Needless to say, both the desert and the sea have always been problematic spaces for the state, as the figures of the bandit or the pirate show, both pointing towards an out-of-bounds beyond the state's representative sovereignty.¹⁵ In fact, it was precisely as romantic pirates that Machado de Assis first described the followers of Conselheiro in an article entitled 'Cançao de piratas' which, as Adriana Campos Johnson has noted, highlights the community as a utopic ideal against the powers of the state:¹⁶

> Imagine a legion of gallant, audacious adventurers, without profession or reward, who detest the calendar, the clocks, taxes, social graces, everything that regiments life, forcing it in line. They are men who are sick of this dull life, the same days, the same faces, the same events, the same crimes, the same virtues. They cannot bear that the world is a secretary of the State, with its appointment book, the fix start and end of his workday, his pay docked for days missed [...] The followers of Conselheiro remembered the romantic pirates, shook their sandals at the gates of civilization, and left in search of free life.¹⁷

As pirates of the desert, as backland bandits, the *sertanejos* conjured the image of an army resistant to enlightened modernity and the progressive historicity which the state tried to impose under the pretence of civilization. The *sertão* – in its etymological association to desert – was seen as the site of a struggle between the state and that excessive other or multiplicity which, following Badiou's terminology, refused to be reduced to the count-as-one of the state's representational apparatus.[18] Not in vain did we see, throughout the nineteenth century, alongside the instauration of the modern republics, a series of state-sponsored crusades directed towards conquering those vast indigenous or native territories which the states could only think of as 'deserts': I am thinking, among others, about the Argentine and Chilean *Conquistas del Desierto*, the Yucatán Caste War and the War of the Triple Alliance. The Canudos Campaign must be understood within this context as part of what Martin Lienhard has called the wave of second conquests.[19] Canudos, with its mismatch of outlaws and minorities, a community composed mainly of pariahs, was seen by the state as a barbaric excess that needed to be domesticated, just as nature had to be tamed through positivist description. The Counsellor's prophetic message – 'The backlands will become the sea and the sea will become the backlands' – can then be read, not merely as divining a future in which the impoverished backlands would gain the position of the wealthy littoral, but also as inscribing within history this catastrophic logic of droughts and floods. His millenarian message then becomes a call to everyone who felt left behind by the Republic's technocracy and positivism, a call to remain faithful to a political event that remained inscribed in the land itself, as a call for an alternative community. It is not surprising, then, that when speaking of the possibility of utopia Slavoj Zizek refers directly to Canudos as an instantiation of a utopic space within the midst of modernity:

> The Canudos liberated territory in Bahia will remain forever the model of a liberated space, of an alternative community which thoroughly negates the existing state space [...] It is as if, in such communities, the Benjaminian other side of the historical Progress, the defeated ones, acquires a space of their own. Utopia existed here for a brief period of time.[20]

The Canudos that appears in da Cunha's *Os sertões* remains a prime example of one of the multiple radical landscapes whose history I will try to follow throughout this book, attempting to trace in turn a counter-history of Latin American modernity where the age of revolutions and the ensuing process of state formation are understood in their true complexity, through the violence of its foundational self-legitimation, as the madness and barbarism inherent in the civilizing process of modernity.

In fact, Walter Benjamin's famous dictum – 'There is no document of civilization which is not at the same time a document of barbarism' – would seem to accompany *Os sertões* as its secret code, illuminating the furtive meaning of a work that exposes how at the very heart of the modern project lies a foundational violence as potent as that which da Cunha so well describes as being emblazoned upon the radical landscape of the backlands.[21] It is a violence which the remaining survivors of Canudos must have witnessed first-hand in the early days of October 1897, when the troops led by General Arthur Oscar de Andrade Guimarães finally arrived to Belo Monte, as the inhabitants called the town, and proceeded to brutally submit by force the few remaining fighters, the counsellor himself having died of dysentery and malnutrition late in September. Having won the war, the republican army seemed adamant in erasing from history the memory of Canudos: the city was bombarded, the houses were burnt and the survivors were murdered, in an act of madness that according to the story told in *Os sertões* ended up with the last four remaining members of Belo Monte – an old man, two full-grown men and a child – facing an army of 5,000 soldiers. Whereas this is probably an exaggeration by da Cunha, who was not present to see these events, the atrocities committed by the army during those final days were so traumatic that they forced the journalist to relinquish description:

> We will forgo describing the final moments. They are impossible to describe. The story we are telling was a deeply moving and tragic one to the very end. We must finish it hesitantly and with humility. We feel like someone who has climbed a very high mountain. On the summit, new vistas unfold before us, and with that greater perspective comes vertigo.[22]

Os sertões therefore ends by both suggesting and veiling the view of a landscape so traumatic that it defies positivist description – a landscape of ruins and suffering that, precisely in being marked by the negativity of death and destruction, defies in its excesses the realm of representation. In the name of progress, the utopia of a city had been reduced to a heap of rubble, reminding us of Benjamin's own idea, suggested in his 'Thesis on the Philosophy of History', that progress is in fact the worst of storms, capable of reducing history to a single catastrophe.

Os sertões could then be said to end with da Cunha, the modernist technocrat, threpublican advocate, yielding to the *vertigo* of a historical landscape so dreadful that the very own grounds of his belief in positivism seem to shake. The infamous two final lines of the book – 'It is regrettable that in these times we do not have a Maudsley, who knew the difference between good sense and insanity, to prevent nations from committing acts of madness and crimes against humanity' – remain an expression of this vertigo and suggest that da Cunha could already foreshadow how the events at Canudos fitted within a longer history of state-sponsored violence.[23] Indeed, looking backwards, his vertigo was not unsubstantiated and his refusal to narrate the ending of the Canudos War in fact seems almost prophetic, as the aftermath of the war was to be long and painful.

After the war, Brazilian soldiers marched to Rio de Janeiro to receive their promised payment. Patiently, they waited by the nearby hillsides for their compensation, which never arrived. Impoverished, they decided to settle in those hillsides, spontaneously constructing in the process a neighbourhood called *Morro da Favela*, in honour of the favela trees in Bahia amongst which the soldiers had camped during the Canudos campaign. This neighbourhood, as the name suggests, turned out to be Brazil's first favela, a precarious settlement that paradoxically mirrored the landscape of Canudos. Still today, when more than 1,000 favelas exist within Brazil, accommodating more than 6 per cent of its population, the *Morro da Favela* stands as a territory hypostasizing the failure of the state to account within its representative apparatus for each and every one of its citizens, an excessive landscape defying the frames through which the modern state wished to portray its modernity – a radical landscape that forces us to rethink how nature and culture interacted within the long process of historical modernization that started in the nineteenth century but whose aftershocks can still be felt today, reminding us of Benjamin's notion that 'the concept of progress must be grounded in the idea of catastrophe. That things are "status quo" is the catastrophe'.[24] A political critique today would then entail analysing the origins of this complex knot throughout which catastrophe, progress, revolution and modernity all reaffirmed themselves in the shaky history of the foundation of the Latin American nation-states as well as in their violent aftermaths. This is precisely the story that *The Literature of Catastrophe: Nature, Disaster and Revolution in Latin America* wishes to tell: a tale that exposes the unredeemed historicity latent within Latin America's foundational landscapes, the political aftershocks of which are still felt today as a call to revise the history of our modernity.

A paradoxical modernity: On Latin America's baroque history

If I have decided to start this book with Euclides da Cunha's *Os sertões* and with his portrayal of the radical landscape of the backlands, it is because his retelling and analysis of the unforgiving history of Canudos already underline the Janus-faced modernity that has marked Latin America's history up until today: a modernity whose positivist self-legitimization rests on its capacity to eradicate, domesticate or tame that same nature upon which it has projected its cultural identity. In the case of Canudos, it was the 'barbaric' nature of the backlands, of which Brazilian identity is in a way a product that had to be erased or tamed. It was precisely this aporia that da Cunha came to understand by the end of his tale and that forced him to describe the final bombardment of the city in the following terms: 'The troops were attacking the very bedrock of our race. Dynamite was the only suitable weapon. It was a tribute.'[25] Nature thus stands in a double position with regard to Latin America's history: both as the agent that defines its cultural difference and as the excessive retrogressive element that must be eradicated in order to give way to the proper progressive historicity of an enlightened modernity. The history told in *The Literature of Catastrophe: Nature, Disaster and Revolution* must be then understood against the background of this broader history of self-definition and effacement. It is a history that perhaps can be said to read Alejo Carpentier's 1975 essay on the 'Baroque and the Marvellous Real' to understand the complex position granted to nature within this history of cultural expression:

> Our world is baroque because of its architecture – this goes without saying – the unruly complexities of its nature and vegetation, the many colours that surround us, the telluric pulse of the phenomena that we still feel. There is a famous letter written by Goethe in his old age in which he describes the place near Weimar where he plans to build a house, saying: 'Such joy to live where nature has already been tamed forever.' He couldn't have written that in America, where our nature is untamed, as is our history, a history of both the marvellous real and the strange in America.[26]

Carpentier's words, by pointing towards an ontology based on the figure of American natural abundance, highlight the ways in which Latin America's untamed nature is seen as the agent of a particular sort of temporality: fluctuating between the circularity of the mythical marvellous real and that of progressivist modernity, Latin America's baroque modernity is marked by a complex temporality that can never be reduced to the homogenous chronology defined by the enlightened calendar. We are far away from Goethe's garden, or at least we seem to have lost the key. As Antonello Gerbi has pointed out, Carpentier was not alone in his attempts to define Latin America in relationship to its baroque or excessive nature.[27] A certain tradition – extending from Columbus to today's tourism pamphlets, and including seminal texts such as Andrés Bello's *Silva a la agricultura de la zona tórrida*, the poems of José María Heredia or the *novelas de la tierra*, without forgetting García Márquez's *A Hundred Years of Solitude* or the reflections of his nineteenth-century precursor Alexander Von Humboldt – has attempted to define Latin America's history in terms of its exuberant nature. Within this tradition, Latin America's sublime nature is seen as being mirrored in its baroque history, a history that while always signalling towards modernity refuses to be analysed through the customary concepts of enlightened politics. Interestingly, even one of its most stubborn modernists, Sarmiento, whose political programme involved civilization and progress at all costs, can't seem to escape the allure of this double movement through which baroque nature is posited both as the basis of our ontological difference and as the obstacle that must be eradicated. In his seminal *Facundo* he describes the Latin American political landscape as a nameless, subaltern volcano:

> Its most skilled politicians have not been able to understand anything of what they saw with their own eyes when they took a quick glimpse at the American power challenging their great nation. Seeing the wave of burning lava roaring in this great focus of intestine struggle, rolling, shaking, and crashing into each other, even those who think themselves most informed have said: "It is just a nameless, subaltern volcano, one of the many that appear in America: soon it will be extinguished".[28]

The nameless, subaltern volcano becomes here a metaphor for Latin America's political panorama: a radical landscape marked by its incommensurability with the enlightened ideals here represented by the European politicians. Even Sarmiento, for whom civilization was the supreme goal of government, the telos of history, can't escape the temptation of defining Latin American history through the supposed barbarism of its unruly nature as the essence that however must be paradoxically transcended in order to become truly modern. For as the subtitle of *Facundo* suggests, nature becomes the political site for the dialectical struggle between civilization and barbarism that marks the history of what he calls the 'Argentine Sphinx, half cowardly woman, half bloodthirsty tiger'.²⁹ If Sarmiento then proceeds, in a fashion akin to da Cunha, to begin the book by sketching the physical features of the land, it is because he knows that the answer to the riddle of the Sphinx remains inscribed within that setting, as the essential hieroglyphic granting us the key with which we could finally enter Goethe's modern garden. The tradition that extends from Columbus to Carpentier via Sarmiento is then one that defines nature as the site of a passionate struggle to be modern. As Alfonso Reyes perfectly puts it in his 1917 essay 'Visión de Anáhuac': 'We are in unison with the race of yesteryear not only through our blood, but more importantly through the effort to dominate the coarse and unyielding nature that surrounds us; such an effort is the foundation of history.'³⁰ The foundation, we must add, of a historical process has since the nineteenth century led us to experience history under the rubric of crisis and nature under the sign of catastrophe.

Following Carpentier, who in novels like *El reino de este mundo* or *El siglo de las luces* explored the place of America's revolutionary history within the broader cartography of the Enlightenment, we could then say that what is baroque about Latin American history is precisely this critical position vis-à-vis modernity. Latin America can only experience its history as crisis precisely because it paradoxically defines itself in relationship to a natural landscape whose exuberance must be eradicated if its dreams of modernity are to be fulfilled. However, rather than seeing this position of historical disjuncture as an impasse, as many of the nineteenth-century *letrados* did, we can say that it is from such a critical position that a critique of modernity first becomes possible. Baroque nature becomes the political site from which, following Derrida, we could say Latin American *différance* is established as the possibility of critical politics.³¹ As Irlemar Chiampi has suggested in *Barroco y Modernidad*: 'The Baroque, crossroad of signs and temporalities, aesthetic logic of mourning and melancholy, luxuriousness and pleasure, erotic convulsion and allegorical pathos, reappears to bear witness to the crisis or end of modernity and to the very conditions of a continent that could not be assimilated by the project of the Enlightenment.'³² It is within this tradition of the critical baroque, which I will later call the historical sublime, that we must place both Carpentier's and Lezama Lima's reflections on history, and the works of Severo Sarduy, Édouard Glissant or Néstor Perlongher. Faithful to the etymological roots linking crisis and critique, links that have been explored by theorists such as Reinhart Koselleck and Paul de Man, their works bear testimony to the capacity to see a political potential in the critical historicity driving Latin American modernity.³³ It is precisely this potential which I have traced throughout *The Literature of Catastrophe: Nature, Disaster and Revolution*, analysing how nature, once suppressed as a symptom of barbarity and underdevelopment, returns once and again, within Latin American modernity with the forced of the repressed, as the catastrophe capable of exposing the fault lines of the Enlightenment.

Bursting the landscape frame: The event of catastrophe

Remembering the ruins of Canudos emerging from within the waters of the *Cocorobó Dam*, thinking about how Latin America's baroque history is experienced as crisis and how nature is seen as the locus of catastrophe, I am reminded of a philosopher whose shadow extends over the whole account told in this book. As will become apparent throughout the coming pages, Walter Benjamin and his philosophy of history serve in a way as the philosophical background upon which many of the reflections here sketched are built. In fact, this book could be said to have sprung from the coincidence of a poem and a philosophical image: its germinal seed could be said to have been born the day I read Jose María Heredia's 1822 poem 'En una tempestad' and thought of the strange coincidence that linked it to Benjamin's well-known image of the angel of history, as it was sketched in his 1936 essay 'Thesis on the Philosophy of History'. I remember reading Heredia's poem, where the poet melancholically confronts in his solitude the winds of a hurricane, and thinking of the strange echoes that made their texts converse. Two thinkers writing in the midst of war – one amidst the landscape of the wars of independence and one battling for survival in the Second World War – both try to reformulate our concept of history through the image of natural catastrophe. Indeed, Benjamin's angel of history would remain for me a crucial image through which to envision the locus of political subjectivity that would emerge amidst the revolutionary landscape that saw the collapse of imperial modes of sovereignty throughout the Americas and the violent emergence of the modern nation-states. Like the *angelus novus*, the subjects that interested me in the long foundational history of Latin American modernity – figures like Alexander Von Humboldt, Simón Bolívar, José María Heredia or François Mackandal – were acting and thinking within a radical landscape where history and nature seemed to conflate, and where the possibility of critique, modernity and revolution coexisted with that catastrophe which Benjamin calls the storm of progress:

> This is how one pictures the angel of history. His face is turned toward the past. Where we perceive a chain of events, he sees one single catastrophe which keeps piling wreckage upon wreckage and hurls it in front of his feet. The angel would like to stay, awaken the dead, and make whole what has been smashed. But a storm is blowing from Paradise; it has got caught in his wings such violence that the angel can no longer close them. This storm irresistibly propels him into the future to which his back is turned, while the pile of debris before him grows skyward. This storm is what we call progress.[34]

Like Benjamin's angel, the political subjects that populate the story told in this book are not afraid to face and tackle the catastrophe of history. 'A great volcano lies at our feet', wrote Simón Bolívar in 1824 to General José Antonio Páez amidst the anarchy of the revolutionary aftermath.[35] His words suggest the way catastrophic imagery intertwined with revolutionary rhetoric during the Age of Revolutions. For him, as for the other political and literary subjects I study throughout the book, catastrophic thinking was never the product of a conservative agenda, but rather a mode of looking at history that allowed them to read modernity against the grain, as a ruinous landscape full of unredeemed potential. For them, catastrophe signals that moment in which the naturalized telos of progressivist modernity, alongside its harmonious progressivism, is finally bracketed and the possibility of critique emerges together with the possibility of historical redemption. Moreover, what Benjamin's philosophy of history allows for, and what remains for me particularly illuminating about it with regard to Latin America, is the way in which this catastrophic historicity is expounded under the rubric of the baroque, understood as a mode of historicity that dialectically confounds the natural and the historical. As Theodor Adorno noted in his essay 'The Idea of Natural History', Benjamin's notion of the baroque is driven by the idea that only through a dialectical understanding of the relationship between nature and history can we understand that what is at stake in baroque allegory is the denaturalization of the status quo through which capitalist modernity perpetuates itself.[36] Reading history against the grain, Benjamin's philosophy of history provides us with the conceptual tools necessary for performing an archaeology of Latin America's baroque modernity.

Catastrophic thinking then implies, first of all, a way of standing critically with respect to history. It is a critical positioning that allows us to counteract the official stories through which the nation-state has attempted to naturalize its history since its emergence in the nineteenth century. If, as we have pointed out, the revolutionary period of 1810–1825 was superseded by the foundational moment of state formation and the ensuing construction of harmonious national imaginaries, viewing history as catastrophe implies exposing the violence inherent in the imposition of this progressivist model of history. As Patrick Dove has suggested in *The Catastrophe of the Nation:* 'The thought of nation and modernity is marked in advance by catastrophe. With regard to the question of national origins, the idea of catastrophe in fact evokes two distinct facets or moments: it describes that fact of annihilation, or the process of violent clearing and reordering that paved the way for the modern nation-state.'[37] It is the evidence of the violence of this inaugural state-of-exception what the nation-state has attempted to erase, either through the dissemination of romantic novels that reflected dreams of national prosperity into the image of the 'natural' heterosexual couple, as Doris Sommer explored in her 1991 book *Foundational Fictions*, or through the construction of imaginary communities formed around newspapers, as Benedict Anderson has noted.[38] Guided by the seminal works of Sommer and Anderson, most studies in nineteenth-century Latin American history have in fact ended up espousing these 'happy narratives' of national consolidation, in the process dangerously replicating the gesture through which the nation-state naturalized its own progressive history. Against such dangers, a proper critical stance is needed: one which blasts open the coherency and harmony of these national histories, showing in turn that there was nothing natural in the process through which the Latin American nation-states posited themselves as the righteous modern heirs to empire. As Phillip Abrams had already stated in his 1977 essay 'Notes on the Difficulty of Studying the State', this naturalization of the state comes at the cost of politics: 'The state is, then, in every sense of the term a triumph of concealment. It conceals the real history and relations of subjection behind an a-historical mask of legitimating illusion; contrives to deny the existence of connections and conflicts which would if recognised be incompatible with the claimed autonomy and integration of the state.'[39] The task then is to unmask the state to show its deep historicity and to denaturalize each of its instances, including its relationship nature.

If romantic novels and newspapers helped the state naturalize its existence around a shared national imaginary, it could be said that visually the nation-state found in landscape the *dispositif* capable of taming its violent periphery. Confronted with the barbaric nature which nonetheless defined what Carlos Alonso has called its claims of autochthony, the nation-state found in landscape a way of harmoniously incorporating peripheral nature into its symbolic regime, projecting a supposed natural order beyond its urban frontiers.[40] As W.J.T. Mitchel has noted, landscape is always an ideological double gesture, through which cultural constructions are projected into nature whilst subjectivities are interpellated with respect to this projection: 'Landscape as a cultural medium thus has a double role with respect to something like ideology: it naturalizes a cultural and social construction, representing an artificial world as if it were simply given and inevitable, and it also makes that representation operational by interpellating its beholder in some more or less determinate relation to its giveness as sight and site.'[41] Landscape therefore marks the site of both a repression and a definition: the historicity of the nation-state is concealed behind the very image that wishes to naturalize and define its political existence. Assemblages of nature and culture, landscapes therefore remain a site of unredeemed political potential, which is our task to unbury.

The Literature of Catastrophe: Nature, Disaster and Revolution in Latin America can be read as an attempt to unbury this latent potential. Reading Latin American modernity against the grain, it sketches a counterstory to that proposed by the romantic novels, newspapers and landscapes through which the nation-state attempted to naturalize its history. Against this landscaping of history, it proposes a new theory of landscape, one which doesn't point back to a naïve return to nature, as preservationist groups would have it, but rather points towards the ideological content repressed within its assumed giveness. As Jens Anderman has noted: 'What we would need to recover would be a notion of landscape that could help us account for its interstitial and oscillating position between image and environment, as that which assembles the perceptive construction alongside the effects that this construction produces.'[42] Be it the sublime natural landscape that confronted Alexander Von Humboldt, the latent secrecy of the pyramids and volcanoes that provoked José María de Heredia, or the swarm of mosquitoes that confronted the French troops of Napoleon in Haiti, landscape is always seen here as the site of political struggle: as the assemblage through which modernity paradoxically reified what has been called the great divide between nature and culture. Following anthropologists like Philipe Descola or Eduardo Viveiros de Castro, what I suggest, instead, is a concept of landscape that is capable of going beyond this distinction, disclosing landscape as the assemblage of nature and culture it is, endowing it in turn with a sense of eventuality. That is to say, the story told in these pages unearths, from the grounds of landscape's conservative origins, its radical potential.

Radical landscapes in the era of the Anthropocene

If, as Jules Michelet suggested, every epoch dreams the one to come, we could say that perhaps we are only now waking up from that long dream through which Western modernity established itself. In fact, there is no doubt that the story told in these pages is only a small fragment within this project of ecological awakening whose echoes resound today stronger than ever.[43] In fact, it was whilst writing this book that its resonance within current debates became increasingly apparent, forcing me to acknowledge its place within the broader history of what in the past two decades, since Nobel Prize winner Paul Crutzen first proposed it as a concept, has come to be known as the Anthropocene.[44] Since then, through its combination of the Greek *anthropos* – designating the human being – and *kainos* – meaning new – the Anthropocene has come to replace the Holocene as the last geological epoch, forcing us to regard humanity as a geological force and imposing upon us a new historical framework for our particular stories of environmental consciousness. It is then against the background of the Anthropocene and its positing of humans as geological agents that we must read the particular story of Latin American modernity proposed by this book. While nature was being exposed as a historical agent, under the discipline of geohistory, history was turning humans into geological agents, tying the perfect knot binding nature and culture under the name of modernity. Moreover, as Christophe Bonnefuil and Jean-Baptiste Fressoz have explained in *The Shock of the Anthropocene* – a carefully told analysis of the concept as well as the historical epoch it describes – we should remain aware that behind the vague generality of the 'undifferentiated Anthropos' that posits humanity as a universal agent, blurring in turn the question regarding environmental responsibility, we have particular microhistories that allow us to understand the specific processes through which the domestication and exploitation of nature were disavowed within that process of modernity.[45] As Bonnefuil and Fressoz state themselves: 'The history of the Anthropocene is not one of frenetic modernism that transforms the world while ignorant of nature, but rather of the scientific and political production of a modernizing unconscious.'[46] The radical landscapes studied in this book should then be understood as what, following the psychoanalytical terminology suggested by the quote, we could call symptoms: political sites where the historical bind tying nature to culture was repressed in the name of modernity's progressivism.

As such, it is not surprising that today we witness nature remerge as the violent return of the repressed. Our nature, if such a thing still exists, is not the Greek *ousía* but rather – as Timothy Morton has recently explored under the rubric of dark ecology – the Lacanian *thing*: the dark substrata puncturing our social reality, forcing us to recognize that fundamental otherness which, nonetheless, renders possible our historicity amidst the proclaimed end of history.[47] Earthquakes, hurricanes, volcanoes, tsunamis and epidemics all seem to conspire daily against the hegemony of the new world order. After all, the history of the Anthropocene, as Jason Moore has suggested, is perhaps best understood as the history of what he calls the Capitolocene: a global history of exploitation that would produce an 'ecological gap between the national economies that generated a great deal of wealth without subjecting their own countries to excessive impacts, and the countries of the rest of the world whose economies were burdened by a heavy footprint on their territory'.[48] It is then symptomatic that this avalanche by which nature floods history usually takes the so-called Third World as its point of departure. Latin America, Southeast Asia, Africa: the eruption of nature takes as its preferred points of expression those sites at the periphery of late capitalism, the precise places that have long provided the *materia prima* for mounting the progressive rails of that enlightened modernity which today we take as a second nature consisting of plantations, railways, mines and future markets.

Latin America, without a doubt, plays a crucial role in this story. Not only because the Conquest of America could easily be taken as the inaugural event of the Anthropocene, marking the prehistory of an epoch that is traditionally dated as starting in 1784 alongside the invention of the steam engine, but more importantly because colonial extractivism was quickly turned into extractivist capitalism at the hands of the modern nation-states. The story told in the following pages then should be read as a signalling crisis within capitalism. After centuries of being exploited, it would seem that nature has finally sprung forth into visibility, fuelled by the discontents of the enlightened project, forcing us to reconsider the ways modernity has negotiated the always-mined relationship between history and nature. If today, after the so-called end of history proclaimed by Francis Fukuyama, it seems that natural catastrophes are our preferred mode of figuring historical events, it is because precisely due to its repression, nature holds a revolutionary potential.[49] To speak then of the radicalism of a catastrophic landscape is to suggest that nature has the capacity to function as a site of historical rupture. As the etymology of the word – in its juxtaposition of the destruction (*kata*) and overturning (*strophe*) – suggests, catastrophe signals the moment in which the destruction of the old makes space for the arrival of the new. Its connections to revolution – understood as the reflexive turning that produces the new – are then clear, leading us to understand how, within modernity, revolutionary history found in catastrophe its preferred trope. As Cuvier's theory of catastrophism made explicit, when it conjectured that the earth's history was marked by the punctual emergence of natural revolutions, this book suggests that since the nineteenth century natural catastrophes have become our preferred tropes for figuring what contemporary philosophers have called the political event. As Slajov Zizek himself defines the term:

> This is an event at its purest and most minimal: something socking, out of joint, that appears to happen all of a sudden and interrupts the usual flow of things; something that emerges seemingly out of nowhere, without discernible causes, an appearance without solid being as its foundation [...] At first approach, an event is thus *the effect that seems to exceed its causes* – and the *space* of an event is that which opens up by the gap that separates an effect from its causes.[50]

Radical landscapes are then landscapes in which, under the sign of catastrophe, nature heralds the advent of the historically new. These are sites of disjuncture where the assemblage between nature and culture is finally exposed. That is, it is exposed as an unnatural construct in relation to which different political subjectivities are interpellated. As Alain Badiou, the great contemporary thinker of the event, has mentioned, events can only exist in relationship to the subjects that are interpellated by the truths that they disclose.[51] As such the story told in *The Literature of Catastrophe: Nature, Disaster and Revolution in Latin America* is that of the radical temporalities opened up and represented by different natural catastrophes as well as the story of the emergence of the revolutionary modes of subjectivities determined by each of these different modalities of the political event. Faithful to the debates concerning the Anthropocene, the characters that populate this book emerge as subjects in relationship to the particular modes of thinking through the historical relationship between nature and culture.

Revolutionary temporalities, revolutionary subjectivities

While, back in Europe, enlightened historiographers – represented by figures such as Kant, Hegel, Ranke and Michelet – were busy founding the discipline of modern historicism, of teleological history, back in the Americas social protagonists were busy 'blasting open the continuum of history', to use Walter Benjamin's words.[52] From Alexander Von Humboldt to Simón Bolívar, from José María de Heredia to Dr Atl, from François Mackandal to an army of diligent mosquitoes, this book sketches the ways in which the political actors and artistic witnesses of nineteenth-century Latin American politics saw in nature a mirror image of the historical violence which surrounded them, a violence which coincided with the foundational period of the modern states. What interests me in this history are the ways in which the political event figured another possible historiography, one which targeted three of the main tenets of enlightened historicism: the idea of representation, the idea of progress and the idea of the sovereign body. Each of the three chapters of the book reads as a critique of these enlightened ideals. The first chapter, which tackles the figure of the earthquake, attempts a critique of the notion of representation in its relationship to the shaky political grounds of Spanish American Empire at the beginning of the nineteenth century. It relates this crisis of representation to the epistemological changes that marked the collapse of natural history and the emergence of a modern, catastrophic temporality. The second chapter, which deals with the figure of the volcano, attempts a critique of the notion of progress, through a study of the emergence of a deep, vertical temporality, which saw in the birth of archaeology its main epistemological proponent. The third and last chapter, which tackles the elusive figure of the epidemic, attempts a critique of the notion of the sovereign body through a study of the biopolitical logic of virality that marked the Haitian Revolution as well as its eventual political aftermath.

This typology of catastrophe has led me to differentiate, throughout the three chapters of the book, between three modes of eventuality. The first, represented by the earthquake, embodies a tradition that perhaps starts with Marx and today finds in Badiou its main contemporary proponent. It suggests that the event is the coming to light of the unpresentable, of that which until now had been invisible. The event, one could say, opens the present to the possibility of an *unforseen future*. The second type of event, represented by the volcanic eruption, sketches a psychoanalytical tradition that could be said to start with Freud and to have found in Jacques Lacan its twentieth-century equivalent. It suggests that the event is the coming to light of a *repressed past*, the emergence of a vertical time that discloses the lost origin of the present. As such, it remains an archaeological endeavour. And lastly, the third type of event would be that which is represented by the viral outbreak and is embodied in a biopolitical tradition that perhaps starts with French sociologist Gabriel Tarde and which finds in the works of Gilles Deleuze and Felix Guattari its twentieth-century culmination. It suggests that the event is the emergence of a multiplicity capable of spreading virally over the body politic. As such, it gives us an image of a *rhizomatic present*. Marxism, Psychoanalysis and Biopolitics are then the three main discursive paradigms that this book proposes as capable of sustaining a reading of the revolutionary event as it emerges at the beginning of the nineteenth century in Latin America.

Each of these modalities of the political event interpellates and marks the emergence of new modes of political subjectivity. In the first chapter, the earthquake comes to figure the shattering event against which the subject arises as *militant* by remaining faithful to that within it which remains unrepresentable. The chapter takes the figure of Simón Bolívar as its exemplary figure. In the second chapter, the volcano comes to figure the explosive event against which the subject emerges as *mournful witness* of an archaic knowledge. José María Heredia becomes the figure of the exemplary mournful, not to say melancholic, historical subject. Lastly, throughout the third chapter, the epidemic comes to figure the sprawling event against which the subject arises as a multitude capable of destabilizing the social contract. François Mackandal becomes the exemplary figure of this sort of viral subjectivity. These three figures – Simón Bolívar, José María Heredia and François Mackandal – are not, however, alone. They are the conceptual personae that make visible three distinct modalities of history against which a multitude of other historical subjects emerge. Always excessive, always exceptional, these subjects trace a history that remains in tension with the history of the state.

However, as the present-day debates concerning the Anthropocene instantiate, this book is grounded in the present. The echoes of this inaugural moment in Latin American politics resound throughout the region's long process of modernization, making it clear that it is precisely the reverberations of this initial founding gesture what we witness today under the apocalyptic imagery of natural catastrophes that assault us daily, be it in the form of high-brow literature or Hollywood blockbusters. The re-emergence of the ruins of Canudos from the waters of the *Cocorobó Dam* is then only the first of a number of aftershocks through which the suppressed memory of this inaugural founding violence is unearthed. Like the earthquake whose expansive waves propagate into the future through the power of the aftershock, the historical event – as Alain Badiou has elucidated – finds reaffirmation in the truth processes through which the event retrospectively marks the emergence of new subjectivities.[53] Perhaps, one could say, it is only today that we are able to witness and comprehend the implications of that which Mary Louise Pratt, in her book *Imperial Eyes*, has called the nineteenth-century 'reinvention of América as nature'.[54] This book takes this consideration seriously, structuring each chapter dually as both a shock and an aftershock. The first part of each chapter, the shock, explores the emergence, in the nineteenth century, of a particular historical discourse regarding catastrophe, while the aftershock provides a theoretical close-reading of a particular twentieth-century novel which explores the present-day ramifications of this catastrophic discourse. These 'aftershock readings' pay particular attention to the ways Latin American nature was reread, in the twentieth century, through the lens of modern technologies such as telegraphy, photography and cybernetics. I would claim that what appears in those technological readings of nature are precisely the discontents of Latin America's project of modernization, as it was conceived throughout the nineteenth century. *The Literature of Catastrophe: Nature, Disaster and Revolution in Latin America* therefore takes the form of a political history of the state *against* the state.

2

Earthquakes: The shaky grounds of Latin American history

*If this is the best of all possible worlds,
what are the others?*

– Voltaire, Candide

Westphalia, Holland, Lisbon, Buenos Aires, Paraguay, El Dorado, Surinam, England, Venice, Paris, Transylvania, Turkey – the errant cartography traced by Voltaire's *Candide, ou L'Optimisme* (1759) shows a contingent world shaken by the power of the first global catastrophe. Two worlds – the Old and the New, the necessary and the contingent – are brought together by a central event: the earthquake that shook Lisbon on 1 November 1755, in an unprecedented manner, leaving the city in ruins and the world out of joint.[1] Although the intellectual debate – which famously brought together enlightened minds such as the young Immanuel Kant, Jean Jacques Rousseau and Voltaire – has been rightly studied in books like Susan Neiman's *Evil in Modern Thought* as a convulsion within the European intelligentsia, one fact must be underlined: the earthquake that struck Lisbon the Saturday morning of All Saint's Day had its epicentre in the Atlantic.[2] Rather than merely as a continental event, the Lisbon Earthquake must be understood as the paradigm of those transatlantic events that in the coming century would shake the imperial foundations of the transatlantic world.

Lisbon, 1 November 1755: from the tip of the Old World and the courts of its empire a seismic wave arises that shatters the static optimism of Leibnizian theodicy. As critics have duly noted, Voltaire's picaresque – in its attack on Leibnizian optimism, in asking, '*If this is the best of all possible worlds, what are the others like?*' – represents an attempt by enlightened thinkers to break into the closed world of enlightened theodicy. A world where evil is let loose is a world where contingency reigns. When the best of all possible worlds collapses, what appears is the historicity of *other* possible worlds. As Pangloss's errant itinerary suggests, a reconfiguration of the relation between ground and representation, symptomatic of a crisis within the empire of letters, is set in motion by the advent of catastrophe. Voltaire's question regarding the possibility and nature of other worlds, implicitly a question about the possibility of a universal history, calls for an American reading. It demands a study of the historical and the discursive repercussions that the emergence of America as an independent region during the Spanish American wars of independence had within European Enlightenment philosophy. In this chapter I wish to explore the role that the earthquake – in its both literal and figurative aspects – came to have within the emergence of a cartography of contingent worlds that shook the continent at the turn of the century: from Humboldt's paradoxical fascination with the natural disruption of his beloved *chain of being* to Simón Bolívar's rhetoric concerning the 1812 Earthquake of Caracas in his *Cartagena Manifesto*, I shall try to sketch how, in the nineteenth century, nature and politics came to be interlinked in such a way that natural catastrophes, understood as political events, came to figure the opening of the world to unforeseen possibilities. The world is out of joint: the play upon Hamlet's worlds describes both the situation of the transatlantic empire at the turn of the nineteenth century and the historicity brought on by the earthquake. Rewriting Reinhart Koselleck's well-known definition of modernity as ongoing crisis, one could perhaps dare say that the nineteenth century sees the emergence of a new mode of transatlantic modernity as the dialectics between catastrophe and restitution, between shock and aftershock. In the advent of catastrophe nature ceases to be natural in order to become historic. Today, when ecological concerns seem to gain pre-eminence and an apocalyptic sense rules the popular imaginary, from video games to blockbuster movies, it seems apt to return to the nineteenth century in order to see how this knot between nature and politics, mediated by the figure of the natural catastrophe, expressed a new paradigm of historical experience.

Tabula Rasa: The quaking of representation

In attempting to uncover the deepest strata of Western Culture, I am restoring to our silent and apparently immobile soil its rifts, its instability, its flaws; and it is the same ground that is once more stirring under our feet.

– Foucault, The Order of Things

The young Alexander von Humboldt who in 1799 prepares to depart from Europe – the land of his early studies – is still a naturalist. Like many of his contemporaries, he sits at a threshold between the taxonomical science of Linnaeus and an extensive, uncharted land of knowledge yet to be deciphered. Like Linnaeus, he dreams of sketching the 'chain of being', an impossible map of a harmonious world, in which reality is interwoven by the swift movement of a tender hand. America, the new continent, remains the blank page upon which he can project such illusions of continuity. As a naturalist, he travels to America with the intention of naturalizing history. He is unable to imagine that to some extent it will be nature that will turn historical. Aboard the *Pizarro*, awaiting his departure, he writes:

> In a few hours we sail around Cape Finisterre. I shall collect plants and fossils and make astronomic observations. But that's not the main purpose of my expedition – I shall try to find out how the forces of nature interact upon one another and how the geographic environment influences plant and animal life. In other words, I must find out about the unity of nature.[3]

History, however, seems to conspire against this vision of unity and harmony. It is the turn of the century: soon, a revolutionary wave that has already begun at Saint-Domingue will extend throughout the whole continent with the same expansive force to which Humboldt refers in his letters as the forces of nature. For the young Humboldt the question remains: can this wave be contained within the limits of unity? Can the forces of nature be organized within the stability of a tableau of knowledge? It is a question of order and stability – a question of politics. Natural history, as the science of observation and measurement, as the science of classification and cataloguing, constitutes a political archive in itself. Humboldt, however, does not know this yet. Prepared with his notebooks, chronometers, telescopes, sextants, pendulums and other scientific instruments, the young naturalist leaves for the tropics with the hope of measuring and classifying the excesses of their exuberant nature. Soon, he would find the volatile reality of a continent whose latent political turmoil would translate into a compulsive recording of natural catastrophes. As he himself states in his diary:

> When shocks from an earthquake are felt, and the earth we think of as stable shakes on its foundations, one second is long enough to destroy long-held illusions. It is like waking painfully from a dream. We think we have been tricked by nature's seeming stability; we listen out for the smallest noise; for the first time we mistrust the very ground we walk on.[4]

Humboldt encounters a convulsive continent. The figure of the earthquake designates the physical phenomenon that so clearly interested a naturalist like Humboldt, while providing a philosophical metaphor for the political events that would end up shattering the historical ground and, with it, the tabula that had theretofore organized the cosmos of naturalists like Linnaeus. In the abyss created between the event and its figure, between the earthquake and the extent of its metaphorical force, lies the true revolutionary potential of the natural catastrophe: a whole system of historical semiotics is set in motion.

'It is like waking painfully from a dream.' The comparison Humboldt makes in his diary between the earthquake and the illusion-breaking moment of awakening evokes the complex metaphorical power of the figure of the earthquake. Catastrophe breaks the illusion of a stable ground of representation, bringing forth the possibility of those 'other worlds' mentioned in Voltaire's *Candide*. By unmasking the illusory nature of the stable tableau of knowledge, it exposes the contingency of that ground of representation under which naturalists had so far archived reality. The emergence of the earthquake metaphor can then be understood as a symptom of the crisis that had assaulted the paradigm of knowledge that until then had determined Europe's understanding of Latin America – *natural history*. As Foucault states in *The Order of Things*, the emergence in the seventeenth century of the classical episteme through the works of Aldrovandi, Buffon and Linnaeus, among others, had been determined by the naturalization of history:

> For natural history to appear, it was not necessary for nature to become denser and more obscure, to multiply its mechanisms to the point of acquiring the opaque weight of a history that can only be retraced and described, without any possibility of measuring it, calculating it, or explaining it; it was necessary – and this is entirely the opposite – for History to become Natural.[5]

In natural history, nature and history had converged within the representative grounds of the tableau: 'The natural history room and the garden, as created in the Classical period, replace the circular procession of the "show" with the arrangement of things in a table.'[6] This naturalization of history, as Foucault goes on to argue, was only able to subsist within a semiotic system that had guaranteed the stability of representation. This stability began to falter at the turn of the century. The tableau could no longer be taken for granted: 'It is in this classified time, in this squared and spatialized development, that the historians of the nineteenth century were to undertake the creation of a history that could at last be "true" – in other words, liberated from Classical rationality, from its ordering and theodicy: history restored to the irruptive violence of time."[7] Rather than the naturalization of history, the nineteenth century sees the opening of nature to the 'irruptive violence of time'. Nature itself, behaving erratically, called for a tabula rasa, a putting into question of the act of representation.[8]

As Martin Rudwick has shown in *Bursting the Limits of Time: The Reconstruction of Geohistory in the Age of Revolution*, the sudden irruption of time within the catalogue of natural history is an event in the history of ideas that coincides with the period historians have called the 'Age of Revolutions'. At the same time that the imperial cartography begins to crumble, the atemporal tableau of natural history begins to totter. As Foucault explains in *The Order of Things*, if the Classical period had naturalized history, modernity responds by introducing time into the atemporal tableau. History regains its place by rendering nature historical:

> It is this configuration that from the nineteenth century onward changes entirely; the theory of representation disappears as the universal foundation of all possible orders; language as the spontaneous tabula, the primary grid of things, as an indispensable link between representations and things, is eclipsed in turn; a profound historicity penetrates into the heart of things, isolates and defines them in their own coherence, imposes upon them the forms of order implied by the continuity of time.[9]

The nineteenth century sees the emergence of a new mode of historicity, of a new relationship between nature and history. Time has violently interrupted the catalogue of knowledge. As Jason Wilson has noted, Humboldt's voyage to the New World must then be understood in its paradoxical complexity: his project sketches the aporias of a naturalist who suddenly finds himself immersed in the trembling grounds of history. His prose, with its frequent allusions to catastrophes and its hyperbolic style, is symptomatic of an era for which the unity of nature, the *great chain of being* of Linnean taxonomy, has become an object of nostalgic desire rather than an object of study. Awoken from the dream of representation, Humboldt witnesses in the constant catastrophes that assault the New World the struggle of forces that battle at the surface of that tabula rasa called history. But he will only realize this in 1834 – as he writes his *Personal Narrative of Travels to the Equinoctial Regions of America*, he remembers with nostalgia the friends that he has lost in the wars of independence. Only then will the figure of the earthquake come to signify for him the natural power of the historical event. The earthquake will signify not only the personal awakening of the naturalist, but also the political awakening of a whole continent.

Waking up from a dream, however, is never easy. As the practice of psychoanalysis shows, waking up is primordially a hermeneutical labour: the subject is given the task of interpreting what his dreams have ciphered. As Hayden White has noted in *Metahistory*, historical experience, as it is transfigured in the nineteenth century, seems to work similarly: it is within this abyss between the event and its interpretation, between the shock and the aftershock, that the semiotic machine of history is put in motion.[10] Humboldt would personally experience the force of this aftershock effect within his own writing. When Humboldt's *Personal Narrative of the Journey to the Equinoctial Regions of the New Continent*, the three-volume memoirs of his travels to the New World, was published in 1834, more than three decades had elapsed since his voyage. The initial impressions of the eager disciple of Linnaeus had traversed the dense web of history. If, as John Lynch claims in *The Spanish American Revolutions*, the revolutions of independence span from 1808 to 1826, Humboldt left America before the revolutions and wrote about his trip after their conclusion.[11] The atmosphere of latent political turmoil that the young Humboldt had experienced as a mere disturbance of his purely scientific pursuit had since become a continental revolutionary wave that led to the wars of independence that would turn many of his former friends, among them Simón Bolívar, into continental heroes. The seemingly abstract nature of the debate regarding the nature of the New World – the famous *Querelle d'Amerique* that brought together thinkers like Thomas Jefferson, the Comte de Buffon, Antonio de Ulloa and even Hegel – had acquired a political dimension.[12] Recounting his departure from Caracas, his memory links revolution and catastrophe, nature and ruins:

> The memory of this period is today more painful than it was years ago. In those remote countries our friends have lost their lives in the bloody revolutions that gave them freedom and then alternatively deprived them of it. The house we used to live in is now a heap of rubble. Terrible earthquakes have transformed the shape of the ground; the city I described has disappeared.[13]

Humboldt's use of the trope of the earthquake is illuminating: political catastrophe turns history into a heap of rubble. From the earthquake that destroyed Cumaná to the volcanic eruptions on the island of Guadalupe, Humboldt's retrospective account seems at times to be more of an encyclopaedia of catastrophes than a catalogue of nature. Humboldt's archive had felt the first tremors: the *chain of being* had been disrupted by a series of political events that deserved to be called natural catastrophes. Nature had retrospectively turned revolutionary. The earthquake becomes a metaphor for the tottering paradigm of natural history itself: it comes to signify the moment of erasure of the tableau, the instant in which the stability of the picture becomes the pure potentiality of the tabula rasa. What is registered here under the name of *catastrophe* is a new relationship between temporality and meaning, a new relationship between nature, history and the archive. Following recent discussions – from Hayden White to Alain Badiou – this retrospective view of history under the trope of natural catastrophe discloses the new structure of the revolutionary event. Discussing the metaphor of the earthquake in Heinrich Von Kleist's 1807 'The Earthquake in Chile', Werner Hamacher argues that 'what first comes to light in the nineteenth century is a simple form of human historicity – the fact that man as such is exposed to the event'.[14] Catastrophe presents itself as the event that disrupts the continuity of the catalogue, the harmony of its taxonomy, leaving in its place a pure multiplicity. This notion of the revolutionary event as pure multiplicity, as interruption, demands a new reading of the canonical texts of the independence movements. One could, however, object: is not a natural catastrophe, and in this case the figure of the earthquake, merely a metaphor, a trope for an event? This objection ignores the power of metaphor: in the absence of the tableau that until then had secured the knot between nature and history, the trope of the natural catastrophe came to work as their mediating force. As Hans Blumenberg has shown, a metaphor is always more than a mere embellishment: it determines a paradigm.[15]

'When shocks from an earthquake are felt, and the earth we think of as stable shakes on its foundations, one second is long enough to destroy long-held illusions': the earthquake metaphor is not, like others, merely a metaphor, merely a rhetorical strategy that leaves the semantic table untouched, but rather the instant in which the whole system of representation – the *tableaux* itself – enters into crisis. Werner Hamacher, in his essay 'The Quaking of Presentation', which delves into the philosophical implications of Heinrich Von Kleist's 1807 *The Earthquake in Chile*, has explored the complexity of the philosophical metaphor of the earthquake as well as its implications for thought. Kleist's story takes place amidst the earthquake that stroke Santiago de Chile on 13 May 1647. It concerns the fortune of two lovers, Jerónimo Rugera and Donna Josephe, who have been sentenced to death by beheading as a result of their illicit affair. As Josephe proceeds to her execution and as Jerónimo plans to hang himself, an earthquake shakes the foundation of the city, reducing everything to ruins. However, not everything is tragedy within the city. The catastrophe has saved the lovers: by a fortuitous coincidence, the collision of two buildings produces the accidental archway upon which Jerónimo can escape in search of Josephe who has escaped her execution amidst the chaos produced by the earthquake. The story continues to explore the ways in which accidents produce and thwart destinies, opening a place where catastrophe takes the place of miracle. Departing from Kleist's story, and placing it in dialogue with the debates concerning the Lisbon Earthquake, Hamacher explores the semantic web unleashed by the conceptual power of the metaphor of the earthquake: from the figure of the happy accident to Kleist's obsession with the act of falling, from the dialectics of contingency to the discussion regarding divine necessity, his essay acts out the ways in which a metaphor comes to produce a change of paradigm. Exploring the relationship between the metaphor of the earthquake and Kant's discourse on the dynamical sublime, Hamacher comes to see the earthquake as a presentation inadequate to all representations, as the *pure negativity* of a phenomenon that defies the representative power of language. The earthquake becomes the paradigm of the modern event: like Descartes doubt it produces the emergence of the modern subject by making its sensual foundation tremble. It forces history to stage its emergency as sublime history.[16]

One question haunts Kleist's story: why stage the story in Chile, when the immediate referent for the story was the Lisbon Earthquake whose shock, according to many, had been primordially a continental event? Kleist's decision to place his story in Chile shouldn't be read as a mere coincidence with romantic undertones, but rather as a significant interpretation of the role that Latin America was having within the reconfiguration of the knot between history and nature. As Mary Louise Pratt has suggested in her essay 'The Reinvention of America', Humboldt's main achievement was to reinvent Latin America as sublime nature, as a landscape that plays with its limits.[17] His *tableaux de la nature*, as he would later call one of his books, was one which constantly played with its frame an attempt to describe a nature that behaved unnaturally as power and force, as nature capable of making history tremble. The earthquake *razes* history. The etymology here is clear. *Raze, erasure, tabula rasa*: the semantic web brings forth the force of negativity within thought. Erasing the status quo of nature, rendering nature unnatural, the earthquake metaphor is able to raze over a territory of knowledge, imposing a certain historicity over nature. Following the intuition opened by our reading of *Candide*, one might say that catastrophe opens history to its own contingency, to the power of its potentiality. Like the subterranean interplay of the tectonic plates, whose potentiality is actualized in the event of the earthquake, history is first understood as something that holds within itself many potential futures, whose face is the task of the subject to record. Like in Kleist's story, nature might bring down the temple of *Natural History*, but it remains the task of the historical subject to cross the accidental archway left by its ruins, walk among the rubble and gather the fragments of sense. Humboldt, who in his trips through America had experienced the latent political discomfort, the atmosphere of a potential revolution, would be later confronted precisely with this paradox: how to describe and register that moment in which nature becomes eventful, that instant in which nature puts on its political face.

The political epicentre: Bolívar's 'Cartagena Manifesto'

And, behold, the veil of the temple was rent in twain from the top to the bottom; and the earth did quake, and the rocks rent
                                                                    – Matthew 27:51

Earthquakes shatter the homogeneity of history: as the ground begins to shake, space and time gain a singular intensity. Nowhere is this more evident than in the rhetorical usage of the figure of the epicentre. The epicentre flags the natural event and inscribes it within the historical archive: here and now something happened. The nineteenth century was to see, under the rubric of geohistory, the consolidation of this discourse interlinking history and nature under the figure of natural catastrophe. As Martin J.S. Rudwick has documented throughout his works, the decline of a natural theodicy marks not only the decline of natural history, but also the emergence of the historicity of nature. Freed from the creationist imaginary of biblical exegesis, challenging their links to the mythical Deluge, natural catastrophes were finally able to establish themselves in a semantic as well as syntactic connection to history. In the wake of the storming of the Bastille, savants across the Republic of Letters such as Blumenbach, Montlosier, Pini and de Luc began to discuss what it would mean to view nature as an archive of revolutions. From Blumenbach's 'total revolution' to Montlosier's 'continuous revolution', *revolution*, along with its semantic web, would slowly begin to claim its place within the realm of nature. Despite its early ties to biblical catastrophism, a growing positivism would eventually lead this discourse to break loose from biblical exegesis and to construct nature as an eventful space inscribed with traces of past revolutions. With the emergence and authorization of the figure of the fossil, the geologist came to be seen as a figure for the historian. As Dolomieu writes in *Discours sur l'étude de la géologie*, nature had burst the limits of time:

> Only the study of nature itself, lifting the imagination to the level of geology's high conceptions, can discover in the combination of circumstances the history of times long before the existence of the peoples who have figured on the world's great stage, long before even the existence of the human race and of all organisms... Bursting the limits [*durée*] of all historical times, and scorning as it were the brevity of epochs relative to the human species, the geologist walks in the immense space that preceded the organization of matter in order to find there the epochs of those great events of which he observes the monuments.[18]

For the savants of the decaying and death-stricken Republic of Letters, fossils were the traces of past revolutions. Their attitude betrayed their conservatism: this focus on the past amidst the trembling landscape opened by the French Revolution was a symptom of the ideological implications that readings of nature would take in the coming century. As members of the old regime, their discourse referred to the past rather than to the future, to fossils rather than to ruins, to origins rather than to contingencies. As Jorge Cañizares-Esguerra has stated in *How to Write the History of the New World*, across the Atlantic, enlightened by many of the same readings, a new generation of creole intellectuals would take this debate in an opposite direction.[19] Rather than seeing in this new connection between catastrophe and revolution a discourse about the past, they found prophecies about the future, possibility and contingency. Alexander von Humboldt, an intellectual divided between two worlds, knew the abyss that could open between a natural catastrophe and its political repercussions. It would be amidst the political ruins left by an earthquake that his friend Simón Bolívar would produce his first major public document, the 'Cartagena Manifesto', a document in which the politics of catastrophe and witnessing, of fidelity and reconstruction, become a prognosis of the state of the patriot revolution.

On 26 March 1812, during the celebrations of Maundy Thursday, Caracas felt the initial shock of an earthquake that would not only pause the services of Holy Week, but also bring down the recently established First Republic of Venezuela. The shock would mark the end of the political structure that had been established two years earlier, precisely on another Maundy Thursday, that of 19 April 1810.

As John Lynch has noted in his recent biography of Simón Bolívar, between the revolution of Maundy Thursday and the earthquake of Maundy Thursday, the movement of independence grew into a confederation amidst the Civil War that flared up after the Congress declared independence. At the moment of the great tremor, the patriots – guided by the intrepid Francisco de Miranda – were celebrating the second anniversary of the Republic and planned to recuperate the region of Guyana from the royalists. The earthquake would bring all of this to an end, with superstitious clergy, partisans of the royalist cause, proclaiming that the coincidence and holiness of the date heralded an ominous truth: god was angry at the triumphs of the independence movements and had brought this catastrophe upon the Republic. The earthquake had, in fact, tilted the tower of the Caracas Cathedral. Working within the frame of biblical exegesis, within the closed world of theodicy, the clergy still belonged to an epoch that viewed natural catastrophes as necessities rather than contingencies. It would take another patriot, the then relatively unknown Colonel Bolívar, to step in and, amidst the ruins, offer a new interpretation. As José Domingo Díaz, a famous doctor and royalist, was to state years later in his 1829 *Memoirs of the Caracas Rebellion*, Simón Bolívar's reaction to the catastrophe was memorable:

> In that moment I was alone in the plaza amidst the ruins, I heard the screams of those dying inside the temple; I went up the stairs and into the enclosure… there, at the highest point, I found Don Simón Bolívar that in his nightgown was going up the stairs to examine the situation as well. Painted upon his face you could see the terror, and the despair. He saw me and he told me the following unholy and extravagant words: 'If nature opposes us, we shall fight against it and force it to obey.'[20]

Behind Bolívar's enlightened words, which removed the catastrophe from the realm of theology, there is a strategy: by claiming that the seism was merely a non-political, natural phenomenon, he performed the first political intervention upon the event. 'If nature opposes us, we shall fight against it and force it to obey.' Politics is finally forced to face nature. These words do not mean that nature was outside of the political realm – years later, Bolívar himself would use the metaphor of revolution as catastrophe in his 'Angostura Manifesto' – but rather that in this first revolutionary moment what was at stake was a freeing of the event from theological necessity, forcing it to yield to the political force of what, following the works of Alain Badiou, we could call human voluntarism. As Badiou himself states: 'The project of the new man imposes the idea that History will be compelled, that it will be forced.'[21] By presenting the earthquake as a purely natural phenomenon, by signalling towards the capacity of the revolutionary subject to whip history into shape, Bolívar was in fact endowing nature with that rightful historicity which would later be evident in his interpretation of the event. As John Lynch has noted, the earthquake of Maundy Thursday was to mark the entrance of Simón Bolívar into the public sphere. His 'Cartagena Manifesto', written on 15 December of that same year, amidst the ruins of the First Republic, departs from the earthquake metaphor of a republic in ruins in order to provide a diagnosis of the disjunction of the political confederation that, according to him, had led to the destruction of the First Republic of Venezuela. As I shall now proceed to expound, it was in this first statement that Bolívar, in a gesture that rendered revolutionary what in the case of his friends from the Republic of Letters had remained conservative, was to first hint at the possible implications that the emerging non-theological discourse of natural catastrophes had upon the revolutionary cartography of the republican movements. An unknown Colonel Bolívar begins his now-famous Admirable Campaign by discussing an earthquake. With this gesture, which would have made his friend Alexander von Humboldt proud, he begins his campaign as *El Libertador*.

Years later, a moribund Bolívar will write, in a disillusioned letter to his friend Francisco de Paula Santander, 'mi época es de catástrofes'.[22] His pessimism will spring from his realization that his megalomania would remain frustrated: the former Spanish possessions of the New World could not be unified. However, thirteen years earlier, amidst the ruins left by the earthquake of 1812, what we find is an enlightened humanist – a reader of Voltaire, Montesquieu and Locke – who passionately believes in the capacity of humans to impose order upon the social disorder released by natural catastrophes. Bolívar's 'Cartagena Manifesto', his first major political statement, attempts to explain what he calls Venezuela's 'physically and politically ruinous state'.[23] In its attempt to read the causes that had led Venezuela to its 'destruction', it reads as a passionate plea for a reformulation of the federalism that, according to him, undermined the achievements of the revolution. After referring to the chaos brought by the clerics reading of the earthquake as damnation, Bolívar proceeds to grant the earthquake a role within the collapse of the First Republic. However, for the young Bolívar, nature – no longer controlled by theodicy – is not superior to the political power of man:

> It is true that the earthquake of 26 March was as devastating physically as it was spiritually and can be fairly said to have been the immediate cause of Venezuela's ruin, but this catastrophe would not have produced such fatal effects if Caracas had been governed by a single authority that could have quickly and virously set

about repairing the destruction, without the complications and conflicts that slowed down the recovery in the provinces, exacerbating the harm until it was incurable.[24]

According to the political scenario sketched out here by Bolívar, the earthquake of Maundy Thursday could only bring the Republic to ruin precisely because the state that the patriot army had won for itself after its first revolutionary wave was already in ruins. The Conquest of the New World had left behind such a catastrophic destruction of the social body that the independence leaders were first forced to testify to the landscape of ruins they had inherited. Bolívar's radical dialectic could then be summarized as follows: the revolutions of independence – understood as a necessary catastrophe – had produced a cartography of devastation, of ruins and fragments, which then had to be politically comprehended as a totality. As Leopoldo Zea has noted in his book on Bolívar, this dialectic between fragment and whole, between ruin and totality, would remain central to Bolívar's political project.[25] Seven years later, in 1819, when Bolívar is asked to address the Angostura Congress, amidst the discussions regarding the new constitution for the emerging nation of Gran Colombia, he will return to the image of catastrophe and reconstruction that had characterized his first political stance:

> The Republic over which I presided during this period was not marked by some new political tempest, or bloody war, or even an outburst of popular anarchy. It was something worse – the upheaval of all disruptive forces combined, the inundation of an infernal torrent ravaging the soil of Venezuela. One man, a man like myself, what dikes could he marshall to hold back the power of such devastation? Adrift on this sea of troubles I was but the lowly plaything of the revolutionary hurricane tossing me about like a piece of straw. I could effect neither good nor ill: irresistible forces.[26]

This interplay between catastrophe and reconstruction will guide Bolívar's political project until his death – the territorial reconstruction of America as totality out of the fragments of post-revolutionary anarchy. Once the tabula rasa had been politically proclaimed, the process of political representation had to begin all over again. As such, his speech should be placed in the context of the romantic notion of the sublime. The notion of the sublime also has to do with the relationship between the fragment and the whole, between ruin and totality – with the tension between the destructive power of nature and its teleological unity. Bolívar, once again, meets his friend Humboldt at that enigmatic threshold where political discourse finds its natural counterpart: in both cases what is at stake is the political implication of what could be called, following Hayden White and Frank Ankersmit, 'the historical sublime'.

The historical sublime: Where history meets nature

World history is to me a sublime object.
– Schiller, On the Sublime

In their introduction to Humboldt's *Views of the Cordilleras and Monuments of the Indigenous Peoples of the Americas*, Vera M. Kutzinski and Ottmar Ette emphasize two of Humboldt's contributions. By portraying the New World as a continent *with* history, Humboldt, they claim, intervened in the centuries-long 'Dispute of the New World' that had until then attempted to portray the New World as a place without history. Alongside this interest in the history of the New World, they underline his second major contribution: an aesthetic vision of history, from the perspective of what they call a 'poetics of the fragment'.[27] Humboldt's work must be understood in relation to the discursive constellation of historical and aesthetics concepts that had emerged in the late eighteenth century and that would concretize itself in the nineteenth century. 'Nature herself is sublimely eloquent': Humboldt's words, as well as his insistence on the aesthetic nature of his descriptions, make him a precursor of sublime historiography.[28]

The sublime, as a concept, has a long history leading all the way back to Longinus, but it is within the properly continental field of aesthetics – famously initiated in the eighteenth century by Baumgarten – that the sublime acquires its proper theoretical and conceptual density in relation to the excesses of the project of the Enlightenment. As Phillip Shaw shows, the history of the concept in the nineteenth century revolves around two main focal points: British Romanticism, represented by figures such as Burke, Wordsworth and Lord Byron, and German Idealism, embodied by thinkers such as Kant, Schiller and Hegel. More importantly, as Shaw also states, the concept has a political dimension and history.[29] Critics like Marie-Hélène Huet, Charles Hinnant and Hayden White have noted that the emergence of an analytic of the sublime at the end of the eighteenth century should be understood in its relation to the political terror unleashed by the French Revolution.[30] The sublime emerges in the late

Enlightenment as a concept that stages the paradoxes of the enlightened project. Perhaps the first relevant contribution is Edmund Burke's 1756 *A Philosophical Enquiry into the Origin of Our Ideas of the Sublime and the Beautiful*. One year after the Lisbon Earthquake, Burke publishes a book in which catastrophic nature is seen as the prime example of sublime astonishment: 'The passion caused by the great and sublime in nature, when those causes operate most powerfully, is astonishment; and astonishment is that state of the soul, in which all its motions are suspended, with some degree of horror.'[31] The sublime, causing both horror and pleasure, is opposed to the pleasing touch of the beautiful upon the senses. As Hayden White notes, it is this opposition between the sublime and the beautiful that would prove so productive for modern politics. To the conservative option of a beautiful historical progression, White juxtaposes the radical gesture of what he calls the historical sublime: 'Romanticism represented the last attempt in the West to generate a visionary politics on the basis of a sublime conception of the historical process ... The domestication of history effected by the suppression of the historical sublime may well be the sole basis for the proud claim to social responsibility in modern capitalist as well as communist societies.'[32] In his diaries, Humboldt would sketch this distinction between the beautiful and the sublime in cartographic terms. America would be to Europe what the sublime had been to the beautiful: 'If men of science who visit the Alps of Switzerland or the coasts of Lapland should broaden our knowledge about glaciers and the aurora borealis, then a traveler who has journeyed through Spanish America should mainly fix his attention on volcanoes and earthquakes.'[33] Glaciers and the aurora borealis, examples of the beautiful, find their counterpart in the sublime catastrophic phenomena of the New World – volcanoes and earthquakes. Europe, the land of the known, of the necessary, projects its excessive shadow upon the New World. As Mary Louise Pratt notes, this catastrophic paradigm of history forces Humboldt to adopt new, non-narrative modes of historical representation: 'So engulfed and miniaturized was the human in Humboldt's cosmic conception that narrative ceased to be a viable mode of representation.'[34] What is at stake in the sublime is a crisis of representation as paradigm of knowledge. The sublime, as Kant so aptly describes in his 1790 *Critique of Judgment*, interrupts representation by presenting the understanding with something excessively great. In fact, Kant's catalogue of examples of the sublime reads as if it had been taken from Humboldt's notes:

> On the other hand, consider bold, overhanging and, as it were, threatening rock, thunderclouds piling up in the sky and moving about accompanied by lightning

and thunderclaps, volcanoes with all their destructive power, hurricanes with all the devastation they leave behind, the boundless ocean heaved up, the high waterfall of a mighty river and so on.[35]

In Kant, the power of the sublime is associated with nature's capacity to break boundaries. The sublime – understood here as event and as action – breaks the fabric of reality by introducing a moment of absolute negativity. Rather than dismissing Humboldt's aesthetics as mere romanticism, we should proceed to read romanticism itself as the excessive shadow of European Enlightenment. Humboldt's work should then be read against the grain: rather than repeating his comments regarding the unity of nature, we should see how his arrival to America was accompanied by a fascination with the destructive aspects of catastrophe. There are numerous political implications of this romantic gesture: unknowingly, Humboldt was participating in a subterranean discourse on the boundaries of enlightened cartographies that would traverse the twentieth century from Sandino to Che Guevara, up to the masked Subcomandante Marcos in the Lacandon Jungle. The question remains: how can the history of these excesses that refuse to assimilate into the hegemonic symbolic regime be narrated? How can the cartography of those regions that refuse to belong to the imperial landscape be traced?

In his 1801 essay 'On the Sublime', Friedrich Schiller tackles a problem that is of particular interest to us: that of the relationship between world history and the politics of the sublime. Schiller starts by sketching the image of a man in a constant battle between freedom and order: 'Freedom, with all of its moral contradictions and physical evils, is for noble souls an infinitely more interesting spectacle than prosperity and order without freedom, where the sheep patiently follow the shepherd and the self-commanding will is degraded to the subservient part of a clockwork.'[36] He then proceeds to state what this search for freedom above order would imply for the notion of world history: 'Considered from this point of view, and only from this one, world history is to me a sublime object. The world, as historical object, is at bottom nothing other than the conflict of natural forces amongst one another and with the freedom of man, and history reports to us the result of this contest.'[37] Like Schiller, Humboldt – as Kutziniski and Ette have shown – was interested in understanding the ways in which the discovery of the New World had complicated the notion of a world history, of a *Weltbild* and *Weltanschauung*, forcing scientists to think of new figures for universal unity. As the erratic cartography of Voltaire's *Candide* makes evident, sublime history poses universal history as a problem precisely because it breaks the order of representation imposed by theodicies and their political embodiment – empires. Once the imperial cartography is fragmented by the revolutionary power of nature, the question of how to regain a common ground for historical representation becomes crucial. Humboldt's work, like Bolívar's, must then be read as a monumental attempt to grasp the sublime dialectic between fragment and totality, between periphery and centre – namely, as an attempt to narrate history after the destruction of the imperial cartography that until then had sustained history's lawfulness. Humboldt's task, like Bolívar's, is one of reconstruction: it enacts the dialectics of fragments and unity, of ruins and totality, that came to characterize American history after the revolutions of independence.

As Mary Louise Pratt has argued in *Imperial Eyes*, the America that Humboldt so effusively described was in fact the enormity of nature, a sublime nature:

> Alexander von Humboldt reinvented South America first and foremost as nature. Not the accessible, collectible, recognizable, categorizable nature of the Linneans, however, but a dramatic, extraordinary nature, a spectacle capable of overwhelming human knowledge and understanding. Not a nature that sits waiting to be known and possessed, but a nature in motion, powered by life forces many of which are invisible to the human eye; a nature that dwarfs humans, commands their being, arouses their passions, defies their powers of perception. No wonder portraits so often depict Humboldt engulfed and miniaturized either by nature or by his own library describing it.[38]

Pratt notes that Humboldt's nature was not the classifiable nature of the tableau but rather a catastrophic nature whose forces conspired against Humboldt's desire for unity. America's nature, in Humboldt's terms, was in constant battle with the frame of its descriptions, always in conflict with the stability of the archive. Although Pratt's arguments regarding 'the miniaturization of men' are correct, what her account seems to ignore is how time and history filter the naturalist's narrative: Humboldt's task was to take a new turn when – while writing the memoirs of his trips – his imagination was filtered by the images of the revolutionary wars. Humans had metaphorically entered the picture posing one question – how should they be placed within this landscape that had originally seemed beyond their grasp, a landscape that had seemed too big for humans to assert their agency? Humboldt's brilliance lies in realizing that the solution lay in nature itself: what he had at first confronted as catastrophic natural phenomena held the metaphorical power to re-inscribe political action within a landscape that now gained the true potentiality of its Janus-faced reality. Under the metaphor of catastrophic history, sublime nature became sublime history. Structurally, the metaphor of natural catastrophe – as his contemporary Schiller understood it – contained all the elements necessary to provide a model for political action: a discourse on power and forces, on fragmentation and unity, on destruction and reconstruction, on the boundaries of enlightened reason. Moved by his romantic drive, faced with the problem of his historical involvement, Humboldt was participating in the emergence of a new mode of historiography as the shadow of enlightened historicism. If, as Frank Ankersmit has noted, sublime history would return in the coming century under the figure of trauma, terror and disaster, it is because the historical sublime, as construed by Humboldt, already signalled towards a critique of the Enlightenment.[39]

The ruins of the Enlightenment: On Bolívar's Elusive Rome

A great volcano lies at our feet.
– Simón Bolívar, Letter to General Páez

'If this is the best of all possible worlds, then what are the others like?' In Voltaire's *Candide*, the great earthquake of Lisbon had opened the Enlightenment to the possibility of other, erratic, peripheral worlds. The cartography sketched by the protagonist's voyage is indeed a political one: from the Grand Inquisitor of Portugal to the slave Candide meets in *El Dorado*, from the Jesuit revolution in Paraguay up to the constant discussion of utopia, Voltaire's picaresque sketches the cartography of an empire in ruins. Deprived of the theological order imposed by divine necessity, the unity of the world is at stake. In this crisis, one question will gain pre-eminence: how can we think of the unity of such a world? Voltaire's political cartography foreshadows the task that Simón Bolívar was to assume in what is perhaps his best known text: *La carta de Jamaica* (1815).[40] The question Bolívar faced also interrogated the politics of territoriality: under what terms could we consider the cartographic and conceptual unity of the revolutionary project that had spread over the whole continent? Once again, the language of catastrophe comes into play: the image repeated once and again is that of an empire in ruins, and more specifically, the image of a heap of rubble that the political subject is meant to reconstitute. As Humboldt had written in his diaries, 'The house we used to live in is now a heap of rubble. Terrible earthquakes have transformed the shape of the ground; the city I described has disappeared.'[41] The figure of the heap of rubble, of the ruinous multiplicity of the shattered ground, comes to represent the problematic nature of Spanish American modernity after the collapse of its imperial foundation. Bolívar's *Carta de Jamaica* sketches a politics of territoriality as the constant negotiation between the ruinous multiplicity of the shattered imperial ground and the sublimated image of a single Latin American nation arising from the imperial ruins.

As John Lynch shows, the ideological life of *El Libertador* had begun ten years earlier amidst a landscape of ruins. In 1805, as part of his trip to Italy with his mentor, Simón Rodriguez, and his friend Fernando del Toro, Bolívar visits Rome. In Rome, the young Bolívar – who in his early years had, in the neoclassical spirit of the times, filled his mind with images of grandeur – gazes with admiration at the sublime landscape of imperial ruins. As legend has it, he then hurries to the Aventine, the *Monte Sacro* where, as part of the *First secessio plebis* of 494 BC, Sicinius led a plebeian revolt against the patrician rulers.[42] There, according to Bolívar's disciple Daniel O'Leary, he vows to liberate Spanish America from its colonial status: 'On Monte Santo the sufferings of his own country overwhelmed his mind, and he knelt down and made that vow [to] whose faithful fulfillment the emancipation of South America is the glorious witness.'[43] Amidst such ruins, as Simón Rodríguez tells Manuel Uribe Ángel, Bolívar reflects upon the past glory of Rome and the status of Spanish America:

> The civilization that has swept us from the East, Bolívar proclaims, has uncovered here all of its phases, disclosing all of its elements; more so when it comes to solving the great problems of the liberty of man, as if the problem was unheard of, and the resolution of such this mysterious enigma had to be solved in the New World.[44]

Amidst the sublime landscape of the Palatine Hill, the discursive relationship between Rome, ruins, freedom and the history of independence is first sketched out. Throughout his writings, the image of ruinous Rome will return, once and again, as an allegory for the disjointed state of that necessary catastrophe that was the revolution of independence.

Nowhere is the image of Rome's ruin and its relationship to the wars of independence articulated with more clarity than in the *Carta de Jamaica*. Written in response to Henry Cullen, a British merchant who had settled on the island in an attempt to get the support of the British Empire, Bolívar's letter returns multiple times to the example of Rome's decadence in order to explain both the decadence of the Spanish Empire and the present state of the revolution:

> I consider the current state of America similar to the circumstances surrounding the fall of the Roman Empire, when each breakaway province formed a political system [...] while we, who preserve only the barest vestige of what we were formerly, and who are moreover netiher Indias nor Europeans, but a race halfway between the legitimate owners of the land and the Spanish usurpers.[45]

In *Discurso desde la Marginación y la Barbarie*, Leopoldo Zea points out that Bolívar's image of a ruinous Rome serves a double purpose. It provides him, on the one hand, with a model for the emergence of a national cartography out of a catastrophic landscape – namely, the emergence of an integrated Europe out of the ruins of the Roman Empire.[46] On the other hand, it offers him a way of explaining the impasses of the revolutionary project – the ruinous state of post-colonial Spanish America as a disjointed cartography without a clear common ground of political representation. The figure of imperial ruins allows Bolívar to rephrase his concerns within the dialectic of catastrophe and reconstruction, of fragment and totality, which we have claimed came to represent Spanish American historiography in the years following the wars of independence. The 'revolutionary storm', as he will later call the wars of independence, functions precisely like Humboldt's earthquake: it shakes the historical tableau of representation, forcing the political subject to reconfigure the relation between fragment and totality. The historical sublime, as conceived by Bolívar, is a search for unity within the ruins left by the collapse of the Spanish Empire.

At the end of his career, exiled in Pativilca, Peru, after the collapse of another constitution, Bolívar would write, in a letter to Francisco de Paula Santander, some of his most disenchanted yet illuminating words:

> Looking around, you can see the disorders of human things: at every point the doings of men have been fragile, but today they seem like the unborn embryos that die before having developed their faculties. Everywhere we are assaulted by horrible noises of decay. My epoch is one of catastrophes: everything is born and dies in front of my eyes as if it were a lightening, everything is fleeting, and how foolish of me if I dared to flatter myself by standing strong amidst such convulsions, amidst such ruins, in the middle of the moral upheaval of the universe![47]

Within Bolívar's letter, catastrophe remains the sign under which history is thought both as contingent potentiality and as tragic reality. Lost within the ruins of Rome, incapable of organizing a coherent narrative for the emerging state, *El Libertador* looks back and sees in history the mere heap of rubble once described by Humboldt. Bolívar's ruinous cartography, his reduction of history to a Humboldtian heap of rubble, foreshadows Walter Benjamin's discussion of allegory and ruin in his book on the *Trauerspiel* as well as his definition of catastrophe in his *Theses on the Philosophy of History*. There history is reduced to a heap of rubble by the storm of progress.

For Benjamin, revolutionary history – figured by the Angel of History – must work through the dialectic of catastrophe and reconstruction that ends up reducing history to a heap of rubble. In his task of sketching out the unity of the cartography in ruins left by the 'revolutionary storm', Simón Bolívar – the political subject who had emerged as such amidst the ruins left by the earthquake of Maundy Thursday – was unknowingly entering into dialogue with a series of future political philosophers who would question the dialectic between progress and ruin, history and catastrophe, within the project of the Enlightenment. As Daniel Castillo-Durante has stated, the heap of rubble comes to represent the negative excess of the First World:

> In the last resort, the rubbish heap is an abstraction of which the hegemonic cultural politics of the techno-scientific world of an industrial and post-industrial capitalism are only able to offer a negative presentation. Inexpressible and unrepresentable, the concept of rubbish heap perhaps makes possible to think of Latin American periphery as the sublime expression of the center. The 'Third World' which terrorizes the centre and sends shivers up its spine functions as sublime object.[48]

Pairing Castillo-Durante's thoughts on the figure of the heap of rubble as the negative sublime that terrorizes the First World with both Humboldt's phrase and Bolívar's discourse of ruins, we get a refracted version of the discourse on the sublime. More than a century before the emergence of a post-industrial society, Bolívar conceives his political journey in terms that foreshadow Castillo-Durante's analysis. Forced to think the unity of a territory whose vastness contains multiple natural and political discrepancies, Bolívar must account for the impossibility of his task. Bolívar's achievement was perhaps to remain faithful to a task he knew to be impossible, that of the utopia of unity disclosed by the figure of the heap of rubble.

The emergence of the state: Representing the multiple

'It would be a folly on my behalf
to stare at the tempest and not seek shelter.'

– Simón Bolívar

The journey of a metaphor can sometimes be the archway of its own demise. In our attempt to grasp the dialectics behind the earthquake-metaphor, we are then driven to a third text by Simón Bolívar: *Discurso de Angostura*. Pronounced 15 February 1819, as part of the Angostura Congress, where twenty-six Congress delegates representing Venezuela and New Granada had been given the task of sketching a new Constitution for the emerging nation of Gran Colombia, the address revisits many of the central images that characterize Bolívar's speeches: the anarchic power of catastrophe, the analogy of America to a Rome in ruins, the enlightened discourse on liberty and will, the constant appeal for a single centralized government. Something, however, has changed. In a gesture that coincides with the disenchantment sketched by Rafael Rojas, Bolívar now faces what he calls 'the political tempest' with the greatest of fears.[49] Not unlike Benjamin's Angel of History, but with a tired spirit, *El Libertador* turns his back to look at history and sees in it an immense catastrophe that awaits political order:

> The Republic over which I presided during this period was not marked by some new political tempest, or bloody war, or even an outburst of popular anarchy. It was something worse – the upheaval of all disruptive forces combined, the inundation of an infernal torrent ravaging the soil of Venezuela. One man, a man like myself, what dikes could he marshal to hold back the power of such devastation? Adrift on this sea of troubles I was but the lowly plaything of the revolutionary hurricane tossing me about like a piece of straw. I could effect neither good not ill: irresistible forces controlled the course of events.[50]

The image of Bolívar that emerges from these lines, that of a man who belittles himself while facing a revolution he himself conceives as a natural catastrophe, is far from that which, according to the memoirs of José Domingo Díaz, had affronted the Earthquake of Maundy Thursday with the dignity of a single phrase: 'If nature opposes our designs, then we shall fight against it, and force her to obey us.' The will of the political subject, empowered by the storm itself, has mutated into a resignation upon which one can find the traces of a secret purpose. Contrary to what it might seem *Discurso de Angostura* remains the statement of a man who is determined to fight against anarchy, a subject determined to give a foundation to history. It is, after all, a constitutional speech and, as such, the metaphors that abound are foundational. Metaphors of base, ground and territory serve Bolívar to construct a basis upon which to run the representational machinery of the emerging state. Bolívar's plea is clear:

'Gentlemen! Let us review the past to discover the base upon which the Republic of Venezuela is founded.' With the force of a single gesture, that of the state, history regains its representational base. However, as Bolívar goes on to explain, this base must remain faithful to the force of nature it wishes to pacify: 'Consider calmly your vote, congressman. Don't forget that you shall spread the foundations of an emerging country that could one day rise to the greatness that nature has marked for it, if you rightly give it the base that its rank awaits.'[51] And so, in this third moment of the dialectics of shock and aftershock, after having erased the *imperial tableaux*, Bolívar proceeds to return to the image of the *tabula* but this time with a difference: his speech performs the transition from empire to state, from the classifying *tableaux* of natural history to the representational archive of the state. The archway sketched by the three moments of the earthquake metaphor describes the way in which one paradigm is displaced by another in a movement that reconfigures the triangle between nature, history and politics. The state however, as Bolívar knew well, remains a hostage to the initial madness of its emergence. Its precarious nature lies in the fact that at any moment the violent nature of its origin could be unmasked, disclosing the empty face that lies behind the set of rules that marks the beginning of its sanity.

At the basis of the state we then find a trembling foundation, a latent multiplicity that threatens at any moment to shake the whole structure. It is precisely this foundational precariousness what the history of the national imaginaries has so far accidentally covered up. From Benedict Anderson's celebrated *Imagined Communities* to Doris Sommer's *Foundational Fictions*, the historiography of the Latin American nineteenth century has found in the nation, understood as imaginary fiction, that is to say, as narrative, the way of sketching a 'happy history' of the transition between the age of empire and the age of the nation-state. It should be no surprise that, within Sommer's account, the figure of the happy resolution, of the resolution of desire within the heterosexual couple, remains the definitive account of the ways nations were able to canalize their internal tensions into coherent national narratives. Recently, this happy historiography has been questioned by intellectuals such as Jeremy Adelman, whose article 'An Age of Imperial Revolutions' questions the national paradigm by uncovering the multiple grounds upon which the transition from empire to nation-state was produced. Adelman's approach is different. Starting from the contemporary discussion regarding the concept of sovereignty, he attempts to plea for a non-narrative history that takes note of the multiple possibilities inherent in the wave of revolutionary wars:

This is now changing, giving way to a view of sovereignty released from the bounded state, and recasting it as a bundle of claims, images, and assertions of authority that can be aggregated at more than one juridical level. This new view takes some distance from the anachronism of identifying national self-determination as the modern genesis of sovereignty, and restores an appreciation for the premodern roots of our transnational political vocabulary.[52]

Released from the bounded state and its narratives, the emergence of the modern Latin American state appears in its original complexity and violence. Beyond narrative, this foundational moment appears in the full complexity of its *eventuality*. To study the nineteenth century from the optics of a politics of the event is then to destroy the imaginary continuity to which twentieth-century historiography has condemned it. Adelman's work, in this sense, forms part of a wider recent interest on the politics of exception. Walter Benjamin's discussion of violence and its relationship to the state has been retaken recently by Giorgio Agamben's discussion of the state of exception as the basis for the foundation of the state's sovereignty. Agamben, following Carl Schmitt, sees the state as being founded upon an initial moment that lies outside the law. The state is always a state of exception:

> The paradox of sovereignty consists in the fact the sovereign is, at the same time, outside and inside the juridical order. If the sovereign is truly the one to whom the juridical order grants the power of proclaiming a state of exception and, therefore, of suspending the order's own validity, then, the sovereign stands outside the juridical order and, nevertheless, belongs to it.[53]

This is the unstable foundation that the state tries to hide behind the masks of its archive. Simón Bolívar's *Discurso de Angostura*, with its initial portrayal of history *as* catastrophe, lends itself to this type of exceptional reading. The state, as Bolívar seems to argue, is never a mere happy resolution, but the suppression of an original chaos by the founding fathers. Against the stereotypical image of Bolívar that wishes to see in him a mere enlightened politician of unity and continental peace, I would argue that we must force this image of the political subject who knows unity is impossible but whose absolute act of sovereignty is to impose order by force of the letter. This is, by no means, to call Bolívar a despot, as became prevalent during his last years, but rather to see, behind his discourse, a deep knowledge of the dynamics of state formation.

The allegories of the state are therefore the broken allegories of catastrophe. In his *Discurso de Angostura* Bolívar returns to the image of Rome in ruins in order to illustrate the precarious state of America after its cessation from Spain. America, like Rome, has become a pure multiplicity whose unity, however, unlike that of Rome, is not guaranteed by any ethnic nature. America, Bolívar writes, is a continent neither of Europeans nor of indigenous people, but rather an unnatural mixture, whose unity and identity are already product of a complex and unnatural catastrophe: that represented by the Conquest of America and the long process of extractivist primitive accumulation that ensued. In addition, one must not forget the tradition of slavery of which Bolívar also takes notice in the language of catastrophe: 'The horrendous slavery covered with its black veil the land of Venezuela and our sky was full of tempestuous clouds that threatened with a deluge of fire. I asked for the protection of God as after the redemption he cleared us of the storms. Slavery broke its chains and Venezuela welcomed its new children.'[54] In the remaining years Bolívar will attempt to think the sublime unity of this continent whose nature exceeds the powers of the archive and its representative machines. Necessarily, he will fail once and again. Failures he will also understand in terms of the precariousness of a state constantly assaulted by the danger of an overwhelming catastrophe. Five years later, exiled in Pativilca, Perú after the collapse of another constitution, he shall write to Francisco de Paula Santander some of his most disenchanted yet illuminating words: 'My epoch is one of catastrophes: everything is born and dies in front of my eyes as if it were a lightening, everything is fleeting, and how foolish of me if I dared to flatter myself by standing strong amidst such convulsions, amidst such ruins, in the middle of the moral upheaval of the universe!'[55] Bolívar epitomizes the political subject in struggle with the state of exception, both as the sovereign and as the *homo sacer*, the subject lost amidst his desire for order. Lost within the ruins of this Rome that was so unlike Rome, incapable of organizing a coherent narrative for the emerging state, Bolívar looks back and sees in history the mere heap of rubble once described by Humboldt.

Aftershock

Cesar Aira's Rugendas: Photographing the earthquake

For some reason, Rugendas and Krause, in their daily conversations on horseback, hit upon a relation between painting and history.

– Cesar Aira

Just like the earthquake only confirms its reality through the concreteness of its aftershocks and the political event is only actualized – according to Alain Badiou – through the retrospective fidelity of its subjects, we could say the foundational violence of Latin American modernity, as it is posited throughout the nineteenth century, finds in its contemporary reverberations the language for its critique. The twentieth- and twenty-first-century re-examination of the nineteenth century past unearths as historical violence that throughout the nineteenth century was naturalized as part of the nation-state's attempt to legitimize its existence. In rewriting the nation-state's foundational fictions contemporary novelists expose the nation-state as the great archival institution it always was, adamant in inscribing both its population and its nature within its all-encompassing representational apparatus.

Against this naturalization of history, what begins to gain form in the nineteenth century under the trope of catastrophe is a new relationship between nature, the political event and the archive: a reformulation of consciousness in its relationship to historical knowledge. Years later, this discourse will find in psychoanalysis its empirical subject. As Walter Benjamin, a prodigious reader of both psychoanalysis and history, knew so well, what I have above called *sublime historiography*, this new relationship between the traumatic event and the archive as totality, already present within the works of Humboldt and Bolívar, would soon find in psychoanalysis its psychic equivalent and in photography its technology. Psychoanalysis and photography reframe the event within its original archival violence as spectral trauma. As Jacques Derrida has explored in *Archive Fever*, while talking about Freud's archive and psychoanalysis as an archival science, the event is always an interruption of the archive, a wound that blasts open its continuity and forces the archive to redefine itself: 'The technical structure of the archiving also determines the structure of the archivable content even in its very coming into existence and its relationship to the future. The archivization produces as much as it records the event.'[56] The event always appears in its truth in the act of rewriting, as aftershock and re-inscription. It is then to no surprise that perhaps the best reading of Humboldt's and Bolivar's earthquake aesthetics wasn't produced during the nineteenth century, but rather by Cesar Aira's 2001 novella: *Un episodio en la vida del pintor viajero*, a counter-historical novel that rewrites a bizarre episode in the life of German painter Johann Moritz Rugendas.

Historical as well as counter-historical rewritings have always been a constant within Cesar Aira's overwhelming literary production: from *Ema la cautiva* to *El Mensajero*, Aira's writing denaturalizes – in the tradition of the avant-garde – what history has naturalized. His operation is usually that of torsion: a historical scene is misinterpreted through the optic of the present conceptual configuration, opening in turn the space for a critical examination of the past. *Un episodio en la vida del pintor viajero*, a short novella published by Aira in 2000, is no exception. There Aira decides to delve into the nineteenth century in order to sketch the figure of he who Simon Bolívar considered the greatest painter of the American landscape: Johann Moritz Rugendas. The novella's fictionalized account of history concerns a fictitious 1837 *episode* that occurs to Rugendas while he treks over the Andes from Chile into Mendoza and from there on to the Argentine pampas in search for what he calls 'other side of his art'.[57] The novella then develops, amidst the sublime emptiness of the Argentine plains which Doming Sarmiento himself had proclaimed paved the way for barbarism and despotism, as an exploration into the mysterious nature of this other side of the art of landscape painting.

But, what could this other side of landscape painting be? As I have explored in the introduction, and as critics like W.J.T. Mitchel have elucidated, landscape painting was used, both in the colonial era and during the foundational period of the Latin American nation-states, as an instrument of cultural power through which both the empire and the nation-state attempted to naturalize certain ideological projections, while simultaneously incorporating peripheral nature into its symbolic regime. The idea of the other side to landscape painting seems then to hint at that which is beyond the state's realm of representation: that excessive other which refuses to surrender to the state's representational apparatus. It is then to no surprise that, within Aira's novella, Rugenda's post-war journey through the Argentine plain is driven by an obsession. The German – originally described as a disciple of Humboldt's physiognomical approach to nature – is obsessed with painting the pure eventuality of an action. Two images fascinate him as (im)possible landscapes: Rugendas is attracted by the idea of painting both an earthquake and an Indian raid. Cesar Aira's historical torsion is already at work: Rugendas's obsession with the other side of his art corresponds to his desire to represent what, by its very nature, remains beyond representation. Within the nineteenth century, the Indian raid, in its barbaric interruption of the codes of civilization, corresponds to the punctual and ungraspable irruption of natural catastrophe, as figured by the earthquake. Both are sublime figures within a radical landscape that marks the frontier where the state encounters its limits.

It is then to no surprise that Rugendas fails once and again in his attempt to paint these figures, for they are from the very get go that refuses to surrender to the domesticating power of the nation-state. At least while he remains within the realm of traditional landscape painting, the earthquake and the *malón*, or Indian raid, are beyond his scope. It is at that point that, within one of those unexpected scenes typical of Aira, a scene where nature meets culture under the sign of science, the novella produces the shocking episode which changes the rules of the game and allows him to finally access the 'other side' of landscape painting. Struck by a thunder, Rugendas is left almost dead, disfigured and monstrous. It is within this altered state, with his face destroyed and his body consumed by the power of morphine, that he comes up with a solution to his artistic ordeal: he shall paint with a black *mantilla* hanging over his face. Rugendas's solution to his personal catastrophe is illuminating: in deciding to paint with a mantilla hanging over his face, he involuntarily mimics the image of the photographic *camera obscura*. Only then, by symbolically entering into the realm of photography, is he able to reach that other side of his art and capture the figure of the Indian raid. By rewriting the nineteenth century from the photographic optic of the twentieth century, Aira is able to illuminate the internal logic of its sublime history as the other side of the process of modernity through which creole history was naturalized through the dichotomy, drawn in Sarmiento's *Facundo*, of civilization versus barbarism.[58] In what follows I shall delve into the consequences of this historical torsion, in an attempt to rethink how photography emerges, within the nineteenth century, as a technology of catastrophe, as short-circuit that reconfigures the political event's disruptive place within the nation-state's archive. Rugendas's other art is then an art of catastrophe.

Un episodio en la vida del pintor viajero: the title of Aira's novella already suggests one of the main conceptual knots at stake throughout the novella. The notion of *an episode* brings forth one of the fundamental problems within romantic aesthetics: that of the fragment's relationship to totality. In fact, Aira's oeuvre, with its multiplicity of *novelitas*, and his poetics of '*la huida hacia delante*', sometimes seems to be a fragmentary poetics of episodes forming a wider body of work whose unity is itself under question. Within the novella, these dialectics between fragment and totality are rendered into a theme. Rugendas's mentor, Alexander Von Humboldt, is described by the narrator as 'el ultimo sabio totalizador'.[59] It is under this image of an all-embracing physiognomy of nature that we are first introduced to Rugendas's procedure: 'Rugendas was a genre painter. His genre was the physiognomy of nature, based on a procedure invented by Humboldt. The great naturalist was the father of a discipline that virtually died with him: *Erdtheorie* or *La Physique du monde*, a kind of artistic geography, and aesthetic understanding of the world, a science of landscape.'[60] The landscape then remains the name for a configuration of nature under the emblem of totality. It remains the ideal of a wholesome representation, of a catalogue under which nature is subsumed and archived. Against this desire for representation, one can then grasp the tension that is at work within the novella between the totalizing notion of a landscape and the fragmentary notion of an episode that breaks free from the totalizing pretences of the archive, redeeming for itself a political sense of historicity.

As we have noted, landscape is to nature what the law is to violence: the imposition of an external measure, the taming of that which threatens to open a gap within the space of the archive. From the aesthetics of Humboldt to Sarmiento's imaginary description of the Argentinean pampas, landscape painting remains a law-making cartographic device, the stabilization of nature as the pillar upon which the state could then begin to represent itself. I am reminded of the parable that Borges recounts at the epilogue of his book *El Hacedor*: a man decides to draw the world, just to find much later that he has sketched the contours of his own face.[61] Like in this parable, the state measures, paints and draws the limits of its landscape, just to find the physiognomy of its own law written over the now mutilated nature. In a violent gesture that is however posited as natural, nature itself is robbed of its historicity. Against this notion of landscape, Rugendas proposes the notion of a radical landscape capable of going beyond representation and towards action. Like the thunder that catastrophically strikes him twice, the landscapes that interest him are rather those – the earthquake and the Indian raid – marked by action: 'Rugendas imagined it. A green field, suddenly smothered by a buzzing cloud, and, a moment later, nothing. Could painting capture that? No. An action painting, perhaps.'[62] His journey towards the other side of landscape is then an attempt to bridge the gap separating representation from eventuality: that is to say, an attempt to make representation itself an event. As Brett Levinson has noted, the novel then moves as a dialectical understanding of novelty and repetition, as the sporadic yet recurring figure of the earthquake or the *malón* suggests: 'Did that mean the Indians were part of the procedure? The repetition of their raid was a concentrated form of history.'[63] How to think both of history and of historical novelty within this world where a logic of repetition seems to underline the possibility of any eventuality.

In this sense, Cesar Aira's rewriting of the life of Rugendas in his novella *Un episodio en la vida de un pintor viajer*, with its historical torsions, remains crucial in order to understand the role of nature within the founding moment of the Latin American states. As the novella recounts, Rugendas came from a genealogy of painters whose task was to document war. Talking about the technique of his great-grandfather, the narrator states: 'An exquisite contrast between the petrified intricacy of the form and the violent turmoil of the subject matter made him unique.'[64] This distinction between the peaceful representation and the violent subject matter remains illuminating, for what is at stake here is the taming of the unlawful outside of knowledge. In Aira's novella Rugendas is described as a disciple of the physiognomic approach to nature, as a landscape painter. And yet, at the very bottom he remains a painter of war, a painter of movement and violence. The novella attempts to negotiate from within this oscillation between the static and the kinetic, between peace and violence, between law and nature, between the novelty and repetition. And so, what drives Rugendas out of the realm of the law is always his desire to reach the outside of representation. His search for the earthquake and the Indian raid are nothing else than his desire to paint history in action. It is a desire that gets fulfilled when nature itself strikes back with the violence of thunder: deformed and in pain, Rugendas is finally capable of painting the outside of the law, the trembling pillars of a shaking state. He who had attempted to sketch the physiognomy of nature finds his own face deformed to the point of being unrecognizable: like a bandit – whose presence, as Juan Pablo Dabove has suggested, is always staged at the limits of the state – he is now forced to wear a mask.[65] A survivor of electricity, as the narrator calls him, Rugendas emerges from the dead as pure other. A masked man, a faceless man, he no longer falls within the realm of state representation; he exists at the very limits of citizenship. Only from that liminal position can he paint the violence that structures the state's self-positing.

Once Rugendas – this great survivor of electricity and therefore a post-enlightened man – puts on the *mantilla*, he crosses the threshold separating painting from photography, representation from action. He establishes, that is to say, a new relationship to the archive which manifests itself in a new temporality. A landscape painter by training, his task had always been that of producing military documents. However, once his vision is blurred, and, with the black mantilla hanging from his face, he becomes symbolically a *camera obscura*, his relationship to the document changes profoundly. He is finally able to record those events which until then had remained outside of his representational realm. We merely have to remember how this elusiveness is portrayed:

> Rugendas would have liked to depict an earthquake, but he was told that it was not a propitious time according to the planetary clock. Nevertheless, throughout his stay in the region, he kept secretly hoping he might witness a quake, though he was too tactful to say so. In this respect and in others, his desires were frustrated. His other cherished dream was to witness an Indian raid. In that area, they were veritable typhoons, but, by their nature, refractory to calendars and oracles. It was impossible to predict them: there might be one in an hour's time or none until next year.[66]

The Indian raid – described here under the catastrophic figure of the typhoon – had until then remained the unfathomable outside of the enlightened chronology, the excessive eventuality that refused to be subsumed within that which Walter Benjamin once called the progression of 'homogenous, empty time'.[67] Struck by thunder, turned into a camera obscura, Rugendas now belongs to a different temporality: that of photography. His relationship to the document has changed, precisely because his perception has been innervated by morphine, producing a mental short-circuit that mimics the automatism of the camera's eye. At the precise moment in which he begins to witness the Indian raids, we have the following description of his mental self: 'From that moment on, like all victims of personalized catastrophes, he saw himself as if from outside, wondering. Why did it have to happen to me? [...] Rugendas, who was going through a particularly critical phase, had attacks of vertigo and cerebral short-circuiting all night.'[68] He has entered the vertiginous temporality of the short circuit of that impossible event of pure instantaneity. It is in this sense that one could claim, following

Rugendas example, that photography as technique reconfigures the sense perception machinery in such a way as to render it adequate to the chronotope of modernity: that chronotope which throughout chapter I have called the *time of catastrophe*. If, playing with Reinhart Koselleck's definition of modernity, I have described this modern temporality as that of an ongoing catastrophe, one could then say that the emergence of photography corresponds to a society whose notion of document goes beyond that of conscious perception.[69] No longer merely a viewing subject, a recording eye, the photographer corresponds to an excessive subject who documents more than he can consciously register. The subject of catastrophe is characterized by that which, following Walter Benjamin, we could call the *optical unconscious*. The genius of Cesar Aira's historical torsion is to show how this all-embracing consciousness is no longer that of a Cartesian subject, not even a consciousness at all, but the optical unconscious produced by the camera. The modern subject, as Benjamin himself stated, finds in the photographer its model and in psychoanalysis its discourse:

> However skillful the photographer, however carefully he poses his model, the spectator feels an irresistible compulsion to look for the tiny spark of chance, of the here and now, with which reality has, as it were, seared the character in the picture; to find that imperceptible point at which, in the immediacy of that long-past moment, the future so persuasively inserts itself that, looking back, we may rediscover it. It is indeed a different nature that speaks to the camera from the one which addresses the eye; different above all in the sense that instead of a space worked through by a human consciousness there appears one which is affected unconsciously [...] Photography makes aware for the first time the optical unconscious, just as psychoanalysis discloses the instinctual unconscious.[70]

Photography reframes the world as sublime world. It challenges subjective representation by hinting towards a utopic out of bounds which remains inscribed within the present as 'that imperceptive point at which, the future so persuasively inserts itself'. A society that takes photography as its paradigmatic happening is one in which the document registers more than it can represent, a society full of that which, following Alain Badiou, one could call exceptional points: points that exceed the representative apparatus, opening in turn sites for political critique.[71] Photography enters into this society both as a symptom and as a salvation, as the technique through which the complex affective structure of this new event – in its indexical, spectral exceptionality – is finally given a body. No wonder at the very beginning of the novella, when describing Rugendas's task, we are told: 'His mission was one that, a hundred years later, would have fallen to a photographer: to keep a graphic record of all the discoveries they would make and the landscapes through which they would pass.'[72] Aira is able to understand that with the emergence of photography the structure of the event changes, and with it the notion of the document and the archive. Thunder struck, metamorphosed into a camera obscura, the delirious Rugendas becomes a subject amidst a landscape of eventuality.

A reality that is more than itself can only be apprehended by the poignant eye of a subject that is more than merely himself: the subject that perceives the photographic event is a subject who exists not in the present instant of conscious perception but rather in the delayed temporality of repetition. Only from there can he look back and discover what his eye had registered without him knowing. Throughout *Un episodio en la vida de un pintor viajero*, these intuitions are channelled through the constant discussions regarding the relationship between art and history that occupy Rugendas in his discussion with his travelling partner Krause, leading him to proclaim: 'Repetitions: in other words, the history of art.'[73] This idea of art as being guided by a principle of repetition becomes predominant after the painter is hit by thunder, leading Rugendas to provide a delirious reformulation of Humboldt's theory of the physiognomy of nature.

Our photographic reading of the novella helps us propose a sense to this otherwise ambiguous motif: history, having moved from the realm of painting to that of photography, is now characterized by the spectrality of its repetitions: 'It [the physiognomic approach] was based on repetition: fragments were reproduced identically, barely changing their location in the picture.'[74] Like the earthquake, whose spectral presence is only confirmed by the aftershock, the photographic event is characterized by the internal difference of its repetitions. This is the logic of Benjamin's dialectical image, as expounded throughout his *Arcade Project*. As Eduardo Cadava has noted in his book *Words of Light*, the temporality of the photographic event is that of repetition, of quoting, of the lighting flash that interrupts continuity and imposes a radical dialectic:

> The radical temporality of the photographic structure coincides with what Benjamin elsewhere calls 'the caesura in the movement of thought'. It announces a point when 'the past and the present moment flash into a constellation'. The photographic image – like the image in general – is 'dialectics at a standstill'. It interrupts history and opens up another possibility of history, one that spaces time and temporalizes space.[75]

The photographic event presents us with the logic of lightning as expounded by the dialectics between potentiality and actuality, the violent logic of interruption and exception that actualizes what in the past had remained a mere potentiality. And so, we could imagine that everything that happens to Rugendas after his accident – his encounter with the Indian raids, his decision to adopt the mantilla, his delirious reflections upon the nature of art – is all an aftershock of that impossible instant in which lighting strikes him in the form of thunder. It is a semiotic response to a pure action: 'What happened next bypassed his senses and went straight into his nervous system. In other words, it was over very quickly; it was pure action, a wild concatenation of events. The storm broke suddenly with a spectacular lightning bolt that traced a zig-zag arc clear across the sky.'[76] The logic then behind Rugendas's method is that practised by Aira: re-inscription, rewriting, repetition. *An Episode in the Life of a Landscape Painter* is a novella about the ends of landscape painting as much as it is about landscape painting: by drawing upon the structural limits of the landscape, by presenting us with that which can't possibly be mere landscape, by rewriting catastrophe under the sign of photography, Aira's novella questions the technical and archival implications of the event in its complex relationship to the changing landscape of Latin American politics and the emergence of the modern nation-states.

3

Volcanoes: Emergencies of an archaeological modernity

'A great volcano lies at our feet... Who shall restrain the oppressed classes? The yoke of slavery will break, each shade of complexion will seek mastery.'
– Simón Bolívar

In one of the decisive scenes of Malcolm Lowry's 1947 modernist novel *Under the Volcano*, the three protagonists – Hugh, Yvonne and the alcoholic Consul – decide to drive out of Quauhnahuac into the Dead of the Death festivities of Tomalín, near Parián. From the window of the 1918 Chevrolet bus that transports them, the Mexican post-war landscape is drawn as scorched earth, as a wasteland in battle with its modernist pretensions. Parallel to the broken, serpentine road in which they travel, they can spot the American Highway, a sign of a linear progress that seems, however, to elude them. Telegraph poles, the other sign of modernity, also seem to lag behind the violence of this catastrophic landscape marked by the presence of the Popocatepetl volcano:

> Nothing but pines, fircones, stones, black earth. Yet that earth looked parched, those stones, unmistakably, volcanic. Everywhere, quite as Prescott informed one, were attestations to Popocatepetl's presence and antiquity. And here the damned thing was again! Why were there volcanic eruptions? People pretended not to know. Because, they might suggest tentatively, under the rocks beneath the surface of the earth, steam, its pressure constantly rising, was generated; because the rocks and the water, decomposing, formed gases, which combined with the molten material from below; because the watery rocks near the surface were unable to restrain the growing complex of pressures, and the whole mass exploded; the lava flooded out, the gases escaped, and there was your eruption. But not your explanation. No, the whole thing was a complete mystery still.[1]

Framed by the windows of the bus, the volcanic landscape becomes a reflection of both Mexico's modern history and the Consul's alcoholic journey. It suggests the subterranean discontents of a culture haunted by the ghosts of a long-buried foundational violence. Like the drunken Consul, like the rocking old Chevrolet bus in which they travel, Mexican modernity seems to stumble its way through history, incapable of walking straight. Against the progressive straight path of the American Highway, its path seems to be constantly derailed by the spectres haunting a landscape that finds in the volcano its Janus-faces symbol: 'Popocatepetl loomed, pyramidal, to their right, one side beautifully curved as a woman's breast, the other precipitous, jagged, ferocious. Cloud drifts were massing again, high-piled, behind it. Iztaccihuatl appeared.'[2] The volcano, both beautiful and ferocious, then hides two facets: a vital side and a deadly side, a forward-looking and a past-looking face. That is to say, the volcano hides within itself a pyramid. Throughout the novel the volcanic pyramid becomes the preferred double symbol for the imminence of catastrophe, as well as for the disclosure of an errant path within modernity, a drunken path leading to modernity's archaic secret.

It should not surprise us, then, that not soon after the protagonist's reflections concerning volcanic eruptions, the reader stumbles upon what remains one of the central scenes of the novel: a scene of violence whose echoes will re-emerge throughout the novel with the force of the repressed, leading directly to the final death of the Consul. As it drags its way through the spectral post-revolutionary landscape previously described, the old bus is once again derailed by an unusual view: lying roadside, by a wayside cross, a dying Indian is discovered, his wounded head covered by a wide hat that serves to disguise his agony. Confronted with this dying man, whose image conjures the ghosts of past historical violence, the three protagonists are shocked by the defeated indolence with which the locals accept their incapacity to save the man.

> Death they knew, better than the law, and their memories were long. They sat ranked now, motionless, frozen, discussing nothing, without a word, turned to stone [...] And yet, in these old women it was as if, through the various tragedies of Mexican history, pity, the impulse to approach, and terror, the impulse to escape, having replaced it, had finally been reconciled by prudence, the conviction it is better to stay where you are.[3]

Against the landscape of volcanoes, death is unearthed as the spectral force propelling forward both the tragedy of the Consul and that of Mexican history.

Incapable of answering the appeal of the dying – incapable of remaining faithful to its call for justice – Mexican history moves forward, like the Consul's bus, propelled by the modern storm of progress, leaving the dying Indian behind and in so doing missing the opportunity to redeem the chain of violence which haunts its historicity as that which, following Michael Taussig, we could call its *public secret*. It is a secret that is generally known but can't be articulated, and whose entrance into the public sphere is always a negative act: an eruption, an excavation, the breaking into a crypt. The archaeology of such secret is then given to art as its political task: that of unearthing the hidden potential buried within the spectrality of the now and whose latent presence is prefigured throughout the novel by the beautiful yet violent, modern yet archaic, symbol of the volcano.

We must then remain faithful to the political paradox illuminated by the scene of the dying Indian. In it, framed by the landscape of volcanoes, the power of negativity is disclosed as the dialectical process that simultaneously drives Mexico's progressive modernity while simultaneously sketching the grounds for its critique. Death is inscribed within Mexican history as both tragedy and redemption, in a double gesture that remits us to Hegel and his idea of tarrying with the negative: 'But the life of Spirit is not the life that shrinks from death and keeps itself untouched by devastation, but rather the life that endures it and maintains itself in it. It wins its truth only when, in utter dismemberment, it finds itself.... This tarrying with the negative is the magical power that converts it into being.'[4] This inscription of death within life, which Claudio Lomnitz has brilliantly explored in *Death and the Idea of México* and which Michael Taussig places at the very heart of his discussion of the public secret in *Defacement*, allows us to read Mexican modernity in relationship to the spectres which seem to haunt it, opening the space for an eventuality that is experienced both as pyramidal excavation and as volcanic eruption. That is to say, the event of ghost can be – as Bruno Bosteels has explored in relationship to the 1968 Tlatelolco Massacre – either conservative or radical, in its attempt to link the past and the future:

> An event, then, appears as a ghost both for what it no longer is and for what it has yet to be. In one case, it ciphers the memory of an annihilated opportunity; in the other, the glimpse of a promise that is perhaps on the verge of becoming real [...] The anchoring point for the figure of the ghost is always a break on the extreme edge where the old bears the new, either to give in to what is gestating there or else to tie it down with the threads of the past.[5]

The ghost's call for justice puts the breaks on the progressivism of enlightened historicity, forcing us to account for the ruinous remnants through which past violence seeks redemption and restitution. Catastrophe then becomes the sign of a particular stance vis-à-vis history: namely, a dialectical stance which, in opposition to the progressivism of historicism, denaturalizes the violence which progress would like to forget, and does so as unredeemed ghost. Like the volcano or the pyramid, it unearths the ruins of a past that bears witness to the 'labour of the negative' through which Mexico has instituted its claims to modernity. Malcolm Lowry, a man torn between the modernity of James Joyce and the ruins of Quauhnahuac, knew it well: modernity sketches its linear path in order to better deviate, in order to be able to dream of archaic ruins.

Attentive to the call of the ghost, conscious that if answered improperly its plea can lead us to the tragic fate of the melancholic, as the indolent faces of the old women in *Under the Volcano* highlight, this chapter proposes itself as a historiographical excavation of the nineteenth century in search for the origins of an archaeological paradigm of history as it emerges in relationship to the concept of Mesoamerican ruins and, in particular, to the notion of an archaeological symbol. It attempts to sketch the emergence of the vertical, not to say deep, temporality of the archaeological symbol as the impasse of enlightened progress. It does so by pursuing how the catastrophic figure of the volcano – a figure of an archaic, buried, emergent knowledge – comes to be articulated, represented and inscribed throughout what we could call the long nineteenth century in Mexico: that period spanning from the Mexican War of Independence in 1810 up to the consolidation of the Mexican Revolution under the *Partido Nacional Revolucionario* in 1929. Three intellectual and artistic figures come forth within this history, determining three distinct yet complimentary modes of tackling the question regarding the past as its comes to be figured by the volcanic pyramid and its spectres: José María Heredia, the Cuban author of *Oda al Niágara*; Augustus Le Plongeon, the British antiquarian and photographer whose work in Yucatán established modern Mayanism; and finally, the infamous muralist, intellectual, philosopher and natural historian Gerardo Murillo, who Leopoldo Lugones baptized as Dr Atl, for the Nahuatl word for water, and whose obsession with volcanoes drove him to lose a leg as part of his project to paint the birth of the Paricutín volcano. Heredia, Le Plongeon and Murillo serve as the three sites of an archaeological excavation within whose millenarian corridors one witnesses the spectral returns of Mesoamerica as a call for political justice.

Spectral as it is, this history refuses to be confined to the nineteenth century. Instead, it moves throughout the twentieth century following the errant itinerary of its foundational symbol, the volcanic pyramid, until Mexico's public secret re-emerges within our days in the mountains of the Lacandon Jungle, through the masked figure of Subcomandante Marcos. From Malcolm Lowry's *Under the Volcano* to Octavio Paz's 1968 *Crítica de la Pirámide*, written in the wake of the Tlatelolco Massacre, all the way to Guillermo Bonfil Batalla's 1987 *México Profundo*, published in the aftermath of the Earthquake of 1985, the volcanic pyramid remains a symbolic site where the creole naturalization of enlightened historicity as progressive modernity is questioned by the ghosts of a repressed indigenous past and their present-day call for justice.

The archaeology of a symbol: Jose María Heredia's volcanic pyramid

Padre de fuego y piedra, yo te pedí ese día
tu secreto de llamas, tu arcano de armonía,
la iniciación que podías dar...

– Rubén Darío, Momotombo

The year is 1823: a young José María Heredia, exiled from his native Cuba, enters the Museum of Natural History in Philadelphia and finds, to his surprise and amazement, the skeleton of a mammoth. The event will be registered in the chronicles of his North American days. Two decades earlier, in 1796, the French naturalist Georges Cuvier had revolutionized the field of natural history with a paper that presented his studies on living and fossil elephants. One of Cuvier's statements had struck particularly hard against the enlightened theory of the best of possible worlds and against the theory of uniform progress: 'All of these facts, consistent among themselves, and not opposed by any report, seem to me to prove the existence of a world previous to ours, destroyed by some kind of catastrophe.'[6] The fossils of elephants evidenced the fact that they were not the same species but rather that we were talking about different species. Under Cuvier's theory, which was later to gain the name of *catastrophism*, extinction was a possibility. As Martin Rudwick has noted, the possibility of extinction disrupted the idea of a great chain of being by posing the troublesome possibility that God might remove some of the necessary links within his divine plan. No longer a homogenous empty space, time appeared under the figure of a discontinuous history divided by catastrophic events – volcanic eruptions, earthquakes, floods – which Cuvier himself, working with the context of post-1789 France, would suggestively call revolutions. At the same time that Darwin's theory of evolution was naturalizing the notion of a progressivist historicity, Cuvier was opening history to its own discontinuities, as part of the geohistorical discovery of that which James Hutton had portentously called deep time.[7] Coincident with the growing neoclassical and romantic discourse on ruins, which saw catastrophe as the point of intersection of natural history and human history, the relationship between past and present was changing with the emergence of a series of 'historical sciences' that were able to read in the present the traces of a past long gone. As Michael Foucault explored in *The Order of Things*, from palaeontology to archaeology, there emerged a science of past signs.[8] The fossil, a natural ruin in itself, had reconfigured the semiotic relationship between past and present in such a way that the young Jose María Heredia who enters the Museum of Natural History in Philadelphia is quick to see in the remnants of the mammoth a natural trope for human history:

> After many centuries these bones have reappeared, just like the naked mast of a ship driven to shore by the waves signal the existence of a shipwreck. And we, we also, shall suffer the same luck the day that an angry page is opened upon the eternal book of destinies, and those who come after us shall look for news from our era just like we fathom the deep darkness that separates us from the epoch in which there existed upon earth this gigantic cadaver.[9]

As the figure of the natural history museum would soon come to attest, human history is here read in relationship to a world where the evolutionary progressivism of animal species is always threatened by the latency of the catastrophic impulse of Cuvier's natural revolutions. The fossil, like the ruin, becomes the site for this dialectic between catastrophe and progress, nature and culture, which would soon lead romantics like Heredia to envision history under the rubric of natural catastrophe.

Who then, was this José María Heredia? Unlike his similarly named cousin Jose María de Heredia, whose European trajectory won him a seat in the *Académie Française*, the story of Jose María Heredia y Heredia was a truly American story. Born in 1803 in Cuba, the young Heredia is arrested in 1823 under charges of conspiracy against the Spanish monarchy. His sentence: a banishment for life from Cuba that forces him to go into exile. At the end of the same year – 1823 – we find him in Philadelphia, the city of the founding fathers, and two years later in Mexico, amidst the anarchy of the recently liberated republic.¹⁰ It is this Heredia, the one who would later become a model in the fight for Cuban independence, leading José Martí, in one of the speeches in New York, to compare his 'volcanic verses' with the revolutionary struggles of Bolívar: 'Heredia only finds his equivalent in Bolívar [...] The first poet of América is Heredia. Only he has loaded his verses with the sublimity, the pomposity, the fire of its nature. He is volcanic like its entrails and serene likes its heights.'¹¹ Martí's comparison of Heredia's sublime verses to the natural dialectic between eruption and serenity, between the urgency to act and melancholic contemplation, makes explicit what we find in the verses that the young Heredia dedicates to the Teocalli de Cholula, or Aztec pyramid, during a visit to Mexico in 1820, in what is considered one of the foundational poems of Latin American romanticism. The poem, entitled *En el teocali de Cholula*, remains one of the best examples of how a discourse of ruins helped recast the past within the revolutionary context of the wars of independence and the ensuing foundation of the modern Latin American nation-states.¹² As we shall soon see, this is a poem that bears inscribed within it many of the contradictory currents that marked Latin American romanticism as both a radical revolutionary movement and a foundational conservative discourse grounding a particularly creole reading of continental history.

As Mary Louise Pratt has explored, in *En el Teocalli de Cholula* Heredia repeats Alexander Von Humboldt's 1803 excursion to the Aztec pyramid, framing his meditations on the ruinous landscape within a profoundly creole rewriting of continental history. Written in the aftermath of the revolutionary period, the poem has been usually read as part of the attempt by creole *letrados* to inscribe within nature a rupture both with the colonial heritage of the Spanish past and with the supposed barbarism of the indigenous legacy. As Gabriel Horowitz has noted, 'the territorialization of nature for Creoles in America is to naturalize a claim of rupture with the past, to make the Spanish and indigenous cultures disappear from view. Turning America into nature – making it seem that deep down, it is an ahistorical space – seems to invalidate both Spanish and indigenous claims to the land.'¹³ Reading the ruins of the pyramid as a remnant of both Spanish and Aztec brutalities, Heredia is able – according to Horowitz – to draw nature as a tabula rasa upon which to draw the dream of creole political autonomy. However, these readings, while highlighting the most evident intention of the poem, fail to account for the way the poem presents ruinous post-war nature as a landscape haunted by the ghosts of past violence, in a gesture that re-inscribes the latency of history within the realm of the natural.

Against this naturalization of history, a properly political reading would try to unearth the modes of historicity which Heredia both proposes and withdraws, in a double gesture that mimics that dialectic between eruption and serenity, activity and contemplation, which Martí used to describe his 'volcanic verses'. In fact, *En el teocalli de Cholula*, an ode to the *teocalli – Nahuatl* for the house of god, namely, for an Aztec pyramid – works through a constant oscillation between precisely these two figures: the pyramid and the volcano. After beginning the poem by praising the fecundity of tropical American nature, in verses that remind us of Andrés Bello's *Silva a la agricultura de la zona tórrida*, the poet proceeds to describe how he sits at sunset in the pyramid to contemplate the landscape amidst the ruins of the Aztec past. In an oneiric setting which reminds us of the pyramidal ascent to heaven by the soul as described in the first lines of Sor Juana Inés de la Cruz's poem *Primer Sueño*, the spectres of history are conjured against a landscape of ruins that at first sight seems to highlight the absolute transience of history. The brutality of Spanish colonialism and, in particular, the superstitious barbarism of the Aztec past are evoked as past realities condemned to oblivion, opening the space for a creole naturalization of history as progress:

> Time runs so quickly, carrying off
> Years and centuries, like the fierce north wind
> Which knocks down a crowd of ocean waves
> Before its breath. You have seen kings
> And people boiling (seething) at your feet, who fought
> Against time just as we fight, and called
> Their cities eternal, and believed
> They could wear out the earth with their glory.[14]

The next verse – 'They passed away: no memory remains of them' – ends up proclaiming their tragic fate: under the scheme of progress provided by enlightened historicity their fate is to be forgotten as mere barbaric echoes of a pre-modern past. Repressing the Mesoamerican past, Heredia therefore attempts to found what Horowitz has called 'a new historical line completely divorced from his cultural and genealogical past, which he saw as decadent and corrupt.'[15] Working within a romantic poetics that posited history as the catastrophic passage of time, Heredia then attempts to naturalize this repression by pointing towards the natural law of decay and death inscribed within a progressivist historicity which condemns everything to the silence of oblivion:

> All things perish
> By universal law. This most beautiful
> And brilliant world where we live is
> Only the pale, deformed corpse
> Of another world which was ... [16]

En el teocalli de Cholula is then, at a first reading, a supreme example of creole romanticism: an exaltation of the post-revolutionary present at the expense of the repression of both the colonial and Mesoamerican past. Every repression, however, produces a symptom, as Freud noticed.[17] Heredia's poem is not the exception. And so, against these reflections regarding the progressive historical development of America, the poem traces the contours of a towering witness that, in its archaicness, refuses to give in to the progressivist arrow of history. Slowly, the poetic voice traces the emergence of the volcano's spectral shadow as a symptom for that repressed past that refuses to be forgotten and instead withstands the passage of time, mimicking in its stubborn yet dormant sublimity the ruinous logic of the pyramid upon which he stands:

> I turned my eyes back to that uplifted
> Volcano which, veiled in transparent
> Vapor, was drawing its black contour
> Onto the occidental sky.
> Giant of Anahuac! How can the flight
> Of rapid ages not imprint some
> Mark upon your snowy face?[18]

Against the storm of progress and the gusts that propel history forward – an image to which Heredia will later return in his 1822 poem 'En una Tempestad' – the volcano acts as the intransigent giant who refuses to conform to the progressive linearity of time: like the pyramid, whose archaic verticality it mimics, the volcano stands firm against the 'quick flight of the ages'. Its temporality is not that of the horizontal arrow of history, but rather that conjured by James Hutton's notion of deep time: the notion of an archaic geological history inscribed in the land itself, contesting the amnesiac forgetfulness of modern human history. Fluctuating between the volcano and the pyramid, Heredia's poem provides the grounds for a reading of the poem against the grain: its attempts to suppress the Mesoamerican and colonial past are counteracted by the emergence of the Janus-faced symbol of the volcanic pyramid as a symptom of that remnant, halfway between nature and history, which refuses to give into the creole landscaping of history through which the poet attempts to naturalize the image of a teleological modernity. Paradoxically, in his attempt to silence what he sees as the violence of history, Heredia ends up uncovering the volcanic pyramid as the founding symbol of the Mesoamerican archaeological imaginary in its spectral call for justice. As we shall see, it is in regard to a constant negotiation with this double symbol that a new mode of historical experience is structured within the thwarted logic of Mexico's archaeological modernity, opening the grounds for a critique of its progressivist historicity and its forgetful claims of homogeneity. The young Heredia who arrives to Mexico in 1920, just when the war is over, unknowingly discerns the logic of the archaeological paradigm: one always produces knowledge the day after the catastrophe, when the war is over, and what is left for the poet is only the excavation of ruins.[19]

Often quoted as Latin America's first romantic poet, whose volcanic verses also bore witness to the neoclassical heritage, José María Heredia's work must be read in the context of the increasing appreciation of ruins that marked both neoclassism and romanticism. In typical romantic fashion, as Antonella Canellier has noted, *En el teocalli de Cholula* proposes history as the catastrophic passage of time that ends up producing the ruins where, simultaneously, the secret essence of the past seems to remain dormant, awaiting the day its spectral call to the future will be heard.[20] As Heredia himself states in his 1825 poem *Placeres de la melancolía*:

> I shall devote myself to extracting high lessons,
> high examples shall my mind find
> in its desolation: ¡how sublime
> is the voice of sepulchres and ruins![21]

Ruins are therefore crypts where history lies dormant, graves where the past lays buried as suppressed knowledge. Looking at history catastrophically, romanticism exposes ruins both as the inevitable product of future-looking progress and as the discontents of such developments, in a gesture that confounds nature and culture. The pyramid – mausoleum for a secret past, inscription of the past within nature – therefore becomes a privileged site, standing as a metaphor both for the poem in itself and for the possibility of historical meaning within a modern world that seeks to condemn the past to oblivion. Heredia, whose poem to the Aztec pyramid was originally called *Fragmentos descriptivos de un poema mexicano*, whose fragmentary work ethic imagined poetry as the production of a subjective ruin against time, recognized this double nature of ruins and produced, in his volcanic pyramid, the foundational symbol for an archaeological modernity whose resonance would soon traverse Mexico's modern history.

A Mesoamerican return of the repressed

'Piramidal, funesta, de la tierra nacida sombra, al Cielo encaminaba de vanos obeliscos punta altiva, escalar pretendiendo las Estrellas': Mexican literature is sometimes said to begin with the pyramidal ascent to heaven by the soul as described in the first lines of Sor Juana Inés de la Cruz's poem *Primer Sueño*. The verticality of the pyramid stands there for the particular spectral and oneiric temporal logic of knowledge, a kinship between the pyramid and knowledge that is reinforced by the fact that the pyramid is merely the external architecture of an internal secret.[22] Like Heredia's *teocalli*, which houses the secrets of the Aztec gods and therefore of the Aztec past, the hermetic pyramid belongs to a tradition of secrecy and veils, of crypts and mausoleums – a tradition that conforms to the logic of negativity, death and mourning. Its figure stands for a knowledge whose origin – whose *arche* – has been lost but whose external face stands unveiled as a call for desire. Namely, the archaeological nature of the pyramid is precisely that of the symbol as it is explained by Hegel in his *Lectures on Aesthetics*, that of a cryptic externality: 'The pyramids put before our eyes the simple prototype of symbolical art itself; they are the prodigious crystals which conceal in themselves an inner meaning... the shape *for* an inner meaning remains just an external form and veil.'[23] Hegel never visited Mexico. Nor did he – unlike Walter Benjamin – dream of Mexico. Unlike his relationship to Haiti and its revolution, of which much has been recently written under the figure of the master and slave dialectic, his links to Mexico would be more remote, if it were not for this passage that continues to explore the site of the pyramid as a semiotic negotiation between meaning, knowledge and death:

> But this realm [the pyramid] of death and the invisible, which here constitutes the meaning, possesses only one side, and that a formal one, of the true content of art, namely that of being removed from immediate existence; and so this realm is primarily only Hades, not yet a life which, even if liberated from the sensuous as such, is still nevertheless at the same time self-existent and therefore in itself free and living spirit. The pyramids are such an external environment in which an inner meaning rests concealed.[24]

As Jacques Derrida has explored in his essay *The Pit and the Pyramid*, what is disclosed here under the figure of the pyramid is the whole architectonic structure of Hegelian semiology. By positing the pyramid as the paradigmatic figure of the sign, Hegel exposes the process of signification as a play between secrecy, archaeology and mourning. We are once again driven back to Heredia's

'En El Teocalli de Cholula' and the Hegelian 'labour of the negative' which is there inscribed within the empty post-revolutionary Mexican landscape as a historical secret which the poet both unearths and represses, in the process turning history into a traumatic past that spectrally returns with the might of the repressed. The young Heredia arrives to a country whose war has barely ended, a country still attempting to settle the anarchic spectres of war, only to realize that instead of recording the epic battles, he is given the task of portraying the ruinous landscape of what was and could be. His poem remains a melancholic ode to a past whose latency resounds throughout the present:

> I found myself seated on the famous
> Pyramid of Cholula. My eyes were
> Invited to divert themselves across
> The immense plain that lay spread out before me.
> Such silence! Such peace! Oh! Who could tell
> That in these beautiful fields barbarous
> Oppression rose up to rule, and that this
> Land has brought forth such rich cornfields
> Paid for with the blood of men, in which
> It was inundated by superstition and war ...?[25]

Nature, under the double symbol of the volcanic pyramid, stands for the subject's opening to a particular sort of eventuality: not the mere horizon of an open future, as progress ridden historicity would have it, but rather the latent presence of a past experienced as the re-emergence of a lost and perhaps traumatic origin. The young Heredia, a man of action who had been exiled from his native Cuba out of fear for his actions, sits among the ruins of the Cholula pyramid in order to melancholically contemplate the sublime landscape upon which the Aztec sacrifices were once executed. The dialectics of the sublime – a play between distance and immersion or between the exteriority of the symbol and its spectral interior – is here sketched in relationship to a logic of mourning that reframes the poet's relationship to both the colonial and Mesoamerican past. Catastrophe, or the latency of catastrophe, becomes, for the romantic poet, a way of rethinking the relationship between past, present and future.

One could then claim the volcanic pyramid stands as the symbol for the possible Freudian 'return of the repressed'. For us, the question would then be: what sort of historicity is here disclosed by the symbol of the volcanic pyramid? What poetics of desire and history are established under the figure of mourning and melancholia, under the figure of a return of the lost origin? Moreover, what would happen if, while opening the pyramid's secret chamber, one fails to find the body, but rather encounters that the lost object, the object of desire and mourning, is nothing else than the figure of Mexico itself? Mexico lost in its desire for Mexico.

The relationship of Freudian psychoanalysis to Latin America has long been marked by what Bruno Bosteels has recently called the logic of a *desencuentro*: a missed encounter based on Freud's impulse to posit his thoughts within an idealist-metaphysical realm rather than exploring them within their concrete-historical context.[26] Recently, however, as Bosteel's *Marx and Freud in Latin America*, Rubén Gallo's *Freud's México* or the growing interest in the work of the Argentine Freudian philosopher León Rozitchner instantiate, there have been multiple efforts to remedy this missed encounter. In the particular case of Mexico, Freud's presence seems ubiquitous. From the dreams of human sacrifice and the pre-Columbian past that appear in *The Interpretation of Dreams* all the way to Octavio Paz's usage of psychoanalytical vocabulary in his conservative critique of what he calls Mexico's underdevelopment: 'The other Mexico, the submerged and repressed, reappears in the modern Mexico; when we talk with ourselves, we talk with it; when we talk with it, we talk with ourselves.'[27] Following Paz's reading of Mexican history, it would seem that what a reading of Freud vis-à-vis Mexican history unearths is precisely the possibility of another Freud: a Freud that provides us with the concepts needed for staging a critique of that same universalist evolutionism which he himself saw as the positivist background against which the tale of psychoanalysis could be read out as the progressive development of the psyche within the history of civilization.

Central to this productive re-reading of psychoanalysis in its relationship to Latin American modernity is its theory of the symptom as spectral remnant. With the introduction of its novel theory of the symptom, psychoanalysis turned the symbol into a ruinous monument for the repression of a traumatic past. As early as 1909, in the first of his *Five Lectures in Psychoanalysis*, Freud recounts the relationship between the neurotics' symptoms, memory traces and monumentality.[28] The neurotic's symptoms are, as Freud states, mnemonic symbols, residues of a traumatic experience. He then proceeds to draw an analogy: 'We may perhaps obtain a deeper understanding of this kind of symbolism if we compare them with other mnemonic symbols in other fields. The monuments and memorials with which large cities are adorned are also mnemonic symbols.'[29] Freud then passes on to discuss this analogy in relationship to *The Monument to the Great Fire of London* – the impressive Doric column with the flaming gilt-bronze urn atop which today stands near the northern end of the London bridge as a reminder of the terrible fire that in 1666 reduced London to ashes and brought on the reconstruction of the city's modern face – in the process elucidating that just like the monument stands as a mnemonic symbol for a past catastrophe, so is the hysterical symptom the symbolic trace of a past personal catastrophe. The analogy, however, closes with one particularly interesting comment. After disclosing the relationship between the symptom and the monument, Freud ends up by underlying the pathological character of hysteria by discussing melancholia:

> But what should we think of a Londoner who paused today in deep melancholy before the memorial of Queen Eleanor's funeral instead of going about his business in the hurry that modern working conditions demand or instead of feeling joy over the youthful queen of his own heart? Or again what should we think of a Londoner who shed tears before the Monument that commemorates the reduction of his beloved metropolis to ashes although it has long since risen again in far greater brilliance? Yet every single hysteric and neurotic behaves like these two unpractical Londoners.[30]

Freud's language, by opposing the impractical figure of the melancholic spectator to that of the efficient working man, exposes the archaic temporality of the symbol: the symbol belongs to a different time, to that unpractical temporality of the monument which interrupts traffic and demands a time of its own. The archaeological symbol, like the neurotic's symptom, belongs to a different topology: it draws a handle within the smooth, progressive surface of modernity. With his analogy, Freud unknowingly adds a third pathological figure to those of the hysteric and the neurotic: the melancholic. Although it would take him a decade to concretize the discovery, what remains implicit throughout these lines is something that would become apparent in his 1917 essay *Mourning and Melancholia*: the insight that melancholia is fundamentally an archaeological disease, a psychological torsion at the very origin of the history of the subject. The melancholic, by refusing to believe that his love object is gone, distances himself from the immediacy of the rushing present and declares himself in war with progress.

As such, Jose María Heredia's *volcanic pyramid* could be read as a symptom of that original repression of the indigenous past through which Mexican modernity is both posited and naturalized. Like in the case of the volcano, where eruption stands as the re-emergence of some repressed original, elementary element – lava, smoke, ash – the melancholic subject repeats history as a way of putting it under parenthesis: it quotes, once and again, from an original scene whose reality has been lost. Melancholia is the disease of a modernity that feels estranged from itself, the pathology of a society that feels exiled from its origin. It should then not surprise us to find that Heredia, an exile, wrote and translated multiple poems on melancholia, many fragments of longer poems that stand today as pyramids among his work. In fact, what renders Heredia a fascinating figure is precisely his position midway between neoclassicism and romanticism. His process of creation, halfway between a revival of the classics and an outburst of inspiration, mimics the volcano's dual nature and posits the process of creation as the paradoxical production of a ruin. Heredia's literary production, which included multiple classical translations from which he took inspiration, could then be best understood not merely as a poetics *about* ruins, but rather as the construction of the poem *as* a ruin. His desire to build his poems as fragments, this conception that the 'final' poem was nothing else than the accumulation of fragments, discloses a certain conception of time: that of melancholy and exile. The exiled subject becomes the paradigm of a subject for whom the only exit from the modern highway is the production of a ruin, the interruption of progress through the emergence of the symptom. The volcanic pyramid then becomes a symbol where Mexican history is unearthed as a ruin that traces the return of its repressed Mesoamerican past as a call for justice. Depending on how the subject relates to this call, it can be a conservative or a radical symbol: its political ambiguity leads both to Octavio Paz's conservative reading of Mexican history or to Subcomandante Marcos's radical politics of emancipation.

In 1968, the year of the Tlatelolco Massacre and the worldwide student manifestations, the same year in which Octavio Paz writes his famous *Crítica de la Pirámide*, two psychoanalysts publish a reading of Freud that revolves around the notion of the archaeological symbol. That year sees the publication of Nicolas Abraham's *L'Ecorce et le Nouyau* and Maria Torok's *Maladie du deuil et fantasme du cadavre exquis*, two articles that, departing from an interpretation of Freud's 1917 *Mourning and Melancholia*, restructure the notion of the psychoanalytical symptom by reading it from perspective of what they call cryptonymy: a science of the symbol as crypt. This arch-psychoanalysis, as Abraham called their approach in his *Introduction to Hermann*, departs from a fascinating intuition: what Freud had hinted at in his article on mourning and melancholia was precisely the idea that psychoanalysis, as the hermeneutical science of anti-semantic symbols, was an archaeological science: a science revolving around the traumatic relationship with regard to a lost origin. Abraham and Torok's theory of the symbol evolves around this insight, modelling itself around the figure of the crypt. Like the crypt, Torok and Abraham suggest, the psychoanalytical symptom is an exterior shell that protects a traumatic kernel that refuses to disclose its meaning. The psychoanalytic symptom, in Torok's words, is a crypt that hides not a body but a phantom, the figure of an unresolved past that haunts the present in search for justice.[31] Every symptom is a pyramid.

Perhaps then, if we read José María Heredia's *En el teocalli de Cholula* from the perspective of cryptonymy, what we see is the establishment of a symptomatic Mexico. Heredia's poetic discourse on ruins – mediated as it is by the catastrophic symbol of the volcanic pyramid – is unearthed as a symptom of Mexico's problematic relationship with the enlightened theory of progress and its archetypal forms of modernity. Heredia erects the volcanic pyramid as a post-colonial crypt within which Mexico can answer the call of its spectral past. As such, Mexico's tradition is a tradition of death, mourning, crypts and phantoms: from Heredia's 'En el Teocalli de Cholula' to Juan Rulfo's *Pedro Páramo*, from Sor Juana's 'Primer Sueño' to Malcolm Lowry's *Under the Volcano*, from Siquiero's *La Gran Marcha de la Humanidad* to Roberto Bolaño's *2666*, the Mexican tradition seems to be guided by the desire to build a monumental crypt in which Mexico can search for its spectres. Be it the holocaust that marked the Spanish conquest or the nineteenth-century repression through which creole *letrados* naturalized the forgetfulness and oppression of its Mesoamerican past, Mexico's modern imaginary seems to be marked by the return of the repressed traumas that marked its violent foundation.

Namely, Mexico's colonial legacy is in itself the founding catastrophe, one which left such destruction of the social body that no national project of reconstruction was able to overcome its racialized, gendered and ethnicized conflicts. A foundational catastrophe whose latent violence gets re-inscribed within post-colonial history not as ontology, but rather as what Jacques Derrida has called hauntology: as the belated temporality through which colonial history and its repressed subjects are said to haunt the so-called modern present in search for justice and restitution.[32] This re-inscription and re-emergence is perhaps best understood in relationship to what Homi Bhabha has called time lag: the past haunting post-colonial history which 'fractures the time of modernity' creating in turn 'a signifying time for the inscription of cultural incommensurability where differences cannot be sublated or totalized'.[33] Disrupting progressivism, exposing the fault lines of the continuum of history, the volcanic pyramid then re-emerges as a symbol that re-inscribes, within the heart of Mexican modernity, the experience of a post-colonial contra-modernity:

> In splitting open those 'welds' of modernity, a postcolonial contra-modernity becomes visible. What Foucault and Anderson disavow as 'retroversion' emerges as a retroactivity, a form of cultural reinscription that moves back to the future. I shall call it a 'projective' past, a form of the future anterior. Without the postcolonial time-lag the discourse of modernity cannot, I believe, be written; with the *projective past* it can be inscribed as a historical narrative of alterity that explores forms of social antagonism and contradiction that are not yet properly represented, political identities in the process of being formed, cultural enunciations in the act of hybridity in the process of translating and transvaluing cultural differences.[34]

It is the spectral temporality of this projective past, or future anterior, what the volcanic pyramid symbolically inscribes within Mexican modernity as the time lag that simultaneously drives Mexican modernity forward while sketching the grounds for a possible critique. As Antonio Gramsci's notion of interregnum showcases, 'The crisis consists precisely in the fact that the old is dying and the new cannot be born; in this interregnum a great variety of morbid symptoms appear.'[35] This temporal disjuncture, characteristic of post-colonial societies, gets concretized in the Mexican case by the volcanic pyramid in gesture that rewrites, within the context of the nineteenth-century post-revolutionary landscape, the myth that states that Mesoamerican civilization had already mysteriously disappeared before the Spanish arrival. Accordingly, the Spanish conquistadors, as Arthur Demarest has explored in *Ancient Maya: The Rise and Fall of a Rainforest Civilization*, did not arrive to the true splendour of the Mesoamerican civilization but to its ruins.[36] The Mesoamerican foundational myth of restitution is that of the flight of Quetzacóatl. When the Spanish arrived the feathered king had already left, leaving nothing behind but a promise: he would return as God. Mexican history, in its relationship to the temporal gap that separates it from Mesoamerica, is experienced as the critical interregnum produced by the delay of Quetzacoatl's promised return.[37]

And so, Mexico's modern historical witness, of which Heredia becomes the paradigmatic example, is always a latecomer: he arrives one day late, when the event is over, and what is left are the catastrophic, spectral and symptomatic ruins of the colonial past as a call for justice. Namely, Mexico stages its post-colonial history as the site of its own historical disjuncture, around the image of a lost origin, in a gesture that belongs to the logic not only of mourning and melancholia, but also of exile: since the very beginning Mexico appears to be exiled from itself. Heredia, an exile himself, a man of letters and politics who arrived to Mexico precisely when the war was over, knew this well: for him the questions of the missing origin, of archaeology, melancholia and poetry were one and the same. If his poetry then turns to nature in look for answers, it is not in terms of a pastoral observation of the smooth fabric of the *natural*, of the uneventful outside of history, but rather of the ways nature is seen as a radical landscape that breaks the so-called natural progressivism of history. Nature is not peace: it is torsion, violence, eruption. It is the site where Bhabha's 'cultural incommensurability' is inscribed as historical latency.[38] What we then end up with is an analogical structure that states the following: catastrophe stands to nature as the pyramid stands to history, the symbol to language and the symptom to the subject. This structural and ecological paradigm, which I have here called the archaeological paradigm, is best understood if we read at once the two faces of Mexico's symptomatic modernity. We are compelled to place Heredia's *A la Gran Pirámide de Egipto* next to his *Al Popocatepl*.

¡Escollo vencedor del tiempo cano,
isla en el mar oscuro del olvido,
misterio entre misterios distinguido,
de un inmenso arenal gran meridiano!

¡Montaña artificial, resto tremendo,
estructura sublime y poderosa,
del desierto atalaya misteriosa,
de la desolación trono estupendo!

Tú que de nieve coronado
Alzas sobre Anahuac la enorme frente,
Tú de la indiana gente
Temido en otro tiempo y venerado,
Gran Popocatepetl, oye benigno
El saludo humildoso
Que trémulo mi labio te dirige.
Escucha al joven, que de verte ansioso
Y de admirar tu gloria, abandonara
El seno del Managua delicioso.

The archaeological paradigm of Mexico's archaeological modernity should be understood in relationship to this constant oscillation between the pyramid and the volcano, between Egypt and Mesoamerica, which ends up comingling the two imaginary worlds of antiquity and reversing the distinction between the Old World and the New World. Years before Augustus le Plongeon sketches his theories about the Mayan origins of Egypt, Heredia's poetry performs a similar torsion. In his poetry, Mexico is understood only in relationship to the Old World of ruins of empires he never knew: Rome, Egypt, Cartago … Heredia's position, half-way between a conservative neoclassicism and romantic rebellion, produces a poetics of history as the latent possibility of emergency. As prefigured by the dormant volcano and the cryptic pyramid, Mexico's modern history sketches itself as the sublime site of a knowledge that has been violently repressed, and for which a symbol now stands as trace, ruin and symptom. Like Torok's crypt, which hides nothing but a phantasm, one finds the image of a nation that has learnt that its true object of desire is nothing but itself. Mexico in search for the *other* Mexico, the *México Imaginario* in search for the *México Profundo*: Mexico as the *objet petit a* of itself.

The politics of mourning

'To write the story of the nation demands that we articulate that archaic ambivalence that informs the time of modernity', writes Homi Bhabha in *The Location of Culture*.[39] It is perhaps this ambivalence which remerges under the symbol of the volcanic pyramid in Heredia's poetry: a symbol that interpellates the subject, staging the grounds upon which his political stance will be defined. For if the volcanic pyramid rewrites modernity as projective past or future anterior, that is to say, as spectral historicity, the danger remains that the subject will either disregard the call for justice of the spectre or melancholically end up giving in to the sublimity of its silence. The line separating redemption from tragedy is here a thin one, just as thin is the frontier separating mourning from melancholia within Freudian psychoanalysis. In a way, this is the trajectory sketched by Heredia himself who, after espousing the revolutionary cause of independence, ends up melancholically giving up to a creole conservatism that would even lead him to become the editor of a Mexican newspaper called *El Conservador*. As the editors of the publication themselves explain in the prospectus to its publication:

> It shall be conservative, because it will seek to sustain the enthusiasm that, since the memorable declaration of the Xalapa Plan animates countries in their struggle to face disorder and immorality; that reflexive enthusiasm which has superseded the imperious, intolerant fanaticism. A calm and decisive will that reclaims with energy the exclusive empire of the law. It shall be conservative because it shall work constantly to tame and moderate the exalted spirits.[40]

As Gabriel Horowitz and Mary Louise Pratt have noted, Heredia ends up giving in to the conservative agenda of the creole *letrados*. In a way that will be echoed by so many of the protagonists of Mexico's archaeological modernity, leading all the way to Octavio Paz's conservative reading of Mexican history in *Crítica de la Pirámide*, Heredia ends up melancholically reifying under the realm of law the past symbolized by the pyramid, at the expense of the archaeological symbol's other side: that of the future-looking, redemption-seeking volcano. In doing so, he fails to do justice to that which, following Michael Taussig, we could call Mexico's *public secret*: that foundational colonial violence which is generally known, but which can't be articulated, and whose presence threatens to plot Mexico's history under the sign of fate and tragedy. For, as Taussig himself has stated, the public secret is precisely that latent presence which refuses to become a positive representation and whose revelation is always a negative act: an eruption, an excavation, the breaking into a crypt. Instead, giving in to melancholia, Heredia ends up imagining Mexican history as a spectre that must be buried under the realm of the law, but only after having already established the symbol that makes that history readable.

Against this conservative melancholia, it is our task to read the symbol of the volcanic pyramid as the truly radical Janus-faced symptom it is: as the emergence of negativity into the public sphere which stages an interruption of the linear progression of time as it had been imagined by the Enlightenment, forcing us to account for the post-colonial persistence of modernity's foundational violence. Against the horizontality of the arrow of progress, its temporality points towards the verticality of archaeology, the depth of strata and excavation. As such, the public secret emerges only as the aftermath of catastrophe, when the fault lines upon which Mexican modernity has been built are finally uncovered: in the aftermath of the 1994 Free Trade Commerce Agreement, in the aftermath of the 1985 Earthquake, in the aftermath of the Tlatelolco Massacre, in the aftermath of the Mexican Revolution, in the aftermath of the Mexican War of Independence. The catalogue of the eternal return of *other* Mexicos so proves it: the Ejército Zapatista's 1994 *Declaración de la Selva Lacandona*, Bonfill Batalla's 1987 *México Profundo*, Octavio Paz's 1968 *Crítica de la Pirámide*, the Mexican Muralism of the 1920s and Jose María Heredia's 1820 *En El Teocalli de Cholula*, all pertain to a tradition of the elucidation of the public secret that emerges in the aftershock of catastrophe, enacting an impasse of progress and claiming justice for another sort of temporality: that deep temporality which, as time lag, opens the space for a critique of the naturalized power structure.

A dream of Atlantis: The Le Plongeon's journey

'Mrs. Le Plongeon and myself, after saving from destruction many important documents and relics, have at last found a key that will unlock the door of that chamber of mysteries. Shall it be allowed to remain closed much longer?'
— Augustus Le Plongeon

In 1873, almost half a century after José María Heredia erects the volcanic pyramid as the archaeological symbol for Mesoamerica's modernity, two Victorian travellers embark on a journey to redefine the bridges already established by the Cuban poet: those between the old and the new world, between ruins and history, between the monuments of antiquity and the languages of modernity. On 28 July 1873, Augustus Le Plongeon, a British-American antiquarian with a passion for photography and theosophy, together with his young wife Alice Dixon, whose passion for spiritism had been coincidentally inherited from his father the photographer Henry Dixon, embark on a trip that will take them to the Mayan ruins of Aké, Chichén Itzá and Utxmal, among others. Freemasonry, photography, spiritism and archaeology: everything amounted to the perfect mix between the modern and the archaic, between technology and history, between science and belief. Indeed, it was a nineteenth-century transatlantic cocktail that would produce some of the most beautiful of delirious theories. On 28 July 1873, from the port of New York, Augustus and Alice board the *Cuba*. One week later they arrive to Heredia's La Habana only to hear that the city is infested with an epidemic of yellow fever. One month later they hear the same news as the ship anchors near the shore of the Yucatán Peninsula. Carrying with them their photographic equipment, alongside books about theosophy and Egyptian archaeology, they arrive to a land secretly afflicted by another social crisis: the *Caste War* that throughout the second part of the nineteenth century confronted the Mayan *Yucatecos* against the European population. From the very start, their travel was to have political implications. Their objectives went far beyond the mere contemplation of ruins: following the intuitions of Charles Etienne Brasseur de Bourbourg, the French archaeologist who had travelled the region during the previous decade, the Le Plongeon couple envisioned something greater – an archaeological theory that would settle the fundamental question regarding the cradle of civilization. Like Brasseur de Bourboug before them, they held that the ruins found in Yucatán were remnants of an original civilization that had disappeared only to re-emerge under a different face in Egypt. As Augustus would later explain in his book *Sacred Mysteries among the Mayas and the Quiches*, their fieldwork into the inscriptions found in the Mayan monuments led them to believe they had found, in Yucatán, the lost land of Atlantis as it had been described by Plato. In the pyramids of Chichén Itzá, Uxmal and Aké, they found linguistic remnants of the land destroyed by a volcanic and tectonic original catastrophe. Augustus, who in the previous decades had lectured on the topic of earthquakes and the origin of civilization, was not foreign to a catastrophic discourse. As such, the idea of a lost continent devoured by an original catastrophe tempted him into thinking that the original civilizations of East and West – the Mayan and Egyptian civilizations of antiquity – were all established by the migrant refugees that escaped the catastrophic destruction of the original continent. From the very beginning the question regarding the origins of civilization is for the Le Plongeons a matter of exile, catastrophe and reconstruction:

> We must not forget that Plato informs us that the priests of Egypt assured Solon, when he visited them 600 years before the Christian era, that all communications between their people and the inhabitants of the 'Lands of the West' had been interrupted for 9,000 years, in consequence of the great cataclysms, during which, in one night, the large island of Atlantis disappeared, submerged under the waves of the ocean. Are we not then right if we surmise that the monuments of Mayax existed 11,500 years ago, and that mysteries, similar to those of Egypt, were celebrated in them? To support that belief we have the symbols existing in chambers.[41]

'To support this belief we have symbols existing in chambers': forced to account for his intuitions regarding the cradle of humanity, Augustus points, not unlike Heredia before him, towards the notion of an archaeological symbol which is best represented by the inscriptions found in the burial chambers of Chichén Itzá. Once again, the pyramid becomes the sign of the symbol, a ruin of language that bears witness to an original catastrophic event: like in the Hebrew story of the Tower of Babel, where linguistic differences are accounted for in terms of a catastrophic origin, the myth of Atlantis comes to explain geographical as well as linguistic multiplicity. More than three centuries after the Lisbon Earthquake, the Le Plongeons provide a new twist regarding the sudden emergence of multiple possible worlds: historical unity can be kept, they seem to say, if one can translate between languages. Like in Babel, we are left, however, with the notion of a symbol that is merely the ruin of a lost origin, the remnant of an original language destroyed by catastrophe and dispersed through the multiplicity of exiled worlds.

As recent studies like Christina Buenos's *The Pursuit of Ruins* or Sara Castro-Klaren's 'The Nation in Ruins' have explored, archaeological ruins were the site of a power struggle throughout the nineteenth century: sites where the modern nation-building projects through which the state attempted to naturalize its creole modernity confronted the resistance of other modes of narrating the national past.[42] Under the figure of cultural patrimony, imperial curiosity had given way to creole reconstruction as a new way of mediating the relationship between nature and history. Natural history had been replaced by archaeology in the long process that, in the case of Mexico, would culminate with the construction of the Museo Nacional de Antropología. It is within this context that we must place the journey of the Le Plongeons as latecomers to a history of transatlantic explorations that was highly indebted to the travels of Von Humboldt and Bonpland, but whose direct influences were the travels and works of Charles-Étienne Brasseur de Bourbourg and Claude-Joseph Désiré Charnay, two French archaeologists whose work attempted to reconstruct the ties between the Old World and the New World, in the context of the failed Second French Intervention in Mexico and its aftermath, which saw the rise of Porfirio Díaz amidst the southern Caste Wars through which the Mayan people reclaimed their autonomy through the declaration of the Chan Santa Cruz State. Within this shaky political context, the delirious theories of the Le Plengeons must be understood as complex allegorical negotiations between the competing modes of historicity that marked the emergence of Mexico as a modern nation within the global political scene.

Published in 1886, *Sacred Mysteries among the Mayas and the Quichés* sets itself as a book about the origins of modern Free Masonry. In the opening pages, Augustus Le Plongeon, a freemason himself, attempts to defy the widespread belief that its origin dates back to the works of Aristotle. The origins of free masonry, he claims, are not to be found in the Greco-Latin texts of the founding fathers of European civilization, but rather in the forgotten lands of the west. His methodology, however, is what interests us: Le Plongeon quickly realizes that his archaeology must be an excavation into the meaning of symbols, of inscriptions, of epitaphs: a study into the power of translation. The book then unfolds as a study of the language of ruins – inscriptions, epitaphs, hieroglyphs – that he had found and visually recorded via photographs in the Mayan monuments. As the title already suggests, *Sacred Mysteries among the Mayas and the Quichés* reads as an excavation into the language of secrecy so dear to the societies of free masonry. As such, Le Plongeon's erects, at the very centre of his study, the notion of the archaeological symbol, paradigmatically represented by the pyramid, as the sign whose meaning remains a secret to us. As ruinous meaning, the symbol remains, to use Taussig's terminology, a *public secret*, an object of desire that calls for the labour of language. This relationship between secrecy and archaeology, between secrecy and modernity, should not come to us as a surprise. In his seminal *Critique and Crisis*, Reinhart Koselleck exposed the central position that secret societies, and in particular free masonry, had in the construction of the crisis consciousness that became fundamental for the construction of our modern notion of the state. At the very heart of the Enlightenment, as some sort of perverse double of it, the dialectic between secrecy and knowledge, paradigmatically represented by the all-seeing pyramid – that same pyramid which years later, in 1968, Octavio Paz was to equate to the history of Mexican power struggles – becomes central for our understanding of the political as well as philosophical implications of crisis as a historical category:

> The political significance of the shift was hidden from the bulk of the society as well – this had its roots in the dialectic between ethics and politics that was provoked by the secret. The political secret of the Enlightenment was not to be shrouded just from the outside: as a result of its seemingly non-political beginnings it was concealed from most of the Enlighteners themselves.[43]

The politics of this paradoxical notion of an enlightened secret, in its relationship to the formation of modern secret societies, remains a symptom of the formation of a new temporality at the very heart of modernity: the notion that at any moment something veiled could come to light, not necessarily as knowledge, but as veiled knowledge. This is precisely what the archaeological symbols stand for according to Le Plongeon: the ruins of an original language – the lost *Babel* – that remains veiled until the reconstructive labour of translation and historical retelling is performed. At the very heart of the enlightened project, within its internal struggle, the notion of an archaeological symbol is the symptom of a modernity that struggles to construct the notion of a *universal history*. In the context of nineteenth-century Mexico, this meant that the archaeological symbol – seen as a fragment of a missing historical totality – was seen as the site of a struggle: the locus of a negotiation between the state's attempt to rewrite the pre-Columbian past according to the creole modernity it wished to naturalize and other attempts to critically examine and counteract this naturalization. As recent studies like Susan Buck Morr's *Hegel, Haiti and Universal History* or Jorge Cañizares Esguerra's *How to Write the History of the New World?* have noted, competing modes of political modernity were at stake in the reconstruction of universal history as it occurred throughout the nineteenth century in Latin America.

Le Plongeon's *Sacred Mysteries among the Mayas and the Quiches* must then be read against this background: as an attempt to posit a secret origin upon which to base a universal history that included both the Mayas and the Egyptians, the Mexicans and the French. As a free mason, Le Plongeon knew that modernity stands upon a delicate triple architectonic foundation: technology, knowledge and desire. As such, his archaeological journey within the Yucatán peninsula must be understood in regard to the tension developed within his theory of the symbol. The archaeological symbol instantiates within language the complexity of a crisis that had marked modernity since the Lisbon Earthquake: the critical tension between the possibility of multiple different worlds, on the one hand, and the necessity, on the other, of a single teleological universal history. As I have explored in Chapter 2, this tension between contingency and universality, paradigmatically represented by Babel and Atlantis, lies at the heart of any modern narrative as the dormant volcano punctuating the otherwise calm landscape. The possibility, so well known to Le Plongeon, that any mountain could be a pyramid, that any mound could turn into a volcano, points towards something essential within the structure of Latin American modernity as it was experienced throughout the nineteenth century: uniform progress was always experienced against the latent presence of a possible catastrophe that would re-enact the foundational violence that gave birth to its traumatic historicity. In the case of Le Plongeon's journey through the Yucatán Peninsula, this must have turned out to be a first-hand experience: in the Caste War conflict that assaulted the region from 1847 to 1901, confronting the Mayan population against the Creole Elite, Augustus and Alice must have seen an instantiation of the same historical, class and racial differences which the state had so badly tried to suppress as part of their foundational nation-building projects. In the diary of their Yucatán trip that Alice Dixon kept, there is a phrase that gets often repeated: '*We discovered a mound…*' This phrase punctuates their narrative endowing it with a sense of possibility. Mounds always appear as a possibility of discovery, as the sign of a latent new symbol, as a call for archaeological work and for the work of translation, but also under the sign of the latency of the negative. More often than not, within Dixon's diaries, mounds turn into truncated pyramids that hold within them chambers. Death inhabits the archaeological symbol as that which refuses to be merely translated into the language of an enlightened progressivist modernity. And so, in Alice Dixon's diary entry for 1 November 1875, written while the couple was exploring Chichén Itzá, we can read: 'Doctor discovered a mound with sculptured slabs, and a statue of a reclining tiger without head half-buried in the ground. The slabs represented tigers, and Macaws eating human heart. This mound is not far from the tiger monument. We took it to be a mausoleum.'[44] Punctuating the landscape of modernity as the archaic secret that can't be subsumed, death discloses itself as the catastrophic interior of the archaeological symbol. Opening the mausoleum, the archaeologist encounters the reclining figure of a nameless effigy.

The stone sculpture found inside the *Platform of the Eagles and Jaguars* in Chichén Itzá, depicting a reclining man with its head turned to one side while it holds a tray in his chest, was soon to find a name. Augustus Le Plongeon, interpreting the statue to be a totemic representation of the mythical warrior Coh, soon christened it as *Chaacmol*, meaning powerful warrior. Years later, the *American Antiquarian Society* inadvertently changed it to *Chacmool*, the archaic Yucatec Mayan for puma. Given the frequency with which the leopard repeats itself across the walls of the monuments in Chichén Itzá, the name seems suitable. The finding was, however, to prove central to the Le Plongeon's archaeological cartography of symbolic possible worlds, serving as the central symbol upon which they would later construct the catastrophic allegory of the lost continent of *Mú*. In fact, the discovery of the statue re-enacts the unveiling of the symbol as it was to be imagined by Nicolas Abraham and Maria Torok: after the supposed mausoleum is open, after the shell-like crypt is uncovered, the statue comes out as the phantasmal kernel of meaning – namely, as the non-modern residue which refuses to play within the smooth economy of translation and equivalence. It becomes the founding stone for the whole edifice of meaning precisely because it, with the negativity inherent in every public secret, refuses to yield its exact value. As it remains clear from the diary of Alice Dixon, as well as from the writings of Augustus Le Plongeon, the discovery of the statue was to jumpstart their desire towards allegory. One is here tempted to hear the echoes of Walter Benjamin's famous dictum: 'Allegory is to the realm of things what ruins are in the realm of thought.'[45] The dictum, which belongs to Benjamin's early reflections on the baroque mourning play and his theory of allegory as ruin, hints at the possible connections between the archaeological symbol, allegory and the problem of universal history. Benjamin's discussion of the baroque, which is in turn a reflection upon modernity as such, removes the allegory from its traditional weak position as direct expression of an idea and complicates the paradigm by rethinking allegory as ruinous meaning. The power of allegory resides, Benjamin seems to say, not in the transparency of a universal meaning but rather in its capacity to reproduce the desire of the particular for such universality. As such, the allegories that we find throughout the writings of Augustus and Alice, all of those attempts at narrating an archaeological history of the origins of civilization, are to be understood within the modern attempt at producing a universal history. One almost feels tempted to rewrite Benjamin's dictum from the perspective of the debates concerning universality. Allegory is to language what catastrophe is to nature: a short circuit that exposes the complex relationship between the fragment and its totality, between the particular and the universal. The archaeological symbol as ruin stands in the middle as the symptomatic condensation of the desire for universality. Throughout their many articles and books, from Le Plongeon's *Queen Móo and the Egyptian Sphinx* to Alice Dixon's epic poem *A Dream of Atlantis* to her longer prose poem *Queen Móo's Talisman*, one finds the many attempts to allegorize the symbol found in Chichén Itzá – *the Chacmool* – into a compelling narrative. Departing from their belief that the Maya hieratic alphabet was easily translated into the Egyptian alphabet, Le Plongeon devised a foundational allegory based upon their readings of the Mayan inscriptions and epitaphs. According to Le Plongeon, the statue of *Chaacmol*, the powerful warrior, stood for the figure of Prince Coh, youngest son of the serpent King Can, and brother of the beautiful Móo who became Queen after the death of their father. It was the law among the Mayas that the youngest son should marry the oldest sister, which would have entitled Coh to the throne. However, Prince Aac, the second son of King Can, was also in love with Móo. In a feat of jealousy and wrath, it is claimed, Aac killed Coh by stabbing him three times in the back, an event that started a civil war in the original continent and led to a social catastrophe. So runs the first of allegorical readings that surround the statue, an allegory that attempts to link itself with the biblical stories found in the book of Genesis: the fratricide of Cain and Abel, the seduction of women by the serpent, the great deluge. Egypt, the sign of civilization, is said to have been founded by the refugees escaping the catastrophe that caused the ruin of the western lands of Mú. Exile, translation, allegory and catastrophe are all linked by the Le Plongeons' attempt to produce a universal history.[46] In fact, as we read a lecture given by Alice Dixon in 1890, we find her go even further, suggesting that the Greek language was also tied to Mayan language through a direct translation. As Lawrence Desmond has explained in *Yucatán through Her Eyes*, a book which explored the Le Plongeons' journey, Dixon even went as far as suggesting that the Greek alphabet, when translated sequentially, narrates the catastrophic disappearance of *Mú*. In a strange feat of allegorical logic, Alice seems to produce a reverse image of Babel:

> The Greek language, according to the Le Plongeon's, derived from the Mayan, and as proof she explained that Augustus had discovered that each letter of the Greek alphabet had a meaning in Mayan. When the letters were translated sequentially, a short poem emerged about the destruction of Mú. Alpha means 'heavily break the waters,' bete means extending over the plains,' gamma means 'they cover the land,' ect, ending with omega which means 'then come forth and volcanic sediments'.[47]

'The come forth and volcanic sediments': the machinery at work in this universal translation is authorized, from the very beginning, by the power of death, exile and dispersal of that first volcanic catastrophe which jumpstarts the desire for allegory under the sign of the impossible return to a catastrophic origin.

Amidst a journey that attempted to bridge a fascination with archaic origins with a modern propensity towards science, it is not surprising that the Le Plongeons' expedition was marked by the usage of a modern technology such as photography. They kept a physiognomic archive of their trip by photographing members of the cities they visited, they taught the natives the mysteries behind the new art, and most importantly, Augustus's translation work – central for his theories – departed from photographs of the inscriptions he found on the Mayan ruins. In fact, as Lawrence Desmond points out, it had been the sales of Augustus's *Manual de Fotografía*, written specifically for the Latin American market, which had helped finance their trip to Yucatán Peninsula. Their lives had, since the very beginning, been touched by the camera: the young Augustus had learnt the art from one of its pioneers, the English photographer Henry Fox Talbot, before going on to open personal studios in the western lands of California and Perú. Talbot himself held a very serious interest in Middle Eastern archaeology and had worked to translate the Syrian and Chaldean cuneiform writings. In the case of Alice Dixon, the connection was immediate: her father, Henry Dixon, held a private studio at 112 Albany Street in London. Working for her father, who had many times been commissioned to photograph the relics of Old London, the young Alice was to learn much of the antiquarian photography that would help her during the days in Yucatán. It is then to no surprise that photography comes to figure, within their work, as the central technology around which the dialectics between archaeology and modernity, originality and translation, repetition and difference, catastrophe and reconstruction gain their relevance.

Photography, as the writings of Walter Benjamin suggest, serves as an allegory for allegory itself: it is a temporal technology that represents the ruin of meaning and time, the catastrophic interruption of the link between the referent and its copy, as well as its multiple dispersal.[48] Like the members of Mú, forced to seek refuge and exile throughout the world, the photograph disperses itself beyond the confines of its origin. Furthermore, as Walter Benn Michaels has explored in his essay 'Photography and Fossils', photography instantiates a technology of time which links the debates concerning the archaeological symbol to a debate concerning another type of archaic sign: the fossil.[49] Like the fossil, like the crypt, the photograph remains an absent presence, a trace for something which once was and no longer is. Following recent theoretical debates we are tempted to say: like the fossil, photography remains an indexical sign standing for an origin that has been catastrophically removed from our modern experience. And so, it is to no surprise that in the introduction to Le Plongeon's *Queen Moo and the Egyptian Sphinx* we find a photography of fossil shells that accompanies the following text concerning the history and marvels of the Mayan ruins as a call for archaeological study:

> Walls covered with bas-reliefs, inscriptions and sculptures carved in marble, containing the panegyrics of rulers, the history of the nation, its cosmological traditions, the ancient religious rites and observances of its people, inviting decipherment, attract the attention of the traveler. The geological formation of its stony soil, so full of curious deposits of fossil shells of the Jurassic period its unexplored caves, supposed dwellings of spirits and elves, creatures of the fanciful and superstitious imagination of the natives; its subterraneous streams of cool and limpid water, are yet to be studied by modern geologists.

In Le Plongeon's text, the archaeological symbol confuses itself with the fossil, in a gesture that forces us to acknowledge the proximity of two contemporary nineteenth-century debates concerning the origins of historical time: those concerning both archaeology and paleontology. Just as Le Plongeon had been forced to revise the biblical theory of the original deluge in order to account for his alternative history of civilization, years before, Georges Cuvier, a French geologist born amidst the anarchy of the French Revolution and its posterior terror, had produced an alternative theory of earth's history departing from his discoveries regarding elephant fossils. Cuvier's theory, which was to eventually gain the name of *catastrophism*, ran as follows: the history of the earth has been punctuated by a series of global catastrophes – which he would later call, in the spirit of the early nineteenth century, revolutions – that had determined the present conditions of dispersal as wells as the variety of fauna and flora. Fossils were the indexical signs of such catastrophes. Namely, what Cuvier developed under the name of catastrophism was another theory for the internal dialectics of the concept of universal history: an explanation of difference that pointed towards a common ground. And so, the nineteenth century sees the emergence of a science of spectral signs – fossils, ruins, epitaphs of gone cultures – that constructs modernity as the other face of a catastrophic allegory. Photography would rise among such ruins as a technology that hinted at how within modernity, the concept of evolutionary progress, necessary for the establishment of a concept of universal history, was only able to establish itself against the background noise of a catastrophic discourse that provided a new mediation between history and nature.

Unintentionally, Augustus and Alice were writing an allegory for the tumultuous political times in which they lived. As they travelled throughout the Yucatán Peninsula, taking photographs of the inhabitants and of the ruins, the region was undergoing a civil war: the *Caste War*, as it grew to be known, consisted of a series of revolts that confronted the indigenous fraction against the population of European descent. The revolts were part of the violent aftermath that followed the Mexican War of Independence, which had inequitably distributed the land among the population, leading to the oppression of the indigenous community, to higher taxation and tougher work hours amidst the boom in production of hemp. The Caste War, spanning from 1847 to 1901, belongs to an alternative history of Mexican modernity which traces the returns of that invisible, untranslatable spectre which refuses to be reduced to the smooth economy of *universal history*: in the promised return of Quetzacoatl, the figure of *el indígena* finds the myth that establishes its repetitive struggle to redefine its place within Mexico's modernity. This history, which is itself a history of Mexico's public secret, of its catastrophic foundation as well as of its archaeological modernity, leads all the way from the arrival of Cortés to the sky masks of the *Ejército Zapatista de Liberación Nacional*. What remains at stake in this history is the negotiation of the non-modern within the enlightened project of a progressive liberal modernity. The Le Plongeons couldn't know it, but their allegories regarding an initial civil war that marked the birth of civilization – their reading of a catastrophic birth of historicity – hinted at something crucial: universal historicity entails, within its structure, the constant struggle to incorporate, without reduction, the non-modern elements of its archaeology. As Lecia Rosenthal has pointed out in her book *Mourning Modernism*, the catastrophic imaginary sketches the boundaries and limits of the capitalist project understood as a homogenous, harmonious, systematic modernity:

> Catastrophe erupts to render visible the ongoing contradictions within capitalism and its commensurating logics of systematization, homogenization, and exchange. At the margins of such systems, catastrophe designates something other to, something other than, the negative moment of an inevitable dialectic of progress and containment. Like the death drive, catastrophe points to a beyond that can never be placed either inside or outside a prior logic of integration, meaning, or futurity.[50]

'*Catastrophe erupts…*': Rosenthal's vocabulary evokes the volcanic eruption in order to highlight the topography of emergency implicit in modern historicity. It is the same volcanic rhetoric that we find, not surprisingly, in *Crack Capitalism*, the latest book of he who has been called the philosopher of the Zapatistas, John Holloway:

> The revolutionary process is a collective coming-to-eruption of stifled volcanoes. The language and thought of revolution cannot be a prose which sees volcanoes as mountains: it is necessarily a poetry, an imagination which reaches out towards unseen passions. This is not an irrational process, but it implies a different rationality, a negative rationality that starts not from the surface but from the explosive force of the repressed.[51]

The volcanic tropology present in both Rosenthal's and Holloway's texts soon shows its Freudian face: the volcanic catastrophe stands, not for any sort of interruption, but for the negative death drive which interrupts the forward-looking temporality of the pleasure principle by staging history as the eternal return of the repressed. History, seen through the spectacles of catastrophic discourse, is seen as the ongoing dialectics between progress and repetition, between the transparency of universality and the ruins of secrecy. As such, it is to no surprise that we find, within Alice Dixon's biography, a progressive politicization with respect to the claims of the indigenous and the Caste Wars, a politicization that culminates with a series of articles on the topic, paradigmatic of which is her 1893 article 'Yucatán since the Conquest' published in the *Magazine of American History*.[52] Departing from Serapio Baqueiro's 1879 *Ensayo histórico sobre las revoluciones de Yucatán desde el año 1840 hasta 1864*, Dixon attempts to construct a history of the conquest as a history of the oppression and systematic destruction of the indigenous population. In the tradition of Bartolomé de las Casas, whose *Historia de la Destrucción de las*

Indias jumpstarts the tradition of catastrophic American historiography, Dixon constructs the modern history of the Yucatán Peninsula as the ruinous history of the survival of the indigenous after the catastrophe of conquest. What is at stake, once again, is the concept of a universal history and its discontents, a history of the allegories of conquest and the instauration of an archaeological paradigm of history. Walter Benjamin once dreamt seeing, while walking through the marketplace at Weimar, an excavation: a Mexican shrine of the times of pre-animism was being extracted from the grounds of the city of Goethe, Schiller and Herder. What this re-emergence of the past within the grounds of the Enlightenment signals is precisely the archaeological modes through which modernity deals with its public secrets. Progress, as Benjamin himself would later point out, bears catastrophe as its pseudonym and works as a storm that impairs us from hitting the breaks on history. Walking amidst the tumultuous landscape of the Yucatán Peninsula, Alice Dixon must have seen, in the battles between the indigenous and the Creoles, the cryptic sign of an urgent call for an impossible universal history.

A thousand time a volcano: Dr Atl, a passion for catastrophe

'Masa piramidal – masa color de cobre oxidado, con reflejos violáceos – desnuda, áspera, terrible – bella como una joya – grande y muda como el recuerdo de una hecatombe […] La solemne montaña surge entre los montes eternamente floridos,
como el sepulcro de un muerto el día de un aniversario glorioso.'

– Dr Atl, Sinfonías del Popocateptl

With Gerardo Murillo, better known as the mythical and infamous Dr Atl – name by which the Argentine poet Leopoldo Lugones baptized him – the volcanic pyramid of Heredia displaces itself once again, in order to settle amidst the anarchic grounds of the Mexican Revolution. The figure of Dr Atl, born on 3 October 1875, traverses Mexican modernity with the impetus of the Nietzschean overman, making himself visible at each of its decisive moments with the elusiveness of his larger-than-life persona: it is hard for us to trace the continuities between the painter and the cultural politician, between the writer and the city planner, between the early anarchist and the later fascist. For Dr Atl was all of these things and many others, all of which remain clouded by the force of his self-mystification. It was of him, however, of whom José Clemente Orozco – one, alongside Diego Rivera and Álvaro Siqueiros, of the three main Mexican muralists – said the following words in his *Autobiografía*:

> He spoke to us passionately about the Sistine Chapel and about Leonardo. The great mural patinings! The immense Renaissance, something incredible and so mysterious as the pharaonic pyramids [...] In those evenings of painting apprenticeship the first artistic revolutionary outbreak appeared in México. In those nightly workshops where we heard the enthusiastic voice of Doctor Atl, the agitator, we began to suspect that all of that colonial situation was merely a trick of international merchants.[53]

Orozco beautifully wraps up his praise of Atl's incendiary rhetoric by sketching their diverting paths: 'Doctor Atl left towards the Popocatépetl, while I began exploring Mexico's worst neighbourhoods.' With such an ending Orozco provides us with a hint to that which would turn out to be the guiding thread throughout the life of this prolific and controversial man: his obsession with the symbolic landscape of the volcano which he must have painted, sketched, and even photographed more than a thousand times. In what follows I aim to read the figure of Gerardo Murillo and his problematic relationship to both the Mexican Revolution and Mexico's process of modernization, through the lens of his volcanic obsession. What arises from this kaleidoscopic view is the image of a multifaceted character whose erratic vitalism embodied the internal conflicts at the heart of the Mexican Revolution.[54] Progress at war with itself: in the erratic pilgrimage of Dr Atl, in that voyage that took him throughout Europe and back to a Mexico in the midst of a war that would bring him to the bridge of death, then to the United States and later again to Europe, all the way to his final return to Mexico, we find the image of a man at war with that same progressivism which in his early years he helped foster. His mystical obsession with the figure of the volcano then becomes a symptom of the impasses of a revolution whose claim to modernity veiled the necessity to come to terms with its spectral past. Like Nietzsche, Murillo – through his ever dislocated and anarchic displacement – becomes symptomatic of an untimely modernity at battle with the ghosts of its founding violence. In his works, the dialectic of the Enlightenment becomes explosive and erratic, always at the verge of danger and contradiction.

At the very turn of the century, on 2 June 1897, a 22-year-old Gerardo Murillo boarded in Veracruz the steamer *Seguraca* on his way to New York. Seventeen days later, after an impactful visit to the *Metropolitan Museum*, a similar boat would take him from New York to Europe, the continent that would serve to consolidate his sentimental education. Paris, Venice, Rome: the journey would expose the aspiring artist both to the great classical works and to the emerging political and aesthetic tendencies of the European fin-de-siècle. With the help of Latin American poets of the calibre of Rubén Darío and Leopoldo Lugones, Murillo would discover the possibilities of modernism without failing to notice, at the same time, the renaissance frescoes of Raphael and Michelangelo, frescoes in which he would find an inspiration for his so-important later adoption of muralism. He would, however, as Olga Sáenz has explored in her book *El Símbolo y la Acción*, also come in contact with the boiling political atmosphere of the Italian artistic circles at the turn of the century. From this early engagement with Italian socialism, with the works of Enrico Ferri and the group that surrounded the publication of *Avanti*, Murillo would grasp the political tension at the centre of the modernist project. One must not forget that it was, as Sáenz points out, from Italian socialism that the two main opposing political tendencies of communism and fascism would later spring. This double, ambivalent tradition would haunt Dr Atl throughout his career. One must remember, also, that the Italy of the turn of the century is the Italy of Marinetti and the futurists, with their almost mystical aesthetization of war and technology. Infected with the Janus faced tradition of Italian socialism, fascinated with the tradition of renaissance frescoes, Murillo returns in 1803 to Mexico. At the outset of the Mexican Revolution, Murillo takes a position as professor of arts in the *Escuela Nacional del Bellas Artes*. From there he will spread with volcanic fervour the teachings of his Italian masters to his students, three of which would later gain a particular place within Mexican history: José Clemente Orozco, Diego Rivera and David Alvaro Siqueiros. At the very outset of the Mexican Revolution, in the years preceding the events of 1810, Dr Atl begins to sketch the problem that will haunt him throughout his life: that of founding a civilization that would remain rooted in the spirit. In other words, he obsessed with a civilization that would remain faithful to the initial catastrophe that gave it rise. It is, as we shall soon see, the problem of the volcanic pyramid, as much as it is that of the cryptic kernel at the heart of the modernist project. With the problem of this spirited civilization in mind, Dr Atl will traverse the anarchic years of the revolution, becoming in turn one of its most effervescent characters. From his initial alliance to the government of Venustiano Carranza to his later involvement with the work of 'national reconstruction' staged by the government of Álvaro Obregón, Dr Atl would remain faithful to his initial civilizing concern. The question for him would remain: how to, amidst the ruins of the revolution, produce a civilizing regime of progress that would not remove from the individual that spirit that linked him with the universal soul? It would be this civilizing project – this project of a spirited universalism – that would later gain for him the density of a symbol: that of the volcano. In *Sinfonías del Popocatepetl*, a beautiful book of poetic prose published in 1921, we can read how Dr Atl weaves the volcano into what he sees as the epic of universal progress:

> Just like, among the works of humans there appear step by step throughout history certain superior and unmistakable ones, just like the thought of Confucius, the religious ideal of Hinduism, Darwin's theory, the laws of Kepler or Newton, the works of Michaelangelo, just like that, over the upheavals of the earth there stand with incomparable beauty and contempt, the great volcanos of México.[55]

Confucius, Darwin, Kepler and Michaengelo: amidst the revolution's programme to reconstruct a national identity, Dr Atl attempts to weave Mexico's history into the universal history of the artistic spirit. Within this historiographical project, the volcano will come to symbolize both the possibility of the great Mexican historical deed and the memory of its founding catastrophe. In this sense, Murillo's project would remain close to that other great cultural promoter of the Obregón administration, José Vasconcelos. In fact, both would embrace a mystical spiritism that would lead them to delve into the myth of Atlantis, in which they would both see the possibility of civilization emerging from catastrophe. Murillo, who throughout his life claimed to have been born in Atlantis, would later publish a book called *Un Grito en la Atlántida*. Vasconcelos's 1925 *La Raza Cósmica* would delve into the myth of Atlantis in order to project upon it his dreams of a universal history.[56] For Dr Atl, as it becomes evident from his book *Sinfonías del Popocatépetl*, this myth of a catastrophic original past would take the symbol of the volcano as its basis. The volcano would become the symbol for a civilization always in battle with progress:

> But the forces of the past kept stalking us and artfully they threw themselves against Civilization, instantly paralyzing the march of progress, destroying lives, annihilating wills and covering the luminous route with inconmeasurable errors and millions of cadavers. It was my task to fight in the same palestra where for centuries barbaric nude men had fought against even more barbaric men dressed in iron and sackcloathes.[57]

'A great and luminous stone fell from the sky, awakening in civilized man an ancestral terror': for Gerardo Murillo, the possibility of universal progress is always threatened by the memory of an ancestral catastrophe. This dialectic is, and this is the point that must be highlighted, intrinsic to modernity itself. The Mexican Revolution was such a catastrophic event, an event that left, in the mind of Murillo, the always imminent sense of an upcoming catastrophe, the Nietzschean sense of living at the end of times and yet simultaneously forming part of the beginning of a new, post-historical, utopian time: 'Above the ruins and the sepulchers plants bloom and animals live – above the tomb, mausoleum of earth's energy, the symphonies of the earth's energy vibrate with the vivifying powers of nature.'[58] We are, once again, reminded of the works of Augustus Le Plongeon and Alice Dixon, as well as of that so often repeated expression of theirs: 'We discovered a mound...' Dr. Atl's mountain always bears within itself the possibility of catastrophe, the possibility of a volcano:

> The mountain has reawakened. Millions of years it slept in deadly silence, millions of years the wind stroke against it, millions of years the forces of nature tried to destroy it, closing its mouth, eating its vertebrae, shaking its formidable body, ripping its lips out of the vibrant and fulminant eloquence it once had... Nothing is old nor dead: at the end of destruction there is life.[59]

'Nothing is old, nor is it dead: at the end of destruction there is life': working within the tradition of José María Heredia, Murillo envisions the latency of the volcano as the imminent possibility of what, following Walter Benjamin, one could call divine violence. That is to say, the radical violence that would final redeem history by doing justice to its past injustices. Moreover, the volcano is portrayed as a literary mouth, whose lips quote a forgotten past: the volcano quotes Mexico's past history in an attempt to bring forth a new life.

One can imagine then the excitement that Dr Atl must have felt the day that he heard from a peasant that from the hills of Quitzocho a volcano had been born. As Dr Atl himself recounts in his idiosyncratic third person autobiographical voice, 'In 1942 the Paricutín emerged. It was logical that the Dr. threw himself against it, a bad comparison perhaps, like a hawk upon a pigeon.' This project would cost Murillo a leg, but in its megalomaniac bet on obsession, we find the passion of a man devoted to thinking emergency as a historical category.

The testimony of Dr Atl's residency as a witness of the Paricutín's birth is narrated, both visually and narratively, in his book *Como Nace y Crece un Volcán: El Paricutín*.[60] After Dionisio Pulido, a peasant of the region, spotted a column of smoke, he informed the authorities at the Municipality of San Juan Parangaricutiro. Murillo must have heard the news quickly, for his account begins a couple of hours after, with the volcanic cone already at a height of 10 metres already 'flaunting a single mouth in its small crater.'[61] For the next months, Dr Atl camped near the volcano, spending his hours documenting the growth of that which he came to call the volcano's 'signos fulgurantes', its fulgurant signs. As he states, he thought himself as a witness to the formation of a new world: 'I felt like I was witnessing the birth of a world.'[62] And so, the book abounds in repetitions: repetitive narratives of the volcanoes descriptions as well as repetitive sketches of the volcano itself. As if he were some sort of Mexican Zarathustra, Dr Atl would stay in the proximities of the forming volcano until 1949, when he would lose a leg as a consequence of the dangerous contact with the volcano's gases. By then he had sketched and drawn the volcano more than a thousand times. The volcano had become the greatest of his obsessions. Murillo had delved into a category that was to be central to modernity: that of emergency.[63] The violent emergence of the volcano amidst the Mexican landscape could be read as a *fulgurant sign* for the Mexican Revolution itself. The revolution had also sprung out of that subterranean layer of discontent that marked the post-colonial period of Mexican independence. From the skirts of that mountain that had suddenly taken a catastrophic face, Atl would sketch the volcano with the terrible patience of he who understands that the project of modernity runs the risk of falling to the temptation of an easy future. Contrary to his fellow revolutionaries, who merely saw in the revolution an open future, a place of immanence and action, Dr Atl – always faithful to his *fin-de-siècle* mysticism – would understand that the dialectic of the sublime that runs the motors of modernity is in itself a tension between two main categories: that of action and that of contemplation, that of progress and that of catastrophe. It is as a dialogue between these two historical categories, between action and contemplation, between immanence and transcendence, that we should try to read a project like Dr Atl's *Como Nace y Crece un Volcán: El Paricutín*. Repetition, one could then say, is precisely the category that knots together action and contemplation, the historical category from which the modern dialectic can be understood in its Janus-faced reality. The act of repeating, perhaps the fundamental political act, lies in a plane that suspends the line of naïve progressivism, puts a break to the run of history and forces us to put the relationship between future and past in quotes. The image of the volcano's crater as a mouth then takes on a different meaning. The volcano becomes a pyramid, a tombstone for quoting a past that suddenly becomes terribly present: 'Like the tomb, the enormous demolished mountain, lies silent above the valleys which the sun has made drowsy; against the blue sky it opens its gnawed and mute crater.'⁶⁴ However, as Murillo so clearly knew, at the end of destruction is life. For him it was clear that he was accomplishing one of his lifelong dreams: that of seeing the construction of a new world, of a new universe, out of the ruins of the old one.

Late in his life Dr Atl would be granted, for one last time, the possibility of sketching such a utopic rebirth of civilization. It was, however, a project that had been fermenting for a long time. Already in 1912, during his stay in Paris, we find in Murillo the will to envision a utopic city where civilization could emerge not by a democratic vision, but rather by a will of universality: 'There is only way to create our civilization: constructing a city of universal culture, where we could then condense the mental potential of humans, directing it not so much towards the common wellbeing, but rather towards the conquest of the Universe, which should be the immediate goal of human progress.'⁶⁵ Born, as he always claimed, in Atlantis, Murillo found himself attracted, from very early on, to the idea of constructing the new Atlantis: the city of universal culture. In him the idea of catastrophe – with the volcanic pyramid as its main symbol and Atlantis as its mythical counterpart – was always linked with the idea of a Nietzschean rebirth. More than forty years after its initial conception, sparked by Murillo's return to Paris, the idea would revive under the name of *Olinka*: the utopian city that, like Borges's aleph, would condense the universe's intelligence.⁶⁶ This time the idea would take off. With the help of Agustín Yáñez, governor of Jalisco, Atl would begin his sketches for *Olinka*, a city which he first envisioned in the Valle de Pihuamo, amidst his two beloved volcanoes, Popocatepetl and Itzaccihuatl, but which soon had to be moved to the Sierra of Saint Catarina, 20 kilometres away from Mexico City. With this project in mind Dr Atl established, in 1952, the *Centro Internacional de la Cultura*, an institute that aimed at gathering the universal intelligentsia. In his essay 'Un Centro Internacional de la Cultura,' the Centre is described as a solution to the problems of modernity's positivism. Murillo begins by claiming that 'the prodigious evolution of the sciences has deorganized the ancestral structure of the world' just in order to call for a 'organizing center, a center of intellectual organization is needed in order to direct evolution towards a new goal. That new goal is the conquest of the Universe'.⁶⁷ Something very profound is then at stake in that megalomaniac project called *Olinka* – something that bridges continents and that points to the very heart of the question regarding the modernity's conception of historical time. *Olinka* discloses the insights of a man who, as both actor and thinker, was able to see –

like Nietzsche before him – the tensions inherent to the historiographical project of modernity. Dr Atl remains, to this day, the embodiment of such tensions, the embodiment of a volcanic modernity, with its effervescence and its dangers, with the suspension of chronological time in favour of another time, a messianic time that spoke in fulgurant signs.

With Dr Atl, Heredia's volcanic pyramid, alongside its criticism of modernity, enters the twentieth century and re-establishes from there its criticism of enlightened progress. In doing so, it also showcases the dangers that from the very get go – like in the case of Heredia himself – threatened to subsume the once radical potential of the symbol into a conservative project of right-wing nationalism. Following Adorno and Horkheimer's intuition – 'Myth is already enlightenment, and enlightenment reverts to mythology' – as it had been sketched in their 1947 book *Dialectic of the Enlightenment*, Dr Atl's volcanic pyramid runs the risk of turning into a fascist mythologizing of war in the name of national purity.[68] As I have mentioned, Dr Atl emerged as an artist in the context of the Italian artistic circles of the early twentieth century, amidst the same ideas which later led artists like the futurist Marinetti to espouse Mussolini's fascism. It took longer for Dr Atl to espouse these ideals but, in the context of the Second World War, and with the government of Lázaro Cárdenas pressing for the secularization of schools and the adoption of what some called a communist agenda, Gerardo Murillo finally gave in to the fascist ideas that had begun to spread throughout Mexican Society. Mimicking the actions and ideals of fascist groups like the Acción Revolucionaria Mexicanista or the Sinarquistas, Dr Atl began publishing fascist-espousing writings in a number of newspapers in which he criticized what he called Cárdenas' espousal of Judaic Marxism. In its criticism of enlightened modernity, Murillo's volcanic thought had completed the arch prophesized by the members of the Frankfurt school: it had turned critique into mythology. His initial politicization of aesthetics had been replaced by an aestheticization of violence that reminds us of Walter Benjamin's own reading of Italian futurism's fascism, while foreshadowing the dangers that would haunt the volcanic pyramid's itinerary throughout the twentieth century.

Aftershock

Malcolm Lowry's *Under the Volcano*: On clouds, telegraphs and volcanoes

In 1925, a young Jose María Heredia begins his poetic homage to the Egyptian Pyramid with the following verses: 'Artificial mountain, great remnant, sublime and power structure, watchtower upon the desert, great throne for desolation!' As I have tried to show in the preceding pages, Heredia's notion of the volcanic pyramid as a *great remnant*, as an artificial mountain of sublime yet ruinous stature, traverses Mexican history sketching the paradoxical crossroads of its archaeological modernity. Nature, culture and history intersect under the figure of that double-faced symbol which is both mountain and crypt, volcano and pyramid. In 1920, almost a century after Heredia writes his poem in the aftermath of Mexico's independence, the Mexican photographer Manuel Álvarez Bravo, working in the aftermath of the Mexican Revolution, concretizes Heredia's words in a photographic piece that plays with the spectator's expectations. 'Arena y Pinitos' presents us with a pictorial representation of the Popocatepetl amidst pine trees, a familiar view to any viewer accustomed to the pictorialist landscapes of Hugo Brehme's photography.[69] In fact, Brehme had, during those years, produced a photograph of the Popocatepetl amidst the trees that comes quite close to Álvarez Bravo's portrayal of the snowy mountain. A second look at the photograph, combined with a reading of its title, however, discloses the photograph as a perfectly executed trick: Álvarez Bravo's camera has tricked us into believing that the close-up to an artificial setup of sand and small branches is actually the Popocatepetl. The pictorialist illusion of a *natural* representation has been broken by a gesture that confounds nature and technology, repeating the image but displacing its content, forcing us to account for the volcano under Heredia's terms: there is nothing there but a *resto tremendo*, a reflection upon artificiality and naturality, a mount of sand that looks as if it were a volcano. We are then reminded of Heredia's poem to the Popocatepetl: 'You, the one crowned with snow/who rises above Anahuac with your great forehead/you of the Indian people/feared once and then venerated,/Great Popocatepetl, hear kindly/the humble greeting/that my tremulous lips pronounce.' Álvarez Bravo's piece, this orientalist bonsai-like production, *quotes* nature and in quoting it, discloses its status as an artificial symbol in constant transit. Between nature and technology, between nature and history, between antiquity and modernity, the volcano becomes for Álvarez Bravo the ruinous symbol for a poetics that highlights the latency of the archaic within the modern.

Álvarez Bravo, however, was not the only artist working in the 1920s interested in redefining, reframing and rethinking the symbols of Mexican history. In the wake of the Mexican Revolution, the first of its kind in Latin America, intellectuals, artists and writers, guided by José Vasconcelos's programme of cultural revolution, were busy rewriting the symbolic history of Mexican modernity vis-à-vis the shaky interwar landscape of global politics. This new wave of national re-imagination was not limited to Mexicans but rather included a series of international figures whose fascination with the country of Rivera and Siqueiros, as well as with its booming revolutionary history, would lead them to cross the Atlantic in search for inspiration or safety. From André Breton to Antonin Artaud, from Trotsky to Eisenstein, the list of public figures that visited Mexico in the aftermath of its 1910 Revolution remains a testimony to its cultural effervescence.[70] Each of them contributed, in their own manner, to the redefinition of national history that was happening in the aftermath of Porfirio Díaz's fall. Few, however, did so in such a striking manner as the British writer Malcolm Lowry, whose modernist novel *Under the Volcano*, published in 1947, remains to this date – in its portrayal of the famous Day of the Dead – a testament to many of the symbols of Mexican history. Central among them, as the novel's title suggests, would be that of the volcano. Inscribing Heredia's symbol within the context of the post-revolutionary landscape, Lowry's novel traces once again the figure of the volcanic pyramid as it appears against the shaky context of the Second World War as a sign of impending catastrophe: 'Popocatepetl loomed, pyramidal, to their right, one side beautifully curved as a woman's breast, the other precipitous, jagged, ferocious. Cloud drifts were massing again, high-piled, behind it. Iztaccihuatl appeared.'[71] A sign of both natural beauty and historical violence, the volcano appears once and again, within the novel, as both a silent witness and a latent omen of the catastrophic fate of the protagonist: 'The old bandstand stood empty, the equestrian statue of the turbulent Huerta rode under the nutant trees wild-eyed evermore, gazing over the valley beyond which, as if nothing had happened and it was November 1936, and not November 1938, rose, eternally, her volcanoes, hear beautiful, beautiful volcanos.'[72] Suspending time, unearthing the past, the two volcanoes of the novel – the Popocatepetl and the Iztaccihuatl – point towards the latency of violence inscribed within a political landscape marked by the spectres of history.

This aftershock attempts, then, to read Lowry's *Under the Volcano* against the preceding reflections concerning repetition and progress, secrecy and symbols, modernity and archaeology, clouds and transparency, addiction and repetition. Reading Lowry's masterpiece alongside the works of José María Heredia, Alice Dixon, Augustus Le Plongeon and Dr Atl, while simultaneously placing it in discussion with Octavio Paz's discussion of Mexican modernity as it appears in his 1968 critical essay *Crítica de la Pirámide*, is like placing Álvarez Bravo's photograph next to Brehme's: the artificiality of the volcanic pyramid as symbol comes forth, allowing us to understand how Mexican modernity has consciously attempted to read itself through the spectral violence inscribed within one of its foundational landscapes, while also pointing to the imminent dangers which – as we have seen from the cases of Heredia and Dr Atl – plague this particular critique of progressivism as its negative shadow, marking the crystal frontier where its call for past justice risks turning into a conservative melancholia.

Under the Volcano is, from the very beginning, a novel marked by the deathly logic of spectrality, repetition and addiction. Towards the sunset of the *Día de los Muertos*, November 1939, two men sit drinking anís on the main terrace of the *Hotel Casino La Selva*, the famous hotel that hosted Dr Atl for many years, reminiscing about an event that had taken place exactly one year before: the fateful and inevitable descent of ex-consul Geoffrey Firmin into the depths of alcoholism in front of the impotent gaze of his former wife and his younger brother. As Mr Jacques Laurelle and Dr Arturo Díaz Vigil remember the Consul's deathly last pilgrimage, a series of images begin to punctuate the landscape as a prophecy of what is to come. From the desolate terrace of the *Hotel Casino La Selva*, amidst the murals of Dr Atl and Diego Rivera, the narrative begins to draw the rhombus that will punctuate the landscape of the novel, its catastrophic topology and its ruinous logic. The ruins of Maximilian's summer villa, immersed in their spectral aura, stand as a catastrophic allegory of what had been the fate of the transposition of the glory of Europe to Mexico's modern landscape. Like the Archduke Maximilian Von Habsburg before him, offered – as part of Napoleon III's monarchic conspiracy – the throne of Mexico just to suffer trial and death at the hands of the troops of Benito Juárez, the Consul's story is one of disappearance amidst Mexico's archaeological modernity. A repetition of Maximilian's founding disappearance, *Under the Volcano* is essentially an exercise in the conjuring of ghosts, as the ruinous landscape of Maximilian's Palace shows:

> The broken pink pillars, in the half-light, might have been waiting to fall down on him: the pool, covered with green scum, its steps torn away and hanging by one rotting clamp, to close over his head [...] France, even in Austrian guise, should not transfer itself to Mexico, he thought [...] Ghosts. Ghosts, as at the Casino, certainly lived here. And a ghost still said: 'It is our destiny to come here Carlota. Look at this rolling glorious country, its valleys, its volcanoes.'[73]

The spectral landscape of Maximilian's Borda Gardens summer residence foreshadows the multiple ghosts that will traverse the novel. This is, however, a novel of ghosts amidst a modern landscape, as the second point in the rhombus is quick to highlight. Beyond the ruins of Maximilian's Palace, beyond the ghosts that seem to inhabit the *Hotel Casino la Selva*, stands the American Highway as another route of escape and disappearance as the sign of a landscape marked by a possible 'return to civilization' which seems, however, to be precluded for the Consul. Symbol for progressivism and linearity, the highway instantiates one of the constant concerns against which the novel stages its plot. The view of modernity as a linear road eventually gets lost amidst the spiralling curves of Mexico's landscape: 'A fine American-style highway leads in from the north but is lost in its narrow streets and comes out of a goat track.'[74] And so, just like the highway stands both for an impossible return to civilization and for the derailment of modernity, the novel abounds with images of misdirected communications: telegraph wires that lead nowhere, letters that never reach their addressee, missed trains and misunderstood telegrams. A logic of spectrality, repetition and melancholia – a logic of death – stages here its battle against the progressive logic of the highway, its speed and its teleology. It is this battle between progress and delay, between the logic of return and that of transit, which gets embodied in the phrase which punctuates the narrative over and over: 'A corpse will be transported by express.'[75] The novel is, as the phrase suggests, the story of an incomplete and delayed delivery of a death foretold: the Consul's journey towards his deathly fate is, like his strayed letters, like the telegraph wires that errantly punctuate its narrative, a spiralling path that refuses to sober up. Following Esther Gabara, we could then claim that *Under the Volcano* traces, already at the level of landscape, the paradoxes of Mexico's 'errant modernism'.[76] One must not forget, as Lowry was quick to point out, that the model for the novel was Dante's *Inferno*: the figure of the circle, not to say the spiral, is therefore here placed in battle with the orderly and speedy straight line. Against the two first points – Maximilian's Palace and the American Highway – a third point comes to punctuate the landscape not only as the pulsating background against which the events take place, but also as that which determines the logic of their eventuality: the presence of the two volcanoes, Popocatepetl and Ixtaccihuatl, distinct as in the paintings of Dr Atl, marks the landscape with a sense of latent imminence that refuses, however, to surrender to the logic of cause and effect. Instead, like the alcoholic Consul, losing himself between drinks, never knowing which one was the first and which one the last, the volcanoes tower above the scenery, underlining the threshold topology of *in-betweenness*, latency and suspense that marks the eventual logic of the narrative:

> Ixtacihuatl had slipped out of sight but as, descending they circled round and round, Popocatepetl slipped in and out of view continually, never appearing the same twice, now far away, then vastly near at hand, incalculably distant at one moment, at the next looming round the corner with its splendid thickness of sloping fields, valleys, timber, its summit swept by clouds, slashed by hail and snow.[77]

The logic through which the two volcanoes slip in and out of sight, escaping the frame and then re-entering, dancing in between the clouds, delineates the clouded locus of an archaeological temporality that is always in transit but which never fully arrives. '*A corpse will be transported by express*': everything in this novel is always in transit but never fully arrives, constantly about to erupt but always in need for something else, like the alcoholic who is never set on merely being drunk but who searches, in a logic of repetition that is also that of death, for the next drink that will finally settle his shaky hands.

And so, it is within the coordinates of this catastrophic rhombus punctuated by the Hotel Casino La Selva, Maximilian's Palace, the American Highway and the two volcanoes that *Under the Volcano* sets off as the retelling of the story of a disappearance: that of European 'civilization' within Mexico's archaeological modernity, that of the Consul upon the anarchic landscape of post-revolutionary Mexico. Inscribed always in relationship to this landscape, which following Jens Anderman we could perhaps call a landscape in trance marked as it is by an errant voyage, the story told in *Under the Volcano* stages world history against what it sees as the imminent catastrophe of Mexican history.[78] It is a novel about the impossibility of reaching a destination, a tragedy about the incapacity to act.

As such, its ending, or lack of ending, is telling: the Consul, completely drunk, is confronted by a group of extreme right wing *sinarquistas*, who accuse him of being a spy and question him regarding an Indian that has been left to die in mid-road. The Consul, feeling guilty about his incapacity to save the dying Indian, answers enigmatically:

> Blackstone, he answered gravely, and indeed, he asked himself, accepting another mescal, had he not and with a vengeance come to live among the Indians? The only trouble was one was very much afraid these particular Indians might turn out to be people with ideas too. 'William Blackstone.' [...]
> 'You are Juden?' the first policeman demanded.
> 'No, just Blackstone.'[79]

Declaring himself to be William Blackstone – in reference to the sixteenth-century Englishman who moved to the Charles River, near present-day Boston, and decided to live in solitude among the Indians – the Consul provides the fascist group with the final misunderstanding that will eventually lead to his tragic death in a gesture that seems to have been presaged throughout the entire novel. Indeed, throughout *Under the Volcano*, the Consul's tragic path towards death seems to be staged against the catastrophe of another tragedy: the tragedy of Mexican history.

Like *Under the Volcano*, Octavio Paz's 1968 essay *Critique of the Pyramid*, written amidst the aftermath of the Tlatelolco Massacre, reads as an attempt to decipher Mexico's public secret. Paz begins the essay by calling forth the tradition whose logic we have tried to deconstruct throughout this chapter: that which assigns a double face, and with it a double geology, to Mexican history. Alongside the official history, Paz points to that invisible history of the *other* Mexico, which Guillermo Bonfil Batalla – in the context of the catastrophic aftermath of the 1985 Earthquake – would later call the *México Profundo*: the subterranean history of the 'underdeveloped' Mexico which refuses to merge into the modern one, and which returns, instead, as its spectral double. This figure is, as Paz is quick to admit, as much geological as it is spectral:

> For me the expression 'the other México' invokes a reality that is made up of different strata and that alternately folds in on itself and unfolds, hides itself and reveals itself. If man is double or triple, so are civilizations and societies. Each people carries on a dialogue with an invisible colloquist who is, at one and the same time, itself and the other, its double. Its double? Which is the original and which is the phantasm?[80]

Like the ghosts that meander around Maximilian's Palace, the ghosts of this invisible *other* Mexico force time to delay its progress and to repeat itself as a cryptic text regarding history and power. Forced to find a figure that embodies Mexico's double history, Paz then decides to draw Mexico's history as the dialectic between crypt and exposure, between invisible history and visible history, present in the truncated pyramid: 'The geography of Mexico spreads out in a pyramidal form as if there existed a secret but evident relation between natural space and symbolic geometry and between the later and what I have called our invisible history.'[81] The pyramid comes to designate the locus of a struggle to control the public secret that re-emerges once and again throughout Mexican history: the known but repressed history of inequality and racism that since the nineteenth century, and even the Conquest, has driven Mexican modernity forward, dragging with it a history of unredeemed violence. Founded upon the millenarian pact between knowledge, power and secrecy, the pyramid sketches the symptoms of a society whose history contains, latent within itself, a repressed counter-history that must be worked through. It is in this way that he proceeds to read the national history that is portrayed in the *National Museum of Anthropology* in Chapultepec. The history of Mesoamerican Mexico is told, Paz argues, in the broken symbols that adorn the Museum's walls, unfolding a history that hides, however, a saga of repressions and power abuse: 'If México's visible history is the symbolic script of its invisible history and if both are the expression, reiteration, and metaphor – on different levels of reality – of certain repressed and submerged monuments, it is evident that in this museum we can find, even though in dispersed fragments, the elements that can serve us to reconstruct the figure we seek.'[82] The archaeological reconstruction that Paz calls forth, this work of translation that inevitably reminds us of Augustus Le Plongeon's work with the *Troano Codax*, brings critique, which Paz himself calls 'crítica', closer than ever to psychoanalysis, and reminds us that the temporality of the archaeological symbol is dual: its Janus-faced reality points both to the future and to the past, in a spiral that refuses to close, but that drags forward with that which, according to Hegel, one could call the spectral labour of the negative. Having read the aporia of Mexican modernity correctly, the problem with Paz's account is that – like Heredia or Dr Atl before him – he ends up naturalizing and mythologizing this power structure. As Bruno Bosteels has explored, Paz ends up tracing this pyramidal structure of power as the inescapable labyrinth that condemns us to experience Mexican history through the lens of a melancholic conservatism:

While he awaits this grand day, the poet continues to unwrite the written and the spectator remains, without a genuine event, as a reminder of that which has already occurred or has yet to occur. The ghost or phantasm is not the point of departure for a process of subjective intervention, but only the unconscious kernel of the whole politico-juridical structure of the Mexican nation-state. Its apparition uncovers the trauma of a constitutive otherness that we must recognize, without exceeding the frame of this structure or the logic of recognition itself. What is more, it does not remit us to the here and now of actual circumstances but to an eternal present, latent in all of Mexican history. The analysis is ultimately geared toward the hidden fixity of a mythical archetypal recurrence.[83]

As Bosteels explains, in the act of mythologizing the pyramid as the unconscious kernel of the politico-juridical structure, Paz ends up naturalizing its eternal recurrence, missing in turn the opportunity to produce a truly political event with respect to which new radical subjectivities would emerge, capable of blasting open the status quo of Mexican politics. Instead, in a gesture that sends us back directly to *Under the Volcano*, Mexican history is perceived, under the tragic rubric of the eternal return of the same, as the naturalization of the stifled volcanoes that punctuate the landscape: 'Here it was, still cluttered up with large grey loose stones, full of the same lunar potholes, and in that well-known state of frozen eruption that resembled repair but which in fact only testified facetiously to the continued deadlock between the Municipality and the property owners here over its maintenance.'[84] As frozen eruption, Paz's pyramid mimics the incapacity of Mexican modernity to respond to the call of its spectral past, instantiated within the novel first by the old women's faces of indolence in the face of the Indian's suffering and then by the Consul's tragic incapacity to first save the dying man, and later to save himself. The Consul's incapacity to escape his tragic fate mirrors Paz's incapacity to see beyond the violent fixity of the Mexican eternal present of inequality. Against this mythical fixity, Bostells suggests that 'instead of merely recognizing the specter, or even standing in awe of the ghost with a properly messianic or visionary outlook, the task would be to traverse the fantasy. Such would be the utopia of a radical emancipatory politics.'[85] In a way, as I will now try to explore, in its portrayal of the Consul's tragedy and its mirror image of Mexican modernity, *Under the Volcano* allows the reader to perform this act of traversing the fantasy, opening in turn the space for an act of radical emancipatory politics.

And so, if we are to read *Under the Volcano* as a proper *travesía*, as the political act of traversing the Consul's and Mexico's modern fantasy, we must perhaps begin by locating its sites of expression. And so, like the promised return of Quetzacoatl, we find, within the pages of the novel, a horse that appears once and again, three times to be precise, with the stubbornness of that tragic secrecy which structures the Consul's otherwise spiralling descent into hell. Conrad Aiken, he who was to be perhaps the only lasting friend of Lowry during his drunken days, he who was to write himself a book about Mexico, *A Heart for the Gods of México*, was the first to notice what he called the *horse theme*. Indeed, with the precision of a symbol, the horse appears from the very start as the figure of a man lead astray, overwhelmed by his passions, incapable of walking in a straight line. Walking back to his house from the *Hotel Casino la Selva*, Jacques Laurelle runs into a drunk horseman:

> The rider of the horse was so drunk he was sprawling all over his mount, his stirrups lost, a feat in itself considering their size, and barely managing to hold on by the reins [...] this too, he thought suddenly, this maniacal vision of senseless frenzy, but controlled, not quite uncontrolled, somehow almost admirable, this too, obscurely, was the Consul.[86]

Even before meeting the Consul, the narrative has already constructed the symbol through which we can understand him: this horse, also a means of transport, incapable of reaching its destination, precisely because the source of agency, the horseman, is incapable of directing it. Like the telegraph poles, or the letters, the horse motif is more an interruption than a delivery. He interrupts Laurelle's walk only to produce the deja vu which will send the narrative one year back to the fateful day of November 1937. Next time we meet the horse he is already stained with the colour of death: he is calmly chewing on the convolvulus in the hedge, innocently standing next to the body of the dying Indian man of whose death the Consul will be erroneously deemed responsible by the *sinarquistas*. The horse returns with the force of death, tattooed with a mysterious number seven on his buttock, only to remind us that what is here at stake is the economy of *the public secret* and its impossible articulation. Like the pariah dogs that follow the Consul, the recurring presence of the horse presages the Consul's tragic destiny. Interestingly, this second appearance of the horse coincides with the crucial event of the novel, the Consul's incapacity to save the Indian.

The horse remains the figure for the impossible return of both the missed opportunity and the incapacity of the Consul to fulfil his diplomatic role: a figure for the untranslatable otherness of the Indian. This is a moment of absolute negativity within the narrative which, precisely because of it, drives the story forward. As such, when the horse reappears for a third time, this time at the very end of the novel, it is under the sign of death and repetition, a figure of an untameable passion that is once again linked to the figure of the dying Indian. The horse comes back, passionately and fatefully, in order to mark Yvonne's death with the sign of catastrophe:

> She heard the wind and the rain rushing through the forest and saw the tremors of lighting shuddering through the heavens and the horse – great God, the horse – and would this scene repeat itself endlessly and for ever? – the horse, rearing, poised over here, petrified in mid-air, a statue, somebody was sitting in the statue, it was Yvonne Griffin, no, it was the statue of Huerta, the drunkard, the murderer, it was the Consul, or it was a mechanical horse on the merry-go-around.[87]

This delirious passage, in which monumental history confuses itself with a certain technology of death – Huerta's statue next to the circular motion of the merry-go-around – encrypts the tragedy behind it: the horse, in its violent act of fleeing the thunderstorm, has killed the Consul's wife. The horse's path, however, doesn't stop there. Ignorant of Yvonne's violent death the Consul runs into the horse by the cantina: 'He could mistake by now neither the number seven branded on the rump nor the leather saddle charactered in that fashion. It was the Indian's horse, the horse of the man he'd first seen today riding it singing into the sunlit word, the abandoned, left dying by the roadside.'[88] The horse returns not only to put an end to it all, a catastrophic end under a clouded sky, but also to put history under the sign of secrecy and conspiracy: it is only then, as he stands by the horse, guilty of not having acted, of having left the Indian man to die by the roadside, that the *sinarquistas* arrive. It is the moment of conspiracy. Confronted with the questions regarding his identity, the Consul refers to himself as a writer, only to be accused – in a memorable linguistic twist – of being a spy: 'You are no a de wrider, you are de espider, and we shoota de espiders in Mejico.'[89] Writers, spiders and spies: the Consul has, without knowing it, immersed himself in the secret life of Mexican politics. He has become a part of the negotiation regarding that *public secret* which dislocates temporality, derailing communication and imposing the logic of repetition and difference. Interrogated regarding his name, the Consul replies with the name of his secret desire: '"Blackstone," he answered gravely, and indeed, he asked himself, accepting another mescal, had he not and with a vengeance come to live among the Indians? William Blackstone.'[90] Lost in this forest where modern politics coexists with the image of another, deeper Mexico, the Consul accepts his fate as he approaches the horse. He is then confronted, just as he is shot to death, with the image of the volcanoes towering over the landscape:

> The Chief of Rostrums pushed the Consul back out of the light, took two steps forward and fired. Lightning flashed like an inchoworm going down the sky and the Consul, reeling, saw above him for a moment the shape of Popocatepetl, plumed with emerald snow and drenched with brilliance. Thunderclaps crashed on the mountains then at hand. Released, the horse reared, tossing its head, it wheeled round and plunged neighing into the forest.[91]

An ending can come, but only under the apocalyptic image of catastrophe, when the subjective world of the Consul gets projected into the landscape of volcanoes as the expression not only of his tragedy, but of the tragedy of Mexican modernity. The linguistic displacement that confuses writers, spiders and spies proves not to be fortuitous. The Consul *writes* his death, he *quotes* history, with a certain passion for secrecy. By refusing to disclose his identity, by misrepresenting himself as William Blackstone, the Consul gives himself up to the logic of secrecy of which he is accused and, like so many before him, disappears amidst Mexico's archaeological modernity. '*Somebody threw a dead dog after him down the ravine*': the novel's final words mark the end under the sign, not of arrival, but of disappearance.[92]

'*You are no a de wrider, you are de espider, and we shoota de espiders in Mejico*': confronted with death and conspiracy, the Consul declares himself a writer. This movement, however, doesn't come out of the blue. Throughout the novel, it is hinted that the Consul has been writing a book about the myth of Atlantis, about secret mysteries and occult sciences. Early on in the novel, Jacques Laurelle remembers, as he walks past the bridge, the moment in which the Consul had disclosed to him his secret project: 'It was on this bridge that the Consul had once suggested to him to make a film about Atlantis. Yes, leaning over, just like this, drunk but collected, coherent, a little mad, a little impatient – it was one of those occasions when the Consul had drunk himself sober – he had spoken to him about the spirit of the abyss, the god of the storm, huracán, that 'testified so suggestively to intercourse between opposite sides of the Atlantic.'[93] Interestingly, and in line with his diplomatic profession, the Consul imagines his movie on the myth of Atlantis as a catastrophic take on transatlantic history: just like the hurricanes that year after year cross the Atlantic, joining the Old World and the New World like those ships which Lowry so much loved, this myth of civilization disappearing into the dark abyss brings forth, in the Consul's film project, the impasses of universal history. Lowry's letters to Conrad Aiken suggest even more. In fact, the third draft of the novel had a Henry James epigraph that ran as follows: 'The plunge of civilization into the abyss of blood and darkness... is too tragic for any words.'[94] In a letter to Whit Burnett, dated 22 June 1940, Lowry clarifies the epigraphs' relationship to the novel: 'You will see how it is both a comment on the bridge between the treacherous years and the years themselves, the past and the present, and upon the Atlantis theme, and how it illuminates the book.'[95] For Lowry, *Under the Volcano* was as much about the collapsed bridge joining past and present, as it was about his own work on the Atlantis myth. Like the *deep, esoteric tradition* which we have conjured throughout the chapter – Heredia, Le Plongeon, Dixon and Atl – it becomes clear, from this quote, that Lowry thought of himself as rewriting Mexican history in relationship to the myth of its catastrophic foundation. The intuition, one could claim, hidden behind Laurelle's claim about the Consul's book on Atlantis is precisely its self-referentiality: that book on Atlantis which the Consul claims to write but nobody sees is precisely *Under the Volcano*, a book on secrecy, on diplomacy and the impasses of a universal modernity. Nowhere is this relationship between communication, transatlantic history and secrecy more prevalent than in the Consul's letter that Laurelle finds hidden among the book of Elizabethan plays. There, among the constant references to telegraphy and the multiple meditations regarding the (im)possibility of communication, we find buried a poetics of secrecy as well as an elucidation of Mexico as the land of the public secret. Writing to Yvonne the Consul states: 'No, my secrets are of the grave and must be kept. And this how I sometimes think of myself, as a great explorer who has discovered some extraordinary land from which he can never return to give his knowledge to the world: but the name of this land is hell.'[96] Mexico becomes the locus of a strange triangle between secrecy, knowledge and death, one that sees itself as culminating in the writing of the book: 'Yes: I can see the reviews now. Mr Firmin's sensational new data on Atlantis! The most extraordinary thing of its kind since Donelly! Interrupted by his untimely death... Marvelous. And the chapters on the alchemists! Which beat the Bishop of Tasmania to a frazzle [...] I might even work in something about Coxcox and Noah.'[97] Interestingly, the book that the Consul fancies writing – this book which is elsewhere referred to as a book on 'secret knowledge' – sounds like a revised version of Le Plongeon's *Sacred Mysteries among the Mayas and the Quichés*. Like his British compatriot before him, Lowry envisions himself as an archaeologist in search for the ruins of the lost garden of Eden, as a man destined to write a universal history of the origins of civilization. One must not forget: Dr Atl's *Un Grito en la Atlántida* dates from 1947, the same year as *Under the Volcano* is finally published. The figure of the lost Atlantis, in fact, becomes crucial to the question regarding Mexican modernity. One merely has to open José Vasconcelos's *La Raza Cósmica*, from 1925, to find a re-emergence of the theme of Atlantis and its importance for the question regarding the impasses of universal history:

> The architectural ruins of legendary Mayas, Quechuas and Toltecs are testimony of civilized life previous to the oldes foundations of towns in the Orient and Europe. As research advances, more support is found for the hypothesis of Atlantis as the cradle of civilization that flourished millions of years ago in the vanished continent and in parts of what today is America [...] This is of great importance to those that try to find a plan in History.[98]

Lowry's great achievement then is to write this journey as the tale of a *disappearance*, a path leading nowhere, like the telegraph wires that punctuate the scenery. The novel is a message sent from America to Europe that never arrives.

If the protagonist's profession is to be taken seriously, the novel must then be read under the code of diplomacy. Written during the years of the Second World War, *Under the Volcano* draws the war as its background. As the novel starts, Mexico has broken its diplomatic relationships with Great Britain as part of President Cárdenas decision to nationalize the country's oil. This broken relationship is a metonymy for a greater rupture: the Consul lies in hostile territory, forgotten and alone, writing telegraphs and letters that never reach their destination. A political catastrophe has broken down the possibility of a progressive, liberal, universal history. Instead, what we are given are telegraphs resembling ruins, a language of rupture writing under the influence of modernity's nightmares:

> Daily Globe intelube londres presse collect following yesterdays head-coming anti-Semitic campaign mexpress propetion see tee emma mex-workers confederation proexpulsion exmexico quote small jewish textile manufacturers unquote learned today perreliable source that Germanic legation mexcity actively behind the campaign etstatement that legation gone length sending.[99]

In the broken language of war, addiction and disaster, we see the Consul in his attempt to tackle the topics of his time as well as its nightmares: the anti-Semitism that soon attracted Dr Atl, the relationship between Mexico and England, the figure of quoting and unquoting a message that is, in itself, an impossible delivery. The fateful paradox surrounding *Under the Volcano* is precisely that its messages are always cut short, that the universality of the symbolic landscape is constantly misread and misquoted. '*A corpse will be sent by express*': something is always in its way, about to be conveyed, lost half-way between culture and nature. One could sketch a brief synopsis of the novel: a drunken Consul errs his way to death amidst a labyrinth of symbols that carry within them the power of death.

One symbol, however, towers above the rest: the volcano. The Popocatepetl and the Ixtacihuatl alternate, like ghosts, in and out of the picture, in a rhythm that determines the spiral of events narrated. The volcanoes appear and reappear with the same frequency with which drinks follow one another, sketching the horizon of eventuality against which the fate of the drunken Consul gains its passionate sense. If we then say that the volcano stands as a sign of the possibility of eventuality as such, as the origin and end of the public secret, under which historical register are we to understand its temporality? One dialectical figure gives us a hint: the clouds that repeatedly block the volcanoes only to later disclose their presence. This dialectic between clarity and obscurity, between the clouded volcano and the visible volcano, marks its strange temporality of in-betweenness: 'The sun shining brilliantly now on all the world before him, its rays picking out the timber-line of Popocatepetl as its summit like a gigantic whale shouldered out of the clouds again, all this could not lift his spirit.'[100] The volcano, always under its elusive dual face – Popocatepetl and Itxacihuatl – comes to represent a landscape in which events are never either real or fictive, actual or potential, past or future. No. The deathly logic of the volcano, its clouded presence, hints towards a conflict at the very heart of enlightened progress: the event is never equal to itself, never merely itself or its recollection. The event, always between times, delineates a space of *latency* and interruption, a space of emergency that is never merely the production of something new, but rather the disclosure of something that was always there as the repressed political potential. This meteorology of history, this history of overcast skies and the possibility of thunder, hints towards a twisted chronology: what the figure of the clouded volcano puts in question, once again, is the precedence of the shock above the aftershock. As a sign of latency, the event belongs rather to the suspended temporality of the aftershock and the photograph. In this archaeology of modernity, time is always in search for its negative, just as in Freud's archaeology of the modern subject, the symptom emerges like the negative of subjectivity. One merely has to think of the shaking hands of the Consul, the symptom of his alcoholism, the hands that shake as a reminder of the tremors that assault history. History then moves forward, with the labour of the negative, in search for that moment of divine violence which will put an end to its essential gap: the thunder that will finally bridge the gap between the actual and the potential, between the past and the future. We must return to the ending of *Under the Volcano*. In that final instant, about to get shot by the *sinarquistas*, the overcast skies concretize the thunder and the Consul, in a gesture of absolute suspension, looks upward to the volcanoes:

> The Chief of Rostrums pushed the Consul back out of the light, took two steps forward and fired. Lightning flashed like an inchoworm going down the sky and the Consul, reeling, saw above him for a moment the shape of Popocatepetl, plumed with emerald snow and drenched with brilliance. Thunderclaps crashed on the mountains then at hand. Released, the horse reared, tossing its head, it wheeled round and plunged neighing into the forest.[101]

It is beautiful to imagine that the snowy volcano which the Consul catches a glance of before his death is in fact not Brehme's, but rather Álvarez Bravo's Popocatepetl, the artificial volcano of sand and pines produced by photography. Only then, if we are able to conjure such an image, can we begin to understand the dislocation that lies at the heart of modernity, guiding the drunken steps of its archaeological double face.

Waking up from the fantasy

The history of the aftershocks of Heredia's volcanic pyramid would remain incomplete if we did not dare follow its itinerary until the present day. As such, we see it remerge in a more radical way in the aftermath of another catastrophe. The earthquake that stroke Mexico City in the early morning of 19 September 1985, razing through the city's modern landscape, fracturing the country's modern spine, would leave the city exposed to the terrible logic of its archaeological modernity. What the earthquake exposed was the end of that phenomenon of economic development that, from the 1940s until the 1980s, saw the entrance of Mexico into the landscape of the neoliberal world as part of a socioeconomic phenomenon that had been called the *Mexican miracle*.[102] It would be in the aftermath of such an event, as an aftershock of the catastrophe, that Guillermo Bonfil Batalla, an ethnologist and anthropologist whose work revolved around the question of indigeneity, would find the grounds upon which to base his concept of a *'México profundo'* in opposition to that of the *'México imaginario'*. The book, *México profundo: Una civilización negada*, was published in 1987, amidst the atmosphere of social unrest produced by the horrible earthquake, as a call – in the natural language of archaeology and geology – for the recognition of the deep indigenous historicity that remained repressed under the official discourse of Mexican identity. Bonfil Batalla's strategy is to bring back, under the geological language of deep time, the concept of Mesoamerica:

> Let us start from a basic fact: one of the few original civilizations that humanity has created throughout all its history arose and developed in what today is México. This is Mesoamerican civilization, from which derives all that is 'Indian' in México [...] Every school knows something about the precolonial world. The great archaeological monuments stand as national symbols [...] That renunciation, that denial of the past – does it really correspond to a total and irremediable historical break? Did Mesoamerica really die, and are the remaining Indian populations simply fossils, condemned five hundred years ago to disappear because they have no place in the present or in the future?[103]

Bonfil Batalla's argument against the fossilization of Mesoamerica, against its petrifaction in national museums, was a wakeup call for Mexico to finally traverse the fantasy through which its official history had been naturalized since the nineteenth century by creole *letrados*, a process that as we have seen continued throughout the twentieth century, leading all the way to Bonfil Batalla's criticism of the naturalization of Mexico's miraculous progressive modernity under the metaphor of depth and burial. What was unearthed by the Earthquake of 1985 were indeed the discontents of a culture that had suppressed its Mesoamerican past, in an event that would lead directly to the emergence of a new political movement when, in the aftermath of the 1994 Free Trade Commerce Agreement, the Ejército Zapatista de Liberación Nacional emerged with their scki masks in a daring act that paradoxically wished to unmask the Mexican state's public secret: the repression through which it had condemned its indigenous population to the state of invisibility the masks symbolized. As Michael Taussig has noted, following Walter Benjamin's dictum – 'Truth is not a matter of exposure which destroys the secret, but a revelation which does justice to it' – the Zapatistas were able to expose that public secret through which the nation-state disavowed a constitutive part of its history in the name of a process of modernization which understood history under the figure of the hurricane of progress.[104]

4

Epidemics: Virality, immunity and the outbreak of modern sovereignty

At the very outset of the Enlightenment, Thomas Hobbes defined the stakes of modern sovereignty under the domestic rubric of the social contract: the modern state was therein defined as the contractual domestication of society's natural side.[1] The fear towards the natural that the Hobbesian state of nature instantiates would haunt the state throughout the coming centuries, to the point that its history could be read as the suppression of its so-called barbaric nature. The phantom of nature's rhizomatic body, its contagious memory and its repressed omnipresence would remain the latent threat against which the state would build its foundations. As Angela Mitropoulos's recent book *Contract and Contagion* explores, nothing can conjure the natural phantoms of modern sovereignty more swiftly than the event of contagion. By bringing down the contractual mediation between society and nature, between the one and the many, epidemics forced the state to envision new modes of sovereignty once the social enemy proved to be, not outside the walls of the medieval city, but rather amidst the social body itself. For Mitropoulous the history of the state is then the history of its *oikonomia*, of its internal administration:

> In any case, that Agamben's negative theology of oikonomia has occasion to turn – by way of a reading of Georges Dumézeil – to the ways in which plagues entail the dissolution of the contractual is not perhaps surprising. Dumézeil had insisted on the structurally foundational and ancient generality of three powers to Indo-European history: ensuring the sanctity of contracts against their breach, the defence of national borders against foreign invasions, and protection against plague and feminine, each of which are, respectively, cast as problems or catastrophes which befall and recompose sovereignty, force, and re-/production. The encounter with contagion, as I argued in the first chapter, translates generation into re-/production.[2]

Sovereignty, force and reproduction: the logic of contagion sketches the impasses of the productive force of labour under the sign of the law and its viral deviations. In what follows I will attempt to show how this fear of nature's contagious multiplicities gave way, within the geopolitical region of the Greater Caribbean, to the emergence of that which I here call the *immunological state*: the modern state as a territory in constant negotiation with its latent viruses. As we will see, the virus, the modern counterpart of the medieval plague, redefined the notion of the sovereign body in relationship to the emergence, in the nineteenth century, of modern sociology and its concern regarding crowds, territoriality, hygiene, citizenship, and so on.

The chapter has three moments: in the first moment, I analyse the epidemiological discourse of suggestion that marked the last years of the Haitian Revolution. After discussing the emergence of radical subjectivities in relationship to the epidemic of yellow fever that struck the colony, as well as its connections with the discursive paradigm set by the introduction of mesmerism to the island, I proceed to expound a first definition of the immunological state. I then proceed to the second moment of the chapter, in which I explore how the nineteenth-century naturalist novel served as an apparatus that helped establish and control the state's immunological system, while at the same time homoeopathically portraying nature's dangers. Through a study of the novels of the Puerto Rican novelist and medical doctor Manuel Zeno Gandía, I attempt to show how the nineteenth-century novel functioned as an immune system capable of extricating the cancerous evils of the social body, providing the colony in turn with a productive body. In the last moment, I travel into the last decades of the twentieth century, as an attempt to explore how AIDS – as a disease of the immune system itself – provided writers with a structural metaphor through which to confront the immunological logic of state power. This third moment takes as its point of departure Reinaldo Arenas's posthumous novel *El Color del Verano*, the polymorphic novel which the Cuban author wrote in his last years while suffering from AIDS. In each case, what interests me is a diagnostic reading of what happens once the unnatural mediation of the natural contract collapses, ensuing the viral decomposition of the social body. Once nature is released from its contractual straightjacket, once it is brought forth in its true multiplicity, what comes forth is the state's paranoic self-inspection, the state as technological system and as computer, always engaged in the process of self-reading.

Contagious states: Saint Domingue and the impasses of modern sovereignty

After the retreat from Saint Domingue and the defeat of Napoleon's forces in 1802, the chief doctor of the expeditionary army, Nicolas-Pierre Gilbert, publishes a history of the ecological and epidemiological reasons behind the defeat of the French forces. The book, entitled *Histoire médicale de l'armée française à Saint-Domingue; ou Mémoire sur la fièvre jaune*, dates from 1803 and shows Paris as its place of publication.[3] Gilbert had been one of the few lucky members to return home out of the more than twenty thousand expeditionary soldiers Napoleon enlisted in 1802 under the command of his brother-in-law, General Charles Victoire Emmanuel Leclerc, as part of his plan to regain control over the island of Saint Domingue. Guided by Toussaint L'Ouverture, slave revolts had wrested the island from French control at the turn of the century. L'Ouverture, allegedly the grandson of a West African king, had one year before – amidst the celebrations of the seventeenth anniversary of the abolition of slavery – declared himself 'governor for life' under the powers given to him by the 1801 Constitution. He then proceeded to pronounce himself loyal to France. Napoleon, however, had other plans. Saint Domingue played a crucial role in his dreams for an imperial cartography in the New World: regaining control over the western part of the island was crucial to his plan of extending the French empire throughout the Americas. Interestingly, as Gilbert recounts in his book, suggestively entitled *Memoirs of the Yellow Fever*, the failed expedition was to be marked by the ravages of disease rather than by that of the sword: the battle for sovereignty at the thresholds of the New World was decided, not by the martial powers of the slave army but rather by the pitiless presence of a plague. As Gilbert recounts, Leclerc's troops arrived at Cap-Français the 14 pluviôse an 10 (the date for 2 February 1802 according to the revolutionary calendar) and quickly took control over the island. However, with control came sickness. Silent, invisible, the plague chose the bodies it would strike with political eloquence: Leclerc's troops soon fell under the power of a sickness of unknown origin, but of recognizable symptoms. By March, with the arrival of the rains, the situation would worsen, decimating the expeditionary forces and turning a triumphal horizon into a catastrophic defeat. Gilbert's *Mémoire sur la fièvre jaune* reads as an attempt to illustrate, for the metropolitan public, the invisible powers of the tropical yellow fever. In his account, the fever 'takes hold' of the soldier's bodies, producing in them a physiological crisis which can't be appeased by enlightened medicine:

> La prostration des forces, qui, dans les premières instans de la maladie, s'était couverte du voile d'une irritation tres-vive, se démasque et marche a grands pas [...] Les dejections sont souvent noires; le visage, qui avait été d'un rouge foncé, se colore d'un jaune plus ou moins saturé : cette suffusion ictérique se répand sur la surface du corps: le malade exhale au loin une odeur cadavéreuse ; il meurt le premier, le troiseme, cinquieme, septieme jour.[4]

Over the next months, LeClerc saw how his troops disappeared into thin air as if by the power of a black magic which, however, left the slave forces untouched. The slaves proved to be immune to the epidemic forces of the disease. As J. R. McNeill has explored, the geopolitics of this differential immunity – the fact slaves were immune to an epidemic that proved to be fatal for the imperial forces – are merely the first of the many political implications such a seminal event had within the history of the Haitian Revolution and, as such, with the rise of the modern nation-state.[5] In fact, what becomes apparent from Gilbert's description of the symptoms of plague-ridden soldiers is precisely the metaphorical extent to which the yellow fever condensed the biopolitical implications of the Haitian Revolution. As Roberto Esposito has argued in *Immunitas: The Protection and Negation of Life*, what remains to be thought out here is the political consequences of the 'immunitary character that the metaphor of the body politic lends to the modern political lexicon as whole'.[6] In this sense, Gilbert's descriptions of the soldier's sick bodies as possessed by electric forces that lead them to unintentional convulsions, to trance-like states, his descriptions of the famous black vomit that overcame soldiers in their last days, as well as his multiple discussions regarding immunity and contagion, allow us to sketch the key concepts for thinking the stakes of the Haitian Revolution. Questions concerning the nature of modern sovereignty, as well as questions concerning the nature of modern radical subjectivities, are all clearly sketched out by the metaphorical as well as terribly physical power of an epidemic that was able to put an end to a war that had extended for over a decade. The epidemiological as well as immunological paradigm sketches out the field of the game.

At first sight, from a simplistic point of view, one could then say, echoing Nicolas-Pierre Gilbert, that the plague, and not the slave army, won the war. The historical account of the Haitian Revolution would be therefore reframed if it were not for the fact that, from the safety grounds of metropolitan France, one hears the voice of a scientist, or perhaps a charlatan, who also claimed responsibility for the triumphs of the New Republic. In Henri F. Ellenberger's *The Discovery of the Unconscious* we read: 'In Saint Domingue, Magnetism degenerated into a psychic epidemic amongst the Negro slaves, increasing their agitation, and the French domination ended in a bloodbath. Later Mesmer boasted that the new Republic, now called Haiti, owed its independence to him.'[7] Ellenberger's account extends the problem precisely where Gilbert's account finishes: according to him, the triumph of the new Republic was partly due to the way in which something called mesmerism spread amongst the slaves, radicalizing them *as if* by the force of an epidemic. The triumphs of the revolution are then displaced once again farther from the individual political subjectivities of the revolutionary heroes – L'Ouverture, Dessalaines, Mackandall – towards an epidemic logic that gains here the density of a proper name: Franz Anton Mesmer. Later, I shall delve into the history of the introduction of Mesmer's magnetic science into the revolutionary grounds of Saint Domingue. For now, however, I will be content with underlying a mere sketch of the 'medical treatment' in an attempt to highlight the similarities that existed between Mesmer's magnetic cure and the trance-like maladies produced upon the body by the yellow fever. In a letter sent in 1784, Jeanne-Eulailie Millet, a colonist from the southern region of Petit Trou, recounts the effects of Mesmer's treatment in the catastrophic language of trance and possession:

> A magnetizer has been in the colony for a while now, and, following Mesmer's enlightened ideas, he causes in us effects that one feels without understanding them. We faint, we suffocate, we enter into truly dangerous frenzies that cause onlookers to worry. At the second trial of the tub a young lady, after having torn off nearly all her clothes, amorously attacked a young man on the scene [...] Magnetism produces a conflagration that consumes us, an excess of life that leads us to delirium.[8]

Mme Millet's description of Mesmer's 'enlightened' cure is illuminatingly paradoxical: its hints at a method of curing which induces upon the body of the patient a crisis so strong that it forces the subject to break loose of its societal boundaries. When she speaks of magnetism as a cure producing an 'excess of life', we are reminded of Nicolas-Pierre Gilbert's descriptions of Leclerc's plague-ridden soldiers. In both cases, under the language of trance, possession and exertion, we are given the image of the sovereign body in crisis, the image of a sick and convulsive subjectivity at battle with the enlightened theories that had produced it.

In fact, as I will later explore, the history of mesmerism and its introduction into the slave economy of Saint Domingue is a fascinating one indeed, full of political mutations. Originally thought of – by the plantation owners – as a possible way of curing slaves and therefore maximizing their labour, mesmerism quickly mutated, as François Regourd has noticed, into a figure for slave resistance. In two rulings from 1786 by the Conseil supérieur du Cap-Français, the authorities highlight the existence of nightly meetings in the northern district of La Mermelade, where they claimed slaves gathered, inducing convulsions and producing, as François Regourd quotes, 'false prodigies due to this would-be magnetism [...] usurped by Negroes and disguised by them under the name of Bila'.[9] As Regourd notices, the name Bila referred to the voodoo practices already shared by some of the slave population. The ruling continues to highlight the 'numerous people' who attended nocturnal events as well as the crossbreeding of mesmerism and occult African practices that characterized them. In the hands of the slaves, mesmerism mutates into a revolutionary science. As I aim to argue in this chapter, in its logic of self-possession and trance, the slaves saw a political tool.

What follows is an attempt to think the dialectical image that sparks once we place, side by side, these two phenomena: yellow fever and mesmerism. Therein, between these two secret poles, I would argue, lies the invisible, epidemic and suggestive history of the Haitian Revolution, its triumph and its consequences.

As of late, in the wake of James E. McClellan's seminal work *Colonialism and Science: Saint Domingue in the Old Regime* and Robert Darnton's *Mesmerism and the Ends of the Enlightenment*, numerous studies regarding the arrival of mesmerism to Saint Domingue have been published: studies such as François Regourd's *Mesmerism in Saint Domingue*, Karol M. Weaver's *Medical Revolutionaries*, and Nathan Gorelick's *Extimate Revolt: Mesmerism, Haiti and the Origin of Pyschoanalysis* have all attempted to read, from different perspectives, the revolutionary turn that mesmerism, or animal magnetism as it was also known, took as soon it disembarked within the already tense political grounds of the New World. Their studies have surged within the new wave of interest regarding the political journeys of enlightened sciences across the Atlantic: whether from the perspective of gender, as in Weaver's case; psychoanalysis, as in Gorelick's case; or history, as in Regourd's case, these studies attempt to answer the complex question regarding the birth and mutations of 'modern science' as they occurred in that two-way street which, following Paul Gilroy, one could call the 'Black Atlantic'.[10] On the other hand, following the resurgence of environmental studies within the humanities, scholars have started to pay attention to the impact that transatlantic routes determined by the slave trade had upon the 'political ecology' of the New World: studies like Stuart McCook's *The Neo-Columbian Exchange* or Debbie Lee's *Yellow Fever and the Slave Trade*, from Robert K. D. Petterson's *Insects, Disease and Military History* to J. R. McNeill's *Mosquito Empires: Ecology and War in the Greater Caribbean*, have all highlighted the repercussions that the ecological mutations introduced by the slave trade as well as by transatlantic mercantilism had upon a political environment that was already ripe for revolution. Some of these studies have further pinpointed the role that the yellow fever, or black vomit as it was also known, had upon the geopolitical history of the Greater Caribbean and, in particular, within the history of the Haitian Revolution. In this chapter I think through what happens when one reads the history of the Haitian Revolution from both perspectives at once. Namely, what happens to the biopolitical history of the Black Atlantic once it is read from the discursive as well as material grounds which mesmerism shared with the yellow fever: a discourse regarding the limits and heightened states of sovereign bodies, the radicalization of subjectivities, and the triple knot between hegemony, subjection and revolution. The biopolitical consequences of such discourse for the history of the late, radical enlightenment are here mediated by a series of *medical* figures at the threshold of positivist science: both the epidemic of yellow fever and mesmerism encourage us to envision social bonds in terms such as contagion, suggestion, excitement and immunity. When viewed from this discursive lens – rather than through a purely materialist conception – the history of the Haitian Revolution, I believe, appears in its true density: as the first clinical case of a wave of political fervour that would soon spread throughout the Americas, exposing the crisis of the imperial modes of sovereignty. The dialectical image joining the plague-ridden bodies of Leclerc's forces to those of the mesmerized bodies of both slaves and colonists gives us the vocabulary through which to sketch many of the crucial questions regarding the role of the Haitian Revolution within modern political theory. What modes of political subjectivities arise out of the structural model of contagion and suggestion proposed by the figures of the plague and mesmerism? What happens to the territorial notion of the 'political body' when it is forced to account for such heterogeneous spaces of intensities as those produced by the plague or by mesmeric magnetism? What happened to the social concept of slavery and empire, in its full semantic density, once it was forced to account for the possibility that a similar logic of the 'possessed body' such as mesmerism could bring the collapse of the slave empire? All of these questions point to the Haitian Revolution as a place in which the Enlightenment encounters itself at its limits, as the condition of possibility of its own collapse. Over a century later, the playwright and writer Antonin Artaud, another Frenchman in battle with his own legacy, would pronounce in his essay *The Plague and the Theater*, some illuminating words: 'He saw himself plague-ridden and saw the disease ravage his tiny state.'[11] Artaud's intuition is precisely right: the logic of contagion and suggestion produces a profound disintegration and reformulation of the state conceived as a body politic. As Roberto Esposito, who perhaps more than anyone else has championed the biopolitical implications of virality and contagion, states: 'Biopolitics [...] by placing the body at the center of politics and the potential for disease at the center of the body, it makes sickness, on the one hand, the outer margin from which life much continually distance itself, and, on the other, the internal fold which dialectically brings it back to itself.'[12] However, this doesn't mean that the threat of contagion means the end of the state. Rather, as I will now attempt to sketch through a very brief history of the Haitian Revolution, what emerged out of such an epidemic crisis would be the modern biopolitical state as a viral body politic in constant negotiation with its latent political viruses.

Revolutionary flights: The invisible territory of the mosquito

Did the mosquito do it?

– Walter Reed

Cuban writer Alejo Carpentier knew very well the role that a mosquito could have in the history of a revolutionary process. Rather than depicting the main fighting years of 1791 to 1804 that frame the revolution's acknowledged chronology, his historical account of the Haitian Revolution in his 1949 novel *El reino de este mundo* centres around an earlier political event that highlights the radical political ecology that characterized the emancipatory process of the first slave revolt of the Americas. In his attempt to uncover the historical logic of the revolutionary process, Carpentier scrutinizes historical records and attempts to find the original source of the revolutionary fever. As the novel's famous prologue clearly states, he finds the source in the outflow of revolutionary fervour and belief that overtook the slave crowd that witnessed the 1758 execution of the famous maroon and voodoo leader François Mackandal. It is at that moment, Carpentier suggests, that history bifurcated the community into two historical groups: on the one hand, the slaves who believed in Mackandal's flight and on the other, the white colonists who returned to their homes believing that he had died in the bonfire. No longer passive spectators, the slaves' faith had transformed them into radical subjects with historical agency.[13] Theirs, however, was not the only transformation. The scene of Mackandal's flight is also a scene of metamorphosis that merges the logic of voodoo with the origins of the yellow fever. In the novel's turning point, Mackandal, a houngan knowledgeable of poisons and occult sciences, escapes the consuming power of fire by metamorphosing himself into the most minuscule of animals: a mosquito. As the narrator, taking the perspective of the slave witness, explains:

> In his cycle of metamorphoses, Mackandal had often entered in the mysterious world of the insects, making up for the lack of his human arm with the possession of several feet, four wings, or long antennae. He had been fly, centipede, month, ant, tarantula, lady-bug, and even a glow-worm with the phosphorescent green lights. When the moment came, the bonds of the Mandigue, no longer possessing a body to bind, would trace the shape of a man in the air for a second before they slipped down the post. And Mackandal, transformed into a buzzing mosquito, would light on the very tricorne of the commander of the troops to laugh at the dismay of the whites. This was what their masters did not know; for that reason they had squandered so much money putting on this useless show, which would prove how completely helpless they were against a man chrismed by the great Loas.[14]

According to this logic of metamorphosis and invisibility, at the precise moment in which Mackandal is thrown into the bonfire a slave voice is heard that yells '*Mackandal sauvé!*' producing a commotion within a crowd that suddenly believes it has seen their leader dissolve into thin air as a mosquito. The scene, presented by Carpentier himself in the book's prologue as the primary example for what he called the 'real maravilloso', gains a particular epistemic density when placed in relationship to recent debates concerning posthumanism, zoopolitics and postcolonial theories of shamanistic transformation. Whether in relationship to what Michael Taussig – in his study of Putumayo shamanism – has called the 'space of death', in regard to Eduardo Kohn's recent work on posthuman anthropology in his book *How Forests Think*, or in the context of the recent debates concerning zoopolitics, from Derrida to Agamben, what the scene stages are the political implications of a 'magical' world where the distinction between culture and nature, between human and animal, has superseded by a chain-like logic of metamorphosis that links the world as cosmos, to quote Isabelle Stengers work on cosmopolitics, or as an assemblage, in the terminology of Deleuze and Guattari.[15] As Deleuze himself has expressed in an interview, the logic of the assemblage is not that of linearity but rather that of contagion:

> What is an assemblage? It is a multiplicity which is made up of heterogeneous terms and which establishes liaisons, relations between them, across ages, sexes and reigns – different natures. Thus assemblage's only unity is that of a co-functioning: it is a symbiosis, a 'sympathy'. It is never filiations which are important, but alliances, alloys: these are not successions, lines of descent, but contagions, epidemics, the wind.[16]

So it should not surprise us that Carpentier, in his depiction of Mackandal's line of flight, foreshadows with decades of anticipation Deleuze and Guattari's conceptual imagery: from his becoming-animal to the line of flight sketched by his deterritorializing metamorphosis, the scene gains political density as soon it is placed side by side with the figural concepts proposed by the authors of *A Thousand Plateaus*. The reader is perhaps reminded of their comments regarding the relationship between becoming-animal and the figure of metamorphosis in their book on Kafka: 'Metamorphosis is the contrary of metaphor. There is no longer any proper sense or figurative sense, but only a distribution of states that is part of the range of the world. The thing and other things are no longer anything but intensities overrun by deterritorialized sound or words that are following their line of escape.'[17] Mackandal's metamorphosis embodies the agitation and destabilization of the status quo that would soon produce the radical states of intensity and belief that would end up shattering the territorial sovereignty of the French empire. As Carpentier correctly portrays, the germ of the revolutionary atmosphere that would later spread over the colony with the ferocity of an epidemic was already condensed in this scene in which a man becomes a mosquito. His insight is illuminating: the history of the revolution could then very well begin and end with a mosquito.

More than half a century before Alejo Carpentier wrote a mosquito into the epic of the Haitian Revolution, another Cuban hypothesized the role of the insect within the complex political history of colonial America. In 1881, three years after the yellow fever epidemic that had devastated the Mississippi Valley, a Cuban physician by the name of Carlos J. Finlay presented a daring hypothesis regarding the propagation of the disease to the Academy of Sciences of Havana.[18]

According to Finlay the agent of transmission of the disease was none other than a particular species of mosquito that would later become known as the *Aedes aegypti*. With his discovery Finlay was uncovering the protagonist of a transatlantic history that had determined the political ecology of the Atlantic for more than three centuries: as J. R. McNeill has studied in his book *Mosquito Empires*, the *Aedes aegypti* was originally endemic to Africa but must have made the transatlantic trip aboard one of the thousands of ships that, beginning in the second half of the sixteenth century and leading all the way to the heart of the eighteenth century, made their way from the coasts of West Africa to the tropical grounds of the Caribbean.[19] The virus probably crossed the Atlantic in its preferred modality: as the latent *stowaway* waiting for the perfect environment in which to proliferate. It soon found the appropriate environment in the economic boom of the Caribbean tropics that, as Antonio Benítez Rojo explains, coincided with the introduction of the slave plantation as a new space of social interaction.[20] The virus proliferated alongside the booming Caribbean economy within that process of ecological globalization that Stuart McCook has recently called the 'neo-Columbian exchange', as a way of differentiating it from the first 'Columbian exchange' as Alfred Crosby had famously termed the ecological exchange elicited by the first imperial impact in the fifteenth century and the early sixteenth century.[21] As McCook and McNeill notice, the logic of 'differential immunity' described by the plague, as well as the history of the virus's relationship to this new environment, helped shape the geohistory of the region. The main event in this invisible history being the introduction, in the seventeenth century, of the sugar cane as a valuable commodity and the emergence of the sugar plantation as the main tropical modality of social life:

> After 1640 sugar and geopolitics set the table very nicely for the yellow fever virus. Sugar wrought an ecological revolution upon dozens of islands and numerous patches of adjacent continental lowlands. Soon, armies of slaves hacked down and burned off millions of hectares of forest in order to plant cane. Their efforts led to multiple ecological changes. Soil erosion accelerated. Wildlife vanished. More important from the human point of view, as plantation replaced forest, conditions came to favor their transmission of yellow fever.[22]

The economic climate surrounding this inaugural moment within the history of capitalism was quickly constructing the ecological as well as political conditions for its eventual demise. As Jason W. Moore has argued in his article 'Capitalism, Ecology and the Nature of our Times', capitalism ends up not only exploiting nature, but rather reconfiguring it: 'Capital's dynamism turns on the exhaustion of the very webs of life necessary to sustain accumulation; the history of capitalism has been one of recurrent frontier movements to overcome that exhaustion, through the appropriation of nature free gift's beyond capital's reach.'[23] For the next century and a half, the population of African slaves blossomed in the colony, while the differential immunity made sure, as McCook illuminatingly points out, to keep the geopolitical status quo untouched: expeditionary invasions during the eighteenth century were all dismantled by the epidemic force of mosquito swarms. Little did the French know that what was truly being built were not the walls of an imperial fortress, but rather an assemblage binding the slave population to the ecological environment of the planation: an assemblage that would later prove capable of radicalizing itself under the form of the revolutionary slave army. *Revolution was in the air*: the expression – which emphasizes the way discourses regarding hygiene, science and revolution coincided within the late Enlightenment – fits perfectly within the case of Saint Domingue. The tropical environment of the island, with its rainy seasons, swamped waters and humid climate – an image of oppression and insularity – was building the grounds upon which it would later show its more radical face. In tune with the pseudo-scientific chitchat that had become fashionable throughout the island in the eighteenth century, we are tempted to say: the air had become electric.[24] What this implies is something crucial: namely, that the territorial grounds upon which the French empire had until then represented its geopolitical power to itself were becoming progressively differentiated by the ecological force of a flow-like political vector that had suddenly interrupted the homogeneity of the territorial status quo. The sovereign imperial body, alongside its territorial representations, was entering into a crisis of unknown precedents.

With its logic of contagion, the expansive proliferation of epidemic diseases was slowly contaminating the hegemonic imperial territory. The political consequences of the not-yet-proposed *germ theory of disease* were being incubated and sketched out with the greatest of curiosities. Regarding this point, medical doctors and military leaders shared a common passion. They both wanted to decipher the propagative logic of these diseases that reproduced without an apparent order. To put the epidemiological paradox in terms that underline their political implications: the paradox regarding epidemics was that they reproduced without a clear representation. Like the slaves, the epidemic logic proliferated in an invisible manner, putting into question the representative realm that had, since the Enlightenment, guided reason. The struggle was then, in all realms, a struggle for representation and visibility. For the slaves, whose population had blossomed to become a distinct majority, it was a struggle for political representation and subjectivity, while for the medical doctors the question was how to represent the invisible, unpredictable and exponential spread of the epidemic. It was both a politics of representation and a politics of scale: it was a struggle to comprehend the political cartography of the newly emerging political ecology. As such, the links between epidemiology, territoriality and empire would become evident in the wave of medical cartography that would keep nineteenth-century medical doctors busy. A prime example of such cartographic enterprises would be that of the French physician and natural historian Jean Baptiste Le Blond, the descendant of the eponymous architect who acted as chief designer of Saint Petersburg under the tsarist rule of Peter the Great. In works like *Observations sur la fièvre jaune*, published in Paris in 1805, Le Blond would record his observations on the disease within a broader concern regarding the ecological cartography of the region. Le Blond's endeavours were not isolated. In fact, they foreshadowed one of the crucial events in nineteenth-century medicine: John Snow's founding works in the field of modern epidemiology. Convinced that the *miasma theory of disease*, the theory that epidemics were spread by bad air, was wrong, Snow set out in the mid-nineteenth century to discover the true source of epidemic diseases.[25] His insight remains an outstanding event in the history of medicine as well as in the history of sociology: confronted with the cholera epidemic that had afflicted London in 1854, he decided to map as dots each of cases that had led to death. His conclusion was surprising: after mapping the deaths produced by the epidemic, he came to the realization that most deaths had occurred in close proximity to the water pump at Broad Street. His investigations led him to believe that it was the water at that pump which had spread the disease rather than 'bad air', a theory he would later confirm when he was able to prove that the Southwark and Vauxhall Waterworks Company was taking water from sewage-polluted sections of the Thames and delivering the water to homes. Snow's discovery proved to be foundational for modern epidemiology and its emerging *germ theory of disease*: the theory that diseases are caused by microorganisms that remain invisible to the naked eye without magnification. More importantly for us what Snow's discovery, with its use of cartography and statistics, proved was that the epidemiological discourse was in fact a political paradigm that linked the microcosm of germs with the macrocosm of visible reality. With its politics of scales, modern epidemiology was inducing a crisis upon the old notions of territoriality: as Snow's map of the Soho cholera outbreak showed, the modern political map was no longer a homogenous representational space but rather a territory infected with dots. Within the walls of the imperial map, there lay latent viruses awaiting a vulnerable body through which to actualize themselves. Nowhere was this new territorial paradigm more evident than in the case of the Greater Caribbean, where the bothersome and miniscule *Aedes aegypti* had set the trap for Napoleon's expeditionary army.

Bodies in crisis: Mesmerism and radical subjectivity

If by chance animal magnetism really existed...
I ask you, sir, what revolution should we not expect?
– Nicolas Bergasse

The territorial body of the empire was not the only body whose hegemony entered into a state of crisis during the second part of the eighteenth century. At the same time that the *fièvre jaune* was setting the ecological stage for the Haitian Revolution, another social epidemic was transforming the way French subjects related to their own bodies. As Robert Darnton has explored, the arrival of *mesmerism* in Paris quickly evolved into a major social event that threatened to radicalize the subjectivities of imperial citizens. In February 1778, a German physician by the name of Franz Anton Mesmer arrived to Paris proclaiming the discovery of 'a superfine fluid that penetrated and surrounded all bodies'.[26] This fluid, Mesmer theorized, was part of a magnetic field of energy transfers that mediated between the realm of animate manner and that of inanimate matter. Rewriting natural history's concept of a *chain of being*, Mesmer saw nature as a universal flow of energy. The Parisian public, fascinated as it was with the possibility of invisible forces such as electricity and magnetism, quickly become intrigued by the possibility of such animal magnetism, as Mesmer called the fluid. A physician himself, he found in medicine the most direct applications: the body, he claimed, was a magnetic field and sickness was the result of an obstacle in the flow of the fluid within this field. His next step was to devise a cure according to this theory. He found such a 'cure' in an alluring performance: by massaging the body's 'magnetic poles', Mesmer claimed to be able to induce a crisis upon the body which, by the way of convulsions and epileptic-like trances, broke loose the obstacles in the magnetic field and restored the health of the patient.[27] Mesmer's cure, acting out a crisis that mimicked the symptoms of an epidemic, was unknowingly producing a new affective concept of the body: the body was no longer the subject of sovereign consciousness but rather a magnetic territory traversed by flow-like intensities. As Robert Darnton explains, in inducing the subject with temporary crises the cure was in itself an alluring social performance. Within what he called his crisis rooms, the performance would take place as a spectacle of truly social dimensions:

> Gossips also found inspiration in Mesmer's apparatus, especially his mattress-lined 'crisis room', designed for violent convulsives and his famous tubs. These were usually filled with iron filings and mesmerized water contained in bottles arranged like the spokes of a wheel. They stored the fluid and transmitted it through movable iron rods, which the patients applied to their sick areas. Sitting around the tubs in circles, the patients communicated the fluid to one another by means of a rope looped about them all and by linking thumbs and index fingers in order to form a 'mesmeric chain', something like an electric circuit.[28]

Both structurally and practically, Mesmer's cure was setting the stage for a radicalized paradigm of social experience that rearranged the relationship between the body, nature and the social medium. The figure of the mesmeric chain gave a radical twist to natural history's *chain of being*. No longer a mere hierarchical structure, the chain was suddenly traversed by the electrical power of a flow capable of producing a social crisis. Mesmer's crisis room set the stage for a new modality of historical subjectivity that embraced the excess of life and attempted to go beyond the limits imposed by sovereign consciousness.

Coincidentally, the story of the arrival of mesmerism to Haiti and its eventual radical mutation at the hands of the slave population begins with a cartographic expedition. Already from the start the territory of the empire is at stake. In June 1784, seven years before the Haitian Revolution, the Comte de Chastenet, a 32-year-old naval officer by the name of Antonine-Hyacinth de Puységur arrives in Saint Domingue aboard the *Frédéric-Guillaume*. His goal was to produce a cartographic survey of the islands north of Saint Domingue. Luckily, the ship had been able to make the transatlantic trip without any major epidemic infecting its passengers. Or so he thought. Puységur, who had studied in Paris with Mesmer himself, probably had an explanation for this. Amidst the cartographic materials that he had brought for the completion of his naval task, he had also brought a series of *bouquets*: in those tubs filled with mesmerized water Puységur had, throughout the trip, administered Mesmer's magnetic cures to his sailors making sure that their health and spirits remained untouched. As he disembarked in the island, he took the tubs with him. Soon, at the *Maison de Providence des Hommes*, Cap-Français's poorhouse, a series of mesmeric treatments were set up. Unconsciously, he had introduced into the already radicalized atmosphere of the colony a machine capable of materializing the latent political tension already present within the colony. However, at first sight, the cure seemed to fit perfectly within the mercantile logic of slavery. Structurally, the cure mimicked the logic of possession, energy and production that characterized slave economies: the mesmerizer, like the slaveholder, took hold of the body of the mesmerized subject, forcing him to release an excess of energy. Understanding the master-and-slave rubric that underlined the cure, colonial slaveholders quickly jumped on the opportunity of maximizing profits. In a 1785 report by plantation owner Jean Trembley we read of the multiple benefits brought by the introduction of mesmerism, among which the author underlines the cure of slaves:

> A cripple brought from the plain to Cap-Français on a liter walked freely afterward. A female slave paralyzed for fourteen years was entirely cured in a short time without her realizing that she was being treated, etc. A plantation owner on this plain made a big profit in magnetizing a consignment of cast-off slaves he bought at a low price. Restoring them to good health by means of the tub, he was able to lease them at prices paid for the best slaves. The rage for magnetism has taken of everyone here. Mesmeric tubes are everywhere.[29]

Trembley's report condenses the biopolitics of the mesmeric tubes as desiring machine: in the economy of expenditure elicited by the cure we find a biopolitical figure that reproduces the discursive paradigm set up by the yellow fever. Trembley's rhetoric – his comments regarding the omnipresence of the cure as well as its capacity to take hold of everyone – already suggest the relationship between epidemics and mesmerism: both phenomena stage a new relationship between the colonial subject and his body, as well as a new relationship between these body and production. What type of economy is sketched therein? Who takes hold of whom, and for what purpose? Like the 'excess of life' with which Mme Millet described the mesmeric crises in the passage previously quoted, mesmerism forces us to see what happens to the subject when its unity is shattered by a multiplicity that knows no boundaries. I am here reminded of Deleuze and Guattari's criticism of Freud's psychoanalytical reading of the crowd in *A Thousand Plateaus*: 'Freud tried to approach crowd phenomena from the point of view of the unconscious, but he did not see clearly, he did not see that the unconscious itself was fundamentally a crowd.'[30] Perhaps, I would claim following their insight, what has been missing from the numerous works devoted to the arrival of mesmerism in Haiti has been a deeper understanding of the ways in which not only was mesmerism an influential element within the Haitian Revolution, but rather a paradigmatic one. As I have tried to elucidate here, it is this paradigmatic aspect that is exposed once the discursive relationship between the biopolitical significance of mesmerism's arrival in Saint Domingue is placed alongside the political role of yellow fever. If, following Ellenberger's image of mesmerism as a 'psychic epidemic', we conceive of it in the biopolitical terms disclosed by our analysis of the yellow fever, then we realize its true historical significance: rather than being merely an influential factor within the history of the Haitian Revolution, mesmerism's radicalization of subjectivity provided a formal model for thinking through the emerging radical subjectivities that would end up shattering the imperial hegemony. It then appears to be no surprise that with the paradoxical logic of Hegel's master-and-slave dialectic, with the traitorous multiplicity of a virus mesmerism suddenly changed hands and became a 'property' of the slaves, as we read in two rulings by the Conseil supérieur du Cap-Français. To some extent it was theirs to begin with, for it was their struggle for a radical subjectivity that the cure mimicked.

Two rulings from 1786 by the Conseil supérieur du Cap-Français allow us to understand the ways in which mesmerism mutated from an imperial science into a political tool used by the slave population. In them, the authorities highlight the existence of nightly meetings in the northern district of La Mermelade, where they claimed slaves gathered, inducing convulsions and producing, as François Regourd quotes, 'false prodigies due to this would-be magnetism [...] usurped by Negroes and disguised by them under the name of Bila'.[31] As Regourd notices, the name Bila referred to the voodoo practices already shared by some of the slave population. The ruling continues to highlight the 'numerous people' who attended nocturnal events as well as the crossbreeding of mesmerism and occult African practices that characterized them:

> The miraculous operator has the subjects who ask to submit to his power brought to him into the circle. He does not limit himself to magnetizing them in the modern sense of the word. After magician has caused the stupor or convulsions in them using both the sacred and the profane, holy water is brought to him since he pretends it is necessary to break the spell that he had previously cast on the subjects.[32]

The counsel's description, in its conflation of mesmerism and voodoo, provides us with the vocabulary through which to think the consequences of mesmerism's mutation at the hands of the slaves: miracles, subjects, power, circles, magnetism, magic, stupor, convulsion, spells, etc. All of these figures allow us to comprehend the introduction of mesmerism into the slave circles within the logic of radicalization that characterized the struggle for subjectivity of the slaves. What comes to light from this description, as well as from Carpentier's description of Mackandal's line of flight, is the fact that in their struggle for political visibility, in their struggle for political subjectivity, the slaves were in fact forcing the enlightened concept of subjectivity to explode from within. As we read in Médéric Moreau de Saint-Méry's 1797 *Description topographique*: 'most of the participants asked for the ability to control the mind of their masters'.[33] Unknowingly, they were casting a spell upon the imperial subject, one that broke it loose of the chains of its imperial unity and brought it forth as a true multiplicity beyond representation. Isn't this precisely the logic of crowds, multiplicity and deterritorialization that is sketched by Mackandal in Carpentier's representation of his final escape? What Carpentier's scene – in its description of the miraculous moment of liberation – suggests is that the true moment of liberation and freedom within the Haitian Revolution was not limited to that of individual subjectivities but rather occurred when the imperial logic of sovereignty was confronted with an epidemic logic capable of decentralizing the subject's self-possession. With the adoption of mesmerism, the slaves were paradoxically gaining advantage of the logic of possession that characterized their situation. As Karol Weaver notes, they were also bringing back the memory of Mackandal's mythic death and with it, the colonial fear of being poisoned: 'These fears are made plain by the court's willingness to apply the 1758 law, which stated, "Prohibited to free men of color and slaves to compose, sell and distribute or buy talismans or macandals."'[34] After conjuring the memory of Mackandal, the declaration of 1786 ends by explicitly forbidding mesmerism between the slaves, as well as among men and women of colour. It also condemned the two main leaders of the mesmeric circles at La Marmelade – Jerôme, Télémaque – to harsh punishments: according to Moreau de Saint-Méry, Jérôme was condemned to the galleys for life while Télémaque was subjected to the iron collar and publicly exposed. However, if we are to believe the records of the counsel, both men escaped. This flight from the territory of the law, despite its historiographic uncertainty, gives an overarching arch to the history here narrated: from Mackandal's flight as a metamorphosed mosquito to the uncertain flight of Jêrome and Télemaque we become witnesses of the logic of deterritorialization produced by a series of material practices that would end up shattering the traditional figure of the historical subject. We are almost tempted, poetically, to think that the mosquitoes that would bite LeClerc's forces more than a decade latter would be precisely the metamorphosed spirits of the two runaways. By forcing upon us a concept of history beyond the sovereign subject, the epidemiological paradigm imposes a question: and now who/what?

And now who/what? New historical assemblages

The body defeats a poison not by expelling it outside
the organism, but by making it somehow part of the body.
– Roberto Esposito

By staging the crisis of the political figure of the sovereign body, both in its territorial as well as subjective moments, the epidemiological events that marked the history of the Haitian Revolution helped sketch, at the very outset, the stakes of modern history from a biopolitical perspective. Both the ecological history of the yellow fever in the Greater Caribbean as well as the disruptive introduction of mesmerism in Haiti became paradigmatic of the 'viral-events' that, in the coming century, would threaten the stability of the Hobessian social contract, forcing the modern state to redefine the nature of its sovereignty.[35] The epidemic, with its complex structure of differential immunity as well as its expansive non-territorial expansion, would become the paradigm for that new political subject whose nature consisted in a constant negotiation with that within him which exceeded life. The plagued subject emerges, as Félix Guattari explains in *The Three Ecologies*, as the protagonist of an animist history that admits of no transcendental subject: 'Today, it seems interesting to me to go back to what I would call an animist conception of subjectivity, if need be through neurotic phenomena, religious rituals, or aesthetic phenomena.'[36] Just like the epidemic logic of contagion, animism, the idea that everything is animated and the cosmos is guided by a flow that puts everything in touch with everything, works metonymically rather than metaphorically. Animism therefore becomes, for Guattari, the structural model for a political system in which individual subjectivities dissolve into large-scale assemblages. The question becomes, as Guattari continues to ask: 'How can it [subjectivity] simultaneously singularize an individual, a group of individuals, and also be assembled to space, architecture and all other cosmic assemblages?'[37] This image of an animist subjectivity, of a subject always at the edge of its dissolution into cosmic assemblages, sketches the contours of a new mode of historical agency. Perhaps, one would argue, the viral subject that supersedes the transcendental one is nothing else than that which Negri and Hardt, in their trilogy, have called the multitude. Interestingly, for Negri and Hardt, as sketched in their book *Empire*, the multitude is both the assemblage that posits the possibility of hegemonic power as well as that which homoeopathically threatens to dissolve it:

> This is another fundamental characteristic of the existence of the multitude today, within Empire and against Empire. New figures of struggle and new subjectivities are produced in the conjuncture of events, in the universal nomadism, in the general mixture and miscegenation of individuals and populations, and in the technological metamorphoses of the imperial biopolitical machine.[38]

According to this logic, the Haitian Revolution would be one of the first irruptions of the modern multitude onto the political stage. In the slaves' struggle for political visibility, in the nightly meetings of the slave crowds at *La Mermelade*, one finds the paradigmatic example of the sociological logic of multiplicity and contagion which comes to characterize the Spinozian multitude for Hardt and Negri. However, like the epidemic and like mesmerism, the nature of this assemblage called the multitude is a paradoxical one: unknowingly, it sketches the biopolitical double face of modern sovereignty. To state it in epidemiological terms, it sketches that which Roberto Esposito has called the immunological paradigm, the state as a viral body in constant negotiation with its latent viruses. The modern biopolitical state, one could argue following Esposito, is the immunological state whose sovereignty is always threatened from within rather than from outside. As Esposito explains in his book *Immunitas*, confronted with a life that aims to exceed itself – as Mme Millet's quote regarding colonial mesmerism reminds us – the state must immunize itself:

> Life is the event, the situation, which by definition tends to escape its own confines – it tends to break down its own limits and turn itself inside out. The mandate of law is to immunize life from its irresistible impulse to overcome itself, to make itself more than simple life, to exceed the natural horizon of biological life (or as Benjamin expresses it, 'bare life,' das blosse Leben) so as to take on a 'form of life' such as 'right life' or 'common life'.[39]

The Haitian Revolution would then mark a threshold in history of modern biopolitics as the moment in which the imperialist logic of territorial hegemony is superseded by the modern state as a heterogeneous assemblage working within the homeopathic logic of contagion.

I would like to end by returning to the initial image of the chief doctor of the naval army, Nicolas-Pierre Gilbert, writing in 1803 the clinical memoirs of his expedition to Saint Domingue from the safety of his Parisian home. *Histoire médicale de l'àrmée française à Saint-Domingue; ou Mémoire sur la fièvre jaune* is a book written in an attempt to calm metropolitan fears regarding an elusive malady whose viral logic escaped the grasp of the French public: 'Je démontrerai, par les faits, que la fièvre jaune de l'Amérique ne doit pas inspirer plus d'alarmes pour l'avenir que toute autre fièvre de mauvais nature [...] On sera forcé d'en conclure que nos Colonies ne seront pas plus désertées par nous, à raison de cette maladie.'[40] The colonies would not be deserted by the imperial army. Gilbert's words emphasize the connection between imperial presence and territorial sovereignty. Little did he know that at the moment of his writing Leclerc's troops were retreating, and the general himself had fallen victim to the fatal yellow fever. Here, once again, the intuitions of Alejo Carpentier's *El reino de este mundo* proves crucial. In the novel, Pauline Bonaparte, sister of Napoleon and wife of Leclerc, seeing the moribund state of his plagued husband, seeks as a last resort the help of a black voodooo priest, a houngan by the name of Solimán. Interestingly, at the last moment LeClerc is forced to resort to the same esoteric practices – creole versions of mesmerism – that, according to the novel, he had made fun of:

> Now she lamented having often made fun of sacred things just to keep up with the trend. The agony of Leclerc, increasing her fear, made her delve deeper into the world of powers that Solimán invoked in his conjures, true master of the island, last possible defender against the lashes of the far shore, only probable doctor against the inadequacy of the traditional chemists.[41]

Pauline's relationship to Solimán is allegorically crucial: her survival is related to her capacity to give in to the new viral logic represented by the houngan. As the novel continues, we find that Pauline Bonaparte – who historically had been infected with the plague herself – carries with her back to France, together with the funeral remains of her diseased husband, the wisdom that she had acquired by her 'contact' with Solimán's contagious presence. Pauline Bonaparte's return had brought within the confines of the metropolis the disease that so far had remained outside its territorial frontiers. As such it remains symptomatic of the transformations endured by the imperial notion of sovereignty. From now on the emerging global state would have to learn how to negotiate with the latent viruses that had suddenly plagued its territory. Little did Nicolas-Pierre Gilbert know that the virus he was writing about was to be found, not across the Atlantic, but outside his door.

The naturalist novel and the social immune system: On Manuel Zeno Gandía's *Crónicas para un Mundo Enfermo*

A brief analysis of the opening pages of Michael Foucault's now famous text on *Panopticism* gives us a first insight into the paradoxical double nature of that which, following the conclusions of the preceding section, I would like to call the modern immunological state. Foucault begins the text by discussing the biopolitics of surveillance that were triggered by the event of a plague in the seventeenth century. In his desire to elucidate the cartography of surveillance and discipline that became operative as soon as the fear of an epidemic struck the community, he proceeds to list the measures that took place in case of the breakout of an epidemic. First, space became partitioned by the sudden emergence of authority: the closing of the town and the prohibition of leaving it was followed by its division into different quarters, each of which was governed by an intendant. Each street was placed under the authority of a syndic whose role was to keep surveillance. The city became a hierarchical space traversed by the presence of the seeing eye and the writing hand of power:

> This enclosed, segmented space, observed at every point, in which the individuals are inserted in a fixed place, in which the slightest movements are supervised, in which all events are recorded, in which an uninterrupted work of writing links the centre and periphery, in which power is exercised without division, according to a continuous hierarchical figure, in which each individual is constantly located, examined and distributed among the living beings, the sick and the dead – all this constitutes a compact model of the disciplinary mechanism.[42]

For Foucault, what the plague discloses is the graphic cartography of power implicit within the city itself: 'The plague stricken town, traversed throughout by the functioning of an extensive power that bears in a distinct way over all individual bodies – this is the utopia of the perfectly governed city.'[43] After this brief introduction, Foucault then goes on to trace a further development in the biopolitics of modern surveillance: the emergence of what, following Jeremy Bentham's panopticon, he calls *panopticism*, the dialectics between visibility, discipline and knowledge that structures modern sovereignty. What remains particularly modern about modern surveillance is not so much its presence but rather its 'generalized model of functioning'. Whereas the plague remains an exceptional situation, panopticism turns the state of exception into the rule as part of the transformation of monarchic societies into disciplinary societies: 'The movement from one project to the other, from a schema of exceptional discipline to one of a generalized surveillance, rests on a historical transformation: the gradual extension of the mechanisms of discipline throughout the seventeenth and eighteenth centuries, their spread throughout the whole social body, the formation of what might be called in general the disciplinary society.'[44] At first, the whole foundation of my argument regarding the role of virality within modern politics seems to be destroyed by the underlining assumption behind Foucault's text: plagues where the biopolitical form of the medieval and classical ages, whereas the formation of the nation-state carries with it the emergence of other, positive, forms of subjection. To some extent, this argument is undeniable: from Boccaccio's *Decameron* to Chaucer's *Canterbury Tales*, from the *Dance Macabre* to Holbein's death, the black death imagery rules the medieval imaginary and only begins to slowly disappear with the emergency of the nation-state. However, what interests me is something that seems implicit in the paradoxical structure of Foucault's argumentation. Not for any reason does Foucault begin with an account of the biopolitical implications of the plague. His strategy is clear. Discussing the plague first allows him to sketch out the power structure which, when later flipped, gives him the reverse image of that which he wants to portray: the positive, generalized state of surveillance and disciplining which rules over the modern social body. What I wish to underline is the *homeopathic* gesture through which Foucault produces the positivity of modern disciplinary society out of the negativity of classical sovereignty. In fact, the plague provides him with that discourse on the invisible hand of sovereignty that he later applies to modernity:

> The plague is met by order; its function is to sort out every possible confusion: that of the disease, which is transmitted when bodies are mixed together; that of the evil, which is increased when fear and death overcome prohibitions. It lays down for each individual his place, his body, his disease and his death, his well-being, by means of an omnipresent and omniscient power that subdivides itself in a regular, uninterrupted way even to the ultimate determination of the individual, of what characterizes him, of what belongs to him, of what happens to him. Against the plague, which is a mixture, discipline brings into play its power, which is one of analysis.[45]

What Foucault attempts to think is the process by which sovereignty as a state of exception became a generalized, invisible, omnipresent, mode of societal functioning: the way in which its negativity became a positive. *Similia Similibus Curantur*, Hahnemann's homeopathic law of similars – *the like cures the like* – is here performed to perfection. The negative of the negative becomes the invisible hand of modern sovereignty. To some extent, to use the epidemiological vocabulary, what Foucault is interested is in the way the modern state inoculated itself against the plague, against its logic of contagion and multiplicity by turning into a disciplinary society that structures itself *as if* it was always under the threat of a plague. The immunological politics of this *as if* must be studied thoroughly. One must not forget that Edward Jenner's smallpox vaccine dates from 1796 and that Louis Pasteur's bacteriological works on the anthrax and rabies vaccines traverse the second part of the nineteenth century with the force of a discursive revolution: his germ theory of disease – the belief that microscopic organisms are to blame for many of our diseases – changed the way society structured itself in relationship to a politics of scales, as well as reinforced what we could call the homeopathic nature of positivism. Regarding the emergence of such homeopathic paradigm, Roberto Esposito, in his 2002 book *Immunitas*, has explored the sociological dimensions of this paradigm. Following the etymological dialectic between immunity and community, Esposito highlights the double nature of the homeopathic cure: 'Immunity, in short, is the internal limit which cuts across community, folding it back on itself in a form that is both constitutive and deprivative: immunity constitutes or reconstitutes community precisely by negating it.'[46] Esposito then goes on to explore, following the work of the father of systems theory, Niklas Luhmann, how the double nature of immunity is itself a new relationship to the law and sovereignty:

> This negative dialectic takes on particular prominence in the sphere of legal language or, to be more precise, in law as the immune apparatus of the entire social system. If, as Niklas Luhmann claims, starting in the nineteenth century, the semantics of immunity have progressively extended to all sectors of modern society, this means that the immune mechanism is no longer a function of law, but rather, law is a function of the immune mechanism [...] this crucial transition constitutes the point of precipitation of an otherwise sharply aporetic path that has its origin in the structural relation between law and violence.[47]

Law, violence, sovereignty and discipline: the nineteenth century sees the emergence of the modern state as the fiction that regulates the entropic flows of a territorial immune system. The modern immunological state regains control of itself by inoculating itself from its own perils. Foucault, in his essay on *panopticism,* speaks of a 'political dream' established by the plague: a dream in which the discerning gaze of the law regulates even the smallest details of everyday life through its hierarchical organization. According to him, as we know, this gaze institutionalized itself in a series of governmental institutions and material practices: the police, the school, the asylum, the prison. Epistemologically, this homeopathic paradigm gave birth to the social sciences.

However, in what follows, I wish to explore another *apparatus* whose internal logic mimicked the state's immunitary logic: the naturalist novel. One merely has to read Emile Zola's programmatic 1880 essay *The Experimental Novel* – where the French author sketches the poetics of the genre – in order to understand its proximity to the logic of immunity and discipline described by both Esposito and Foucault. Taking the physiologist as his model, Zola envisions a mode of writing characterized by observation and analysis:

> He (the naturalist writer) should be the photographer of phenomena, his observation should be an exact representation of nature... He listens to nature and he writes under its dictation. But once the fact is ascertained and the phenomenon observed, an idea or hypothesis enters his mind, reason intervenes and the experimentalist comes forward to interpret the phenomenon.[48]

In what follows, I will attempt to show – through the study of the works of the Puerto Rican doctor and writer Manuel Zeno Gandía – how the naturalist novel functioned as an apparatus whose internal dynamics mimicked the homeopathic logic of the state's immune system. The naturalist novel acted as an apparatus whose desire to portray the logic of contagion in all its modalities served a homeopathic function: that of containing nature's rhizomatic multiplicity within the territorial boundaries of the empire's sovereign gaze.

A bacterial colony: On the naturalist novel as culture medium

La novela naturalista extirpa los cánceres sociales, ocultos
en su mayor parte tras la pulcra vestimenta de la humanidad.
–Matías González

History has its paradoxes. If by the end of the eighteenth century Haiti was already on the verge of declaring itself a free Republic, by the end of the nineteenth, almost a century later, Puerto Rico was still a colony of Spain. Alongside with Cuba, the island remained the last colony under Spanish rule at the end of a tumultuous century that had erased and redrawn the political cartography of the Americas. By the last decade of the century, however, the prospects of independence must have looked promising amidst the internal collapse of the Spanish empire that would culminate in the catastrophic losses of 1898. However, as the atmosphere of the island boiled with desire for autonomy, intellectuals feared that the social body was not ready to assume the task of citizenship. The arrival of the naturalist novel to the island must be understood against this background of fears concerning the health of the social body. As Fernando Feliú Mantilla has sketched in his genealogy of the genre, the naturalist novel arrived to the island mainly thanks to the translations of the works of Emile Zola that, starting from 1885, Manuel Fernández Juncos began including in his newspaper *El Buscapié*, among them excerpts from *Germinal*, *Eugene Rougon* and *La Ventre du Paris*.[49] By 1887 we have record of a lecture by Alberto Regúlez y Sanz del Río about realism and naturalism, and by 1889 the genre had produced its first intellectual polemic. That year *El Boletín Mercantil* published a series of articles entitled 'El Naturalismo en el Arte' in which José Arnau Igarávidez highlighted the achievements of the genre while at the same moment condemning some of its excesses. The polemic would reach its culmination some years later when the writer Matías González García, in the prologue to his 1893 novel *Cosas*, proclaimed the naturalist novel as the only appropriate vehicle capable of both developing a reading public as well as of building up its moral dimension. The words that González García would choose to portray the task of the genre remain illuminating: 'The naturalist novel excises the social cancers that lie occult beneath humanity's clean clothes.'[50] Social tumours: it would be against this background of medical discourse and social preoccupations that the doctor and writer Manuel Zeno Gandía would conceive his novelistic project *Crónicas de un Mundo Enfermo* as an attempt to reform the social body by portraying its sickly state. As I will now attempt to show, Zeno Gandía, a medical doctor trained in Spain and an avid supporter of the independence movement, conceived the naturalist novel under the homeopathic rubric provided by the immunological logic of vaccination: his narrative project attempts to inoculate the body politic from the danger of that which we could call, following González García, social cancers. Namely, if we are to borrow the vocabulary of microbiology, Zeno Gandía uses the form of the naturalist novel in order to conduct a social experiment: the naturalist novel serves as the culture medium through which the writer studies the behaviour and logic of the spread of social disease, its causes and its structure. The insular space of the island mimics the perfect ecological environment of the *Petri dish* and imagines it as a bacterial colony under observation. Paradoxically, by dissecting the rationality behind the logic of contagion, by illustrating the causality behind the apparent multiplicity, the naturalist novel ends up providing the social body with an image of itself as a healthy immune system. This didactic paradox, which I here call the immunological paradox, traverses the medical discourse of Zeno Gandía's *Crónicas de un Pueblo Enfermo* serving as the driving force behind its rehearsal of citizenship. As Juan del Salto, the cultured landowner and representative of the *ciudad letrada* in Zeno Gandía's 1894 novel *La Charca*, suggests, the task is that of giving a form to the masses, that of turning the rhizomatic *gentío* into cultured citizens for the coming state:

> It was a tomb for the living. The red blood cell, in its struggle with the white cells, had forever escaped from that great pale multitude. That great mass of people was a multitude of vague silhouettes, dregs ... a bundle of twisted vines with the vices and virtues so tangled that they were inseparable. Ah! How can one define them?[51]

'Ah! How can one define them?': the task of the writer is conceived as that of drawing distinctions amidst the swarming multiplicity of the social body. Juan del Salto's panoptic vision of his plantation, his territorial gaze as well as his reflections concerning the working classes provide an image of the naturalist writer as a doctor of the social body. This social body is not, however, any social body: as the above image of the battling red and white cells suggests, Zeno Gandía envisions the social body of the colony under the sign of *anemia*. His task is inoculating the anaemic body from its own vices, from its tendency towards contagion, mixture and indistinction. Namely, making it a productive body. As Gabriela Nouzeilles has noted in her essay 'La Esfinge del Monstruo' this emphasis on a hygienic modernism must be understood within the broader politicization of the body and its metaphors within the nineteenth century.[52] The clinical discourse that Nouzeilles had already sketched out in her book *Ficciones somáticas* belongs to the biopolitics of desire that became central within the foundational projects of nation-state in the nineteenth century.[53] However, if in the foundational romances studied by Doris Sommer what mattered was the harmonious resolution of desire within the image of the heterosexual couple, in the case of the naturalist novel, as Nouzeilles suggests,

what matters is portraying the dangers of a viral catastrophe: the degeneration of the political body into a formless infertile monster. Both Sommer and Nouzeilles depart, however, from the same intuition: nineteenth-century realism, as Leo Bersani has shown, takes as its main concern the regulation of desire.[54] Whereas foundational romances attempt to solve the problem by narratively resolving desire, the naturalist novel attempts to cure the malady by exposing its dangers. The paradoxical nature of its homeopathic logic is evident from the above quote by Juan del Salto: there one gets an image in which vice tangles itself around virtue with the same rhizomatic logic with which white cells snarl around red cells. The figure of the social body as anaemic body sketches the main concerns of the immunological state: the relationship of the body to itself and its capacity to interact with that within itself that seems to exceed it. Moreover, the figure of the *anaemic body* remains crucial since it exposes the naturalist novel as the stage where questions regarding labour and productivity in their relationship to the expenditure of energy are negotiated: the writer's double task is that of invigorating the anaemic social body at the same time as detaining the contagious proliferation of unhealthy desire. The naturalist novel negotiates the distribution of energy within the social body. In the agricultural context of nineteenth-century Latin America, this task would prove crucial. After the abolition of slavery, the plantation would see the emergence of the creole worker as the main proletariat force driving the economy: namely, for the first time in history, the body of the colony was also the body of its labour force. Sociological concerns regarding the proletarian class, its health and its productivity would become, as a consequence, a common thread throughout the century. In the case of Puerto Rico, these would lead to a series of sociological studies that would take as its main concern the figure of the creole working man, the *jíbaro*: from the 1882 novel of customs *El Gíbaro* by the medical doctor Manuel Alonso to sociological essays like *Las Clases Jornaleras* by Salvador Brau, the question regarding the health and productivity of the *jíbaro* quickly became synonymous with the question regarding the future of the colony as well as its possible economic future as an independent state.[55] It then comes to no surprise that both *Garduña* and *La Charca*, the two pre-1898 novels in Zeno Gandía's *Crónicas de un Pueblo Enfermo*, read as novelized versions of the sociological concerns expressed in essays such as Brau's *Las Clases Jornaleras*. In them the plantation becomes the ecological locus for a sociological experiment regarding the dangers of an unproductive expenditure of energy. The omnipresent narrator of the naturalist novel – writing from an all-seeing perspective not unlike that of Juan del Salto in *La Charca* – observes, records and regulates the flow-like dispersion of energy in an attempt to make sure its deployment is optimized. His greatest fear is the logic of contagion that deterritorializes energy in nonproductive manners. He fears that which Georges Bataille would latter call *expenditure*.[56] And yet nothing fascinates him more than portraying the unproductive expenditure produced by such viral behaviour and vices:

> In studying the people of the mountains, Juan was witness to the evolutionary development of a race: its prehistory, its obscure origin, its migrations, and then – upon contact with the Europeans – its mixtures and transformations. He was well acquainted with the life these people led in the colony. He saw them descend in a straight line of ethnic mixtures whose end product was contaminated with a deadly, invincible weakness, leaving its arteries anemic, the brain sluggish, the arms without strength.[57]

In Juan del Salto's vision the anaemic body of the country is the product of unhealthy racial miscegenation. As Gabriela Nouzeilles has noted, the racial miscegenation that characterizes the 'clases obreras' was feared as being unhygienic and therefore unproductive. The contaminated ontology of the proletariat classes characterized them as an unproductive '*gentío*' rather than as productive citizens: 'Were those poor people clustered on the spurs of the mountain human beings, or merely shreds of life launched forth by chance? Were they rabble? Were they swine? Were they sheep? What moved them? [...] No, it was not the spirit. The contaminated, the feeble, the deformed, was the body.'[58] Zeno Gandía's novelistic project *Crónicas para un Mundo Enfermo* must then be placed alongside the great treatises of sociology which at the end of the nineteenth century began to think through the characteristics of that new viral subject called the crowd: *La Charca* was published one year before Gustave Le Bon's 1895 *La Psychologie des Foules* and five years before J. M. Ramos Mejías's *Las Multitudes Argentinas*.[59] In fact, the opening reflections by landowner Del Salto foreshadow many of Le Bon's reflections regarding the viral psychology that characterized the crowd as subject: its contagious inclination towards suggestions, its vicious spontaneity, its tendency towards crime, among others. Zeno Gandía's crowd belongs, however, to the tropical plantations rather than to the urban centre: his *gentío* is composed, not of urban proletariats, but of agricultural workers. As such the relationship to nature and dirt is more apparent. In fact, throughout the novel moments of contagion appear constantly as the great fear, as the reason behind the social *anaemia* that prevents the country from subsisting by itself. Namely, on the eyes of Zeno Gandía, the country's incapacity to reach independence was largely due to its incapacity to sanitize itself. The author, a medical doctor who had been trained in Spain, would himself write, in the custom of the nineteenth century, a hygienic manual aptly entitled *Higiene de la Infancia al Alcance de las Madres de Familia*.[60] In the introduction to the manual, the author begins by sketching the naturalist analogy between humans and plants: 'The human is perfectly comparable to a plant: the atmosphere surrounds it and feeds it, assimilating what it needs and giving back what is not needed for nutrition, substances it ingests to reinvigorate the organism and to protect itself against hazards.'[61] However, as he so well knew and as the imagery in *La Charca* makes evident, the problem was precisely in the organ of nourishing: the colony had a sick stomach. In this sense, fears regarding social contagion and blood contamination must be understood with regard to the epidemic of *hookworm* that struck the colony's working classes throughout the nineteenth century. By the end of the century, as becomes evident in *La Charca's* ever-present image of the sick stomach, the small worm-looking intestinal parasite had infected more than 90 per cent of the workers, leading to a widespread of anaemia. The *jíbaros* working in the mountains, being mostly of white origin, were not immune to the disease that had been brought two centuries before by the slave trade. As such, the image of the infected stomach leading to an *anaemic state* quickly becomes the leading image for a state whose workforce is limited:

> They were like a 'giant stomach,' perishing from malnutrition. 'If that giant stomach would nourish itself,' he said, 'the race would improve, future generations would be healthy and robust. We must not ask a poor starving man for his tithe, for his alms; we must offer him free bread, not stinginess.'[62]

One could then claim that, confronted with the atrophy of its operating organ, the body of the nation found in the naturalist novel a transplant. The naturalist novel becomes the technological *dispositif* that comes to regulate the energy distribution and immunological operations of the social body. Through the construction of a sovereign causality, it acts as an implantable immune system, reterritorializing the energy that had been inadequately dispersed. Its relationship to the law comes then as no surprise: the naturalist novel stages the law as its main concern and finds in crime fiction its structural model. As the above image of the anaemic body suggests, following the thread of vice one might find virtue. The naturalist novel stages the outbreak of disease as the crime it must solve: it unknots the thread of social evils until it finds, at the very end, perhaps not the resolution of desire or the exaltation of virtue, but rather the possibility of the law as such, its subsistence within the otherwise entropic realm of social phenomena. Both *La Charca* and *Garduña* stage themselves as juridical novels: in the case of *La Charca* the novel deals with the aftermath of the killing of Deblás and in the case of *Garduña* with the legality of an inheritance. The possibility of a law without necessary justice sketches in both cases the possibility of a territorial unity devoid of unhealthy multiplicities.

Unknotting nature's crime: The lawful labour of naturalism

Así urdida la trama, se aseguraba el secreto.
Secreto muy hondo de una intriga muy negra.
– Manuel Zeno Gandía, *Garduña*

Garduña, the first novel belonging to *Crónicas de un Pueblo Enfermo*, begins by staging the production of visibility from the heights. Three horse riders climb the mountains, making their way through the rough vegetation, until they reach a plateau nested between two hills that 'opens' for them the view of a valley. Only then are we introduced both to the lawyer Hermógenes Garduña whose name gives the novel its title, as well as to the valley of *Paraíso* whose legal ownership seems to be at stake. The reader quickly realizes that what lies in front of him – the landscape now drawn from the perspective of the *abra* – is the object of a legal dispute. This beginning marks the delimitation of the territory of fiction as that which must prove capable of being traversed by the lawful eye of writing: 'That's why, once the eviction was decreed, I decided to come here myself. I was afraid he would change the limit points. That way, as you can see, I have been able to delimit myself the boundaries of the estate, which is now mine.'[63] In a single gesture the novel begins by knotting together many of the main dichotomies and concerns that traverse the naturalist novel as genre: the relationship between nature and law, between the act of observing and that of living, between transcendence and immanence, between the cultivated land and uncultivated nature. The territorial limits of naturalism – 'los límites de la finca' – are set as the reterritorialized grounds upon which the contractual law of literature must prevail. What is at stake, we hear, is the outcome of a 'pleito'. This legal dispute is not, however, any dispute, but one regarding a very special type of legal document: the will of the moribund landowner Tirso Mina. This specificity must not be ignored. What the will, as the mediator between life and death, as the mediator between father and children, between generations as such, highlights is the contractual sense of naturalism. With the force of nineteenth-century Darwinism, the will binds the progeny to the law. Like the social contract before it, it legitimates the possibility of historical unity and continuity by reassuring that after the death of the father the estate does not fall back upon the civil war that marked the Hobessian state of nature. The sovereignty of the father's testamentary word becomes the fundamental biopolitical oath by reassuring the continuity of the 'natural' status quo: the property of the father should be that of the progeny. The will, as contract between the citizen and history, makes sure that nature behaves within the limits of the law in order to avoid historical degeneration. Unless, and here lies the secret crime at the very core of naturalism, something comes to disturb the stability of the natural law: perhaps, one could say following Zeno Gandía, an illegitimate child. Next thing he knows the reader finds himself far from the initial panoptical perspective of the *abra*, locked within the close doors of a house in which the landowner Tirso Mina prepares to die from tuberculosis. His close family joins him, not out of a desire to help, but rather out of the fear that in his final moments, the landowner might decide to produce a will. Their fears have a reason. Tirso, who had no legitimate progeny in life, is believed to have had an illegitimate daughter:

> The inheritance! Only the inheritance mattered there, even at the expense of the poor sick man to whom, from time to time, they even forgot to medicate [...] Maybe, kneeling down, he had begged Tirso to produce a testament and he, half unconsciously, has agreed. He could see something in the midst of confusion and indecision. He knew that Tirso was the father of an abandoned girl who lived with Ocampo.[64]

Against such fears, Leonarda, Tirso's sister and lawful inheritor, has sketched a plan with the help of Garduña: to make sure that he dies without producing a will, in which case she, as closest legally acknowledged family member, will receive the inheritance automatically. However, the plan collapses as they see Ocampo – an old friend of Tirso who is believed to be the father of the woman with whom the landowner had the illegitimate daughter – enter the room and leave. Only then, against the fears that Ocampo might have taken with him a will, Leonarda, with the help of Garduña, storms into the room and forces Tirso to produce a last will in which he declares them the legal inheritors of the sugar plantation Mina de Oro. *Garduña* unfolds against such an initial crime, as an exploration of the biopolitical relationship between the law and life. It stages the fictional writing of a natural law.

Naturalism, one could then say, posits the natural law as its foundational fiction: like the social contract, it writes, against the multiplicity of the social, the rationality of a natural law. Within this paradigm the emergence of illegitimate others, of the dirty parasite or atrophied cell, is seen as the social evil that must either be written into the representative realm of the law or removed from the picture. What *Garduña*, through the triumphs of the eponymous character portrays, is the very paradox at the core of the genre itself: the fact that there is nothing natural about naturalism. Naturalism deprives nature of its rhizomatic, not to say violent essence, by imposing upon it the structure of an overarching rational teleology. It deprives nature of its spirited multiplicity by rendering everything within it necessary. As Toni Negri has pointed out in his discussion of Spinoza: 'The social contract theory is an explicit sociological fiction that legitimizes the effectiveness of the transfer of Power and thus founds the juridical concept of the State.'[65] What the naturalist novel, through its adoption of the formal structure of crime fiction stages, is the capacity of the self-organizing modern state to reform the non-rational multiplicities that arise within its social body. More than narrating the search for the truth behind the enigma of the illegitimate child Casilda, *Garduña* unfolds as the story of the main protagonist's Machiavellian scheming against the involved parties in order to gain control of the plantation. At the end, with both Leonard and Casilda tricked by the protagonist's false rationale, what we are forced to acknowledge are the triumphs of a formalist ratio written under the sign of the law. The triumphs of licenciado Garduña, here thought in terms of naturalism's determinism, portray the triumph of the possibility of the law as such. Interestingly, this paradoxical lawful ending – paradoxical since justice is never attained – is visualized in the novel in geometrical manners, as the territorial correction of the '*ángulo del mal*' that had so much bothered Garduña:

> Garduña did as he wished. Placing his property side by side to Mina de Oro, he was able to regulate its limits, keeping for himself a good piece of the land and erasing... finally, that entrance angle which so much worried him [...] Good, justice, the rights of the weak to receive the protection of the strong, everything had been realized.[66]

With this ending *Garduña* actualizes what in the beginning had only been sketched as prophecy: the possibility of a reterritorialization devoid of thwarted paths, of illegitimate others. The possibility of a landscape. No wonder this ending coincides with the expulsion of Casilda, the illegitimate child, from Mina de Oro. Like the bad cell which must be either written into the law or expelled from the social body, the last scene of the novel presents us with the image of Casilda's convoy leaving Paraiso and its infected mud: 'stepping over – without staining her angel-like gallant dress, adorned as it was with lightful colors – the infected mud of the land'.[67] The ending of Garduña, however, is not alone in this respect. In the ending of *La Charca*, as the fatal conclusion to the crime fiction, we are presented with the death of Silvina as she falls from the height into pure nature:

> She collapsed by the edge of the slope as she writhed about, a victim of the sickness of her organism, shaking under the stimulus of her convulsions, she momentarily moved away from the edge of the Cliff; but after an instant's calm her body shuddered spasmodically, her face contracted in a horrible grimace, and she writhed close to the edge of the abyss [...] She was life returning to its origin, the borrowed breath giving itself back to earth.[68]

The teleological structure of naturalism, not to say its determinism, is perfectly sketched out by the image of Silvina's final image. As we see Silvina being devoured by nature we are reminded of the etymology of her name: Silvina, Silva, selva, jungle, uncultivated land. The bacterial colony sketches for itself the image of the final degeneration of its parasitic components into a formless mass. But in the meanwhile, and here lies the achievement of the naturalist novel as genre, this same teleological arch sketches the possibility of an 'evolutionary ratio' that guarantees the survival of the social body as immune system. We are presented with the very possibility of historical lawfulness.

The germ of laziness: Hygiene and neocolonialism after 1898

What if these people were merely innocent victims of a disease, modern only in name?

– Bailey Ashford

The year 1898 proved to be a decisive year in Puerto Rico's history: the Spanish-American War shattered the colony's dreams of autonomy, as the island saw itself transformed from being a Spanish colony to being an American colony. In accordance with the political ecology of the times, the territorial rigidity of the Spanish empire had finally crumbled against the neo-liberal, self-generating flexibility of North America's emerging empire. Transatlantic relationships would soon be displaced by relationships between North and South, a political cartography that would frequently be understood in terms of northern consumption and southern production. It would be amidst this geopolitical and ecological reconfiguration of the Americas that many of the concerns expressed by Manuel Zeno Gandía's *La Charca* would finally be systematically tackled. Preeminent among them would be the *Puerto Rico Anemia Commission*, an attempt by the emerging colonial government to tackle the so-called *germ of laziness* which had left the colony's working classes, as Zeno Gandía had pointed out, in a state of anaemic misery. The commission was led by Bailey K. Ashford, a professor at Georgetown University and an assistant surgeon at the United States Army. Throughout the first decade of the century, the commission would conduct field research into the causes of the anaemia epidemic among the working classes, also known as *jíbaros*. The sociological as well as medical results of the field research would serve as the basis for Ashford's 1911 report entitled *Unciniariasis (Hookworm Disease) in Porto Rico: A Medical and Economic Problem*.[69] What remains striking about Ashford's report is that it reads not only as a scientific document, but rather as a socioeconomic history of the island. In fact, from the very start Ashford begins by declaring himself a reader of the tradition of nineteenth-century sociological literature that had taken the problem of the *jíbaro* as its topic: he declares himself in debt with the writings of Salvador Brau, Cayetano Coll y Toste, Dr Francisco del Valle Atiles as well with the writings of poet Manuel Fernández Juncos. Fascinatingly, Ashford begins by declaring himself a reader of the socio-literary medical tradition that, throughout the nineteenth century, had attempted to build a healthy nation out of its collapsing labour force. With a precision characteristic of Zeno Gandía, Ashford quickly locates the problem as a historic problem: 'With the threatened extermination of the Indian slave, the Spanish saw the necessity for importing labor, and in the coming of the negro slave we can see the beginning of what later proved to be the greatest curse Puerto Rico has ever suffered, epidemic uncinariasis, or "La Anemia".'[70] This great curse – '*La Anemia*' – is not, however, understood to be an intrinsic defect of the working classes – a defect of its vicious nature as Zeno Gandía would have claimed – but rather as the result of a purely natural disease: hookworm, scientifically known as *unciniarisis*. As he states throughout the report, what must be understood is the man behind the pandemic: 'The jíbaro is a type to be well studied before we essay to interest him in bettering his own condition. Many have written of his virtues, many of his defects, but few, even in Puerto Rico, have seen through the mist of a pandemic the real man beyond.'[71] With such words then begins a new chapter in the history of the colony, a new relationship between medicine, labour and consumption written under the sign of foreign intervention. What the *Puerto Rico Anemia Commission* foreshadows is the complex political ecology that would bind the island to its new metropolis for the next century: an experimental ecology within which the island would function as a perfect bacterial colony for the emerging empire. Two decades later, funded by the Rockefeller Foundation, another doctor, Cornelius Roads, would arrive to the island to study, once again, the anaemic nature of the island. His studies would soon turn to oncology, and a scandal would soon erupt regarding a letter in which Roads claims to have injected cancer cells within the body of Puerto Ricans: 'The Porto Ricans [sic] are the dirtiest, laziest, most degenerate and thievish race of men ever to inhabit this sphere ... I have done my best to further the process of extermination by killing off eight and transplanting cancer into several more... All physicians take delight in the abuse and torture of the unfortunate subjects.'[72] Independently of its veracity, Road's statement perfectly captures the logic of the bacterial colony and with it, all its consequences: the emphasis on laziness and labour, the colonial subject as experimental subject, the island itself as a laboratory within which the metropolis could conduct its experiments in view of paradoxically constructing a healthier immune system.

Aftershock

Reinaldo Arenas's *El color del verano*: AIDS and the end(s) of the immunological state

Muchos de entre nosotros han muerto de la plaga que no cesa. Nosotros somos los sobrevivientes de una sobrevida que hay que pagar al precio de nuestras vidas; vidas que además estamos siempre a punto de perder.

– Reinaldo Arenas, *El color del verano*

An early draft of Reinaldo Arenas's posthumous novel *El color del verano* contains an epigraph that reads as follows: 'I dedicate this work to AIDS because without that experience I would have never written it.'[73] Arenas, who had been diagnosed with the disease in 1987, knew that he was not only writing *against* the virus, but also *through* it: the disease had begun inhabiting his work as the invisible spirit driving the proliferation of writing against time. Paradoxically, it had become the invigorating catalyst of proliferation and force within an otherwise weakened body. One could even claim that Arenas was never more prolific than in those final years after the diagnostic, when the problem regarding the end and endings must have become terribly pressing. *El color del verano* reads, in this sense, as the culmination and exaltation of the viral character of his oeuvre. Arenas's works are never self-contained stories, but rather parasitical works that give way to a contagious proliferation of desire, of imagery, of laughter. Like Deleuze's *desiring machines*, his novels question the territorial unity of plot, replacing it instead with the agitating force of vital rhythms that traverse the plot's structure, interrupting the flow of sense and deviating it, perverting the web of meaning in ways that question the authority of the nineteenth-century omnipresent narrator. His are transvestite fictions – assemblages of theatre, short stories, poetry, tongue twisters, songs – always in the process of mutation, displacing their narrative strategies so as to make it impossible for the reader to establish observational positions from which to regulate them. *El color del verano* is then, to no wonder, a novel about endings, a novel about social malaise, a novel about sexual repression, but also a novel about pleasure, about humour, about sex, about all of those elements which end up corroding the immune system of the state. Writing against the imminence of a death that had taken AIDS as its signature, Arenas ends up producing a novel that stages the end(s) of the immunological state as the modern paradigm of political sovereignty. *El color del verano* is a novel about the possibility of a final flight towards freedom. Staged ten years into a future that had been taken away from its author, staged against the very end of the millennium, Arenas's literary assemblage mounts itself around a very particular event: the carnival that the dictator Fifo – i.e., Fidel Castro – sets up to celebrate his fiftieth year in power. From the very beginning, the question regarding sovereignty, power and censorship is at stake. In fact, Arenas begins the novel by placing himself in front of the law through a prelude entitled *To the Judge*:

> Whoa, girl, just hold it right there. Before you start going through these pages looking for things to have me thrown in jail for, I want you to remember that you're reading a work of fiction here, so the characters in it are made up – they're concoctions, denizens of the world of imagination (literary figures, parodies, metaphors – *you* know), not real-life people. And another thing, my dear, while we're at it – I wrote this novel in 1990 and set it in 1999. I mean think about it – how fair would it be to haul me into court for a bunch of fictitious stuff that when it was written down hadn't even happened yet?
>
> The Author[74]

This false start begins by staging the conditions of possibility of the novel as genre: the legitimization in front of the law, the staging of its hypothetical character as well as of its figural nature are all part of the strategies by which Arenas as 'the author' puts on the table the problems he wishes to tackle: the relationship between literature and freedom, literature and sovereignty, the complex notion of a literary activism, as well as the generic boundaries of historical fictions. From the very start his targets are set. Next thing we know, the prelude in front of the law gives way to a theatre where the main characters of Cuban cultural history witness the flight of literature away from the law: the body of the novel begins by staging the attempt of a resurrected Gertrudis Gómez de Avellaneda to escape the island amidst the celebrations of Fifo's fiftieth year in power. In 'La Fuga de Avellaneda', the play that jump-starts Arenas's desiring machine, Gertrudis de Avellaneda, the nineteenth-century Cuban poet, plunges into the sea in her attempt to escape the oppressive climate of the island. The machine is then set in motion as an attempt to stop her flight. The cast of characters include

José Martí, Halisia Jalonzo, Zebro Sardoya, Delfín Proust, Raul Kastro, Cynthio Methier. From the very beginning it becomes clear that *El color del verano* is a delirious literary artefact where Arenas, writing under the sign of AIDS, feverishly hallucinates Cuban modern history. A viral allegory where history goes mad.

To say that *El color del verano* begins with a flight and the ensuing attempt to recapture the fleeing element is not enough. For what is at stake in Arenas's novel is something much more perverse: the flight of allegory itself outside the territory of circulation. Traditional allegory, we could claim, is an *insular* genre. It stages language as the circulation of signification. In the genre's conventional sense – in the sense that was debunked by early twentieth-century modernism – it imagines language as a healthy body insuring the circulation of meaning through a general system of equivalence. Within a healthy allegory, meaning circulates with the calming knowledge that its stability is guaranteed by the promise of a happy resolution within its closed circuit. Like an island, allegory forbids the flight of meaning by remaining a territory without exits. As such, it is as much hygienic as it is lawful. *El color del verano*, we could then say, stages the heterotopia of an allegory gone wild, of a wasteful, open flight of meaning that marks the discontents of an oppressive insularity. As Arenas suggests in the recurring passages entitled 'La Historia' which constantly punctuate the novel, the idea is not to merely escape the island but to stage the escape of the island itself:

> The dream of the entire population of the island was no longer to be free, but rather that someday they be able to escape from the island, which was a perfect prison. But how was one to escape from the island, which was a perfect prison? [...] So great was their desperation that people finally decided that the only way of escape was by using the island itself.[75]

As such, the novel not only sketches a series of flights outside of the island, but the flight of the island itself. Throughout the novel we hear that a subversive group is working on corroding the island's foundation in an attempt to allow it to flee from itself. The same could be said of the role of allegory within the novel: Arenas contaminates the genre from within, providing it with a grotesque plasticity that allows it to deviate constantly. To say it differently: once the immunological, not to say insular, logic of allegory is weakened – in a manner that inevitable leads us to AIDS – desire is able to circulate, mutate, grow and eventually produce that final catastrophe which according to Arenas paradoxically leads to historical freedom.[76] Arenas seems to write or, if we are to use his words, paint with this catastrophe in sight: 'The last part of the painting will be very dark, almost black. In it, all those who have been expelled will huddle together [...] and if they come closer they'll be able to hear explosions and screams and the muted sound of the city collapsing. They will see the panicked flight and the final disaster.'[77] *El color del verano* then reads not only as an allegory of historical catastrophe but rather as catastrophic paradigm of allegory that takes, as one can imagine, AIDS as its founding trope. But how does one write or, even better, 'paint' the catastrophe of allegory? Arenas hides an answer behind the novel's subtitle.

'I will paint the cracked and peeling walls of my body': if, while reading Arenas's novel, we are reminded of the grotesque imagery of medieval paintings we are in the right path. The subtitle of the novel, *Nuevo jardín de las delicias*, outlines the tradition within which Arenas envisioned his project. *The Garden of Earthly Delights* is the title of Hieronymus Bosch's most famous painting, a triptych that portrays, in the sprawling style of the Dutch master, the history of mankind as the corrosive progression of sin. Central to the piece is the body as the site of both pleasure and sin. The sinuosity of the bodies portrayed, their amorphousness that hints at formlessness without fully embracing it, brings forth the imagery of the plague-ridden body. The memory of the *Black Death*, still in the air at the end of the sixteenth century, gets transformed within Bosch's painting into the great carnival of history. It then comes as no surprise that Bosch, perhaps the greatest of all plague painters, decided to paint history itself as a viral procession. Beyond being a mere representation of the sick body or even of the body as sickness, *The Garden of Earthly Delights* stages itself *as* a sick body: the triptych, when closed, portrays the globe in the third day of creation, as if it were the external profile of humanity understood as historical body. Later, when opened, one has the sense that, like the anatomist, one has been granted access to the entrails of a sick body: the multiplicity and polymorphousness of the bodies that punctuate the painting mimics that of cells struggling for preeminence within a body at battle with itself. One could then say that *The Garden of Earthly Delights* stages human history under the carnivalesque sign of the viral body. Arenas's decision to honour Bosch through the subtitle of his last novel then gains a particular density: it foreshadows that what is to come should be read under the sign not only of the body, but of the viral body and its discontents. *El color del verano*, like Bosch's painting, stages history as a sprawling carnival that portrays the unsubsumable multiplicity of the social body. Within it, painting reaches that humorous threshold where figuration itself is conceived as catastrophe.

A linguistic carnival: The neo-baroque allegory as desiring machine

Solamente quisiera apuntar que no se trata de una obra lineal,
sino circular y por lo mismo ciclónica, con un vértice o centro que es el carnaval,
hacia donde parten todas las fechas.

– Reinaldo Arenas, *El color del verano*

El color del verano stands within a broader constellation of Caribbean novels that, after the second wave of the avant-garde in the 1960s, began to envision the novel as an entropic machine rather than as lawful observation. From Luis Rafael Sánchez's *La guaracha del Macho Camacho* to Guillermo Cabrera Infante's *Tres tristes tigres*, from Manuel Ramos Otero's *La novelabingo* to Severo Sarduy's *Colibrí*, all of these novels implode the classical novel from within, infecting it with flows of desire that challenge its disciplinary order. Interestingly, many of them stage themselves as allegories of insularity and its discontents. Following Severo Sarduy, one could then give this tradition a name: the neo-baroque allegory.[78] In this sense, the neo-baroque allegory stands as an inversion of the nineteenth-century novel. If, according to Leo Bersani, the nineteenth-century novel stages the suppression of desire, then the twentieth-century neo-baroque allegory, of which *El color del verano* is a prime example, stages its boundless proliferation. Like in Bosch's *The Garden of Earthly Delights*, the body here becomes the contagious presence that virally disrupts the law, propagating itself like a pure multiplicity, weakening in turn the internal classificatory apparatus of the novel. Namely, with the baroque novel, the body stops acting as a unity of sovereign action and begins to act like a crowd. This is perhaps the great discovery of that which, following Susan Sontag, we could call the discursive realm of modern medicine: in each of its modern variations, the modern 'plague' – with cancer and AIDS as its main figures – converts the body into a society itself alongside its misbehaving crowds.[79] The body becomes a multiplicity. It is around this discovery, facilitated by the microbiological discovery of germs, cells, parasites and viruses, that the possibility of thinking the society as sick body is latter constructed. What the baroque allegory then stages is the endless proliferation of bodies, its fractal multiplicity, as well as its grotesque debauchery. One must not forget that *El color del verano* stages itself not only as a novel, but rather as a carnival: a carnival that celebrates the fiftieth anniversary of Fifo, the dictator which allegorical comes to represent

Fidel Castro. As such, one should read the novel under the carnivalesque sign of the never-ending masquerade. As Arenas himself suggests:

> Our wet, razor-sharp bodies slice through this frightening quietness, which echoes, silently, in our every fiber – and we defy the heavens to fall upon us as we try to find a response out there in the glowing splendor of the sea. But all there is bodies – writhing, squirming, coiling about one another, hooking to one another in the midst of a Carnival without shadows, in which every person wears the mask he feels like wearing, in which betrayal and ass-wiggling are part of the official system, part of our most fundamental tradition.[80]

Within this great carnival of masks no name can remain merely itself, just as no body can remain untouched. The neo-baroque allegory provokes the deviation as well as proliferation of the proper name. If *El color del verano* shows itself to be, at moments, a highly autobiographical novel, it does so only under the constant displacement of the author's name: the proper name – Reinaldo Arenas – traverses the novel, in the process mutating, masking and unmasking itself, participating in the erotized atmosphere of cross-dressing that surrounds the carnival and its cloud of anonymity. Throughout the novel Arenas refers to himself, allegorically, as both Skunk in a Funk and as Gabriel, in a fight within the self that provides the novel with a multiplicity of authors: 'Don't pay attention! Reinaldo shouted at Skunk in a Funk from somewhere deep inside Skunk in a Funk, just keep working on your novel!'[81] Whereas the realist novel posited the omnipresent narrator as the locus from which the law itself became a possibility, the neo-baroque allegory – understanding that the body itself is a crowd – multiplies the author and his masks in an attempt at subverting this same law. One may ask, what happens then to the novel as genre when it is forced to confront the carnivalesque polymorphousness of its author? Following Arenas's suggestions, one might answer that the novel that emerges from this viral catastrophe of sense is no longer a book, but an assemblage, a cyclonic machine that removes the possibility of transcendence.

Machines abound in *El color del verano*: from the computer lab at the end of the novel to the small linguistic fugues that Arenas disperses alphabetically across the novel, the neo-baroque allegory stages itself as an assemblage composed of small transistors whose task is to deviate sense, increasing in turn the momentum of pleasure. If, following Deleuze and Guattari, we think of *El color del verano* as a desiring machine, then we must pay attention to the formal machines through which Arenas the author tricks himself. One of the 'name fugues' – most of which are tongue-twisters that take the name of his friends as basis – seems to me of particular importance. That which the author dedicates to himself:

> In a chain gang in a cane field in the rain, in-your-face gay tale-teller Reinaldo Arenas is constrained by hyenas to raise cane. Unswayingly praying to Ares to pave the way to his release from this chained travail, escapist Arenas entertains himself by telling himself tales he's spun of penises seen in urinals and train terminals until, flayed by the hyena's maces, he's returned to the traces. [...] Escaping the hyenas, escapist escape-artist Reinaldo Arenas hastily hails a plane for Spain, where his daydreams of unprosecuted penises seen in urinals and train terminals are realized.
>
> *For Reinaldo Arenas*[82]

Small fugues like this one interrupt the plot constantly, guiding sense towards the line of flight of pure sound, wildly multiplying the connections within the allegorical machine itself. The above fugue, however, seems crucial. By taking the name of the author itself as point of departure it discloses many of the themes at play within the novel itself: the dissolution of the author into a rhythmic multiplicity, his entanglement within a broader web of pleasure production, his incapacity to achieve a transcendental position. Everything gets folded back into Arenas's viral allegory, even himself. Everything flows back into the entropic rhythms of this desire machine that weakens the immunological logic of the social law and allows pleasure to explode in all directions. This establishment of allegorical machine as the absolute place of immanence is fundamental for it prohibits a transcendental position from which the regulation of the machinery might operate. This is perhaps what is at stake in a novel like this: the belief that language might actually be beyond the panoptical power of the state, even beyond the immunological logic of the novel itself. For Arenas, and this is crucial, the body is not the body of the law, but rather the absolute viral body, the body that is undistinguishable from the viral logic itself. And moreover, as we are led to understand, this viral logic is precisely the logic of language. As we read in his final linguistic fugue:

> Let us march, then, militarily, down to an emaciated sea where a marmo-real marmot murmurs myriads of mistreatments... And yet we find that we have come, finally, to the finest fuckup of them all, the great floating flophouse where a photographer forever flutes its philanthropic fluff and an unphotogenic, fetid, syphilitic mephitic proffers us, frothing at the mouth, his furious physiognomy. Ay-y-y-y-e-e-e-e. *To all of us*.[83]

Confronted with his imminent death, Arenas writes this play upon endings that serve as a condensation of the main motifs of the novel. For *El color del verano* can be read, at the very core, as a voice summoning the multitudes towards that sea that marks the horizon of an unhappy insularity. This flight towards the sea, towards the ever-receding horizon of pleasure and freedom, is however understood under the ever-present yet silent sign of AIDS: the corrosion of the body from within, the body weakening its own immune system, the island eating away its own foundation: 'So tacitly they decided to gnaw away at the platform that bound the island to the seabed until they had separated the island from its base.'[84] It is this final flight, this corrosion of the system itself, that marks Arenas's final reflections upon the law under the sign of viral catastrophe in all its modes: humour, sex, disease.

An endless summer: Learning to live amidst the crowds

> *Esta es la historia de una isla que mientras aparentemente se cubre*
> *con los oropeles de la retórica oficial,*
> *por dentro se desgarra y confía en la explosión final.*
>
> – Reinaldo Arenas, *El color del verano*

El color del verano is, in many ways, a novel about endings. Arenas's decision to set the novel in the vertiginous future, at the very turn of the millennium, must then be read alongside its neo-baroque impulse towards problematizing the figure of the end in all its allegorical modes: the end(s) of the state, the end(s) of the body, the end(s) of the novel, the end(s) of insularity. Moreover, as Alexander García Duttman has highlighted in his well-known essay on the topic, AIDS – as the paradigmatic disease of the end of the millennium – was from the very beginning conceived as a polemic regarding the figure of the end: an inscription of death within life that marked the spiralling descent of sovereignty and identity under the sign of a catastrophic latency.[85] *El color del verano* is, as such, a novel written against time under the sign of survival: 'A lot of us have died of The Plague, which is raging, my dear. So those of us who are left are the survivors of an afterlife that we pay for with our very lives – lives we are literally about to lose.'[86] The novel carries with it all of the signs of the posthumous: it is a novel written not only from the perspective of the future, but rather as a prophecy for the future. A prophecy that must be written before time expires. We are then tempted to ask: how should we read the final explosion that constitutes the ending of the novel? Like in the last triptych of Bosch's *The Garden of Earthly Delights,* the ending of *El color del verano* paints the final convergence and explosion of a carnivalesque historical procession. The final exposure of the reader to Fifo's *Garden of Computers,* in which the monitoring power of the state is exposed; the attempt by virgin Tedevoro of finding someone who will take his virginity; a multitude of dwarfs at the orders of Fifo; the funeral of Virgilio Piñera, all of these possible endings open up the space within which the novel finds its crowded resolution. They set up the stage for the last line of flight. That of the island itself:

> It was drifting, drifting, drifting away. The Island was drifting away […] This time it was the whole country – and it was floating away, in geographical, geological flight. This was exodus like any other in the history of exoduses – the Island of Cuba, unmoored from its foundations, was sailing out of the Gulf makings its way toward the open sea. It was leaving behind the great catacomb-palace as it sank into the ocean, computers howling, to the sound of muffled explosions of fury […] And as the Island floated away, the people of the Island, seized by the euphoria of flight and therefore of freedom, began to shout with joy, and with their hands, like oars, they tried to steer the Island… each one to a different place.[87]

The final flight of the island out of its foundation is here staged against the power of the multitude. However, as Arenas seems to suggest, the rise of the power of the multitude comes at the price of the greatest social confusion: El Pueblo battles over the direction the island must take. Catastrophe ensues the island, incapable of finding a stable direction, begins to sink within the sea. It is at this moment that Arenas's politics gain their definitive density, forcing us to see his relationship with the popular crowds in its true complexity: although he seems to find in the crowds the element of subversion, he also seems to condemn its arbitrariness. What then is left? The novel seems to respond: what is left is the power of writing, the never-ending spiral gesture of a minor literature committed to corroding its own foundation. At the very end, in a chapter called 'Botellas al Agua', Arenas stages his final will: amidst the sharks that devour the masses, amidst the sharks that devour the body of the state as well as its territory, Arenas, in all of his masks, is seen finishing this novel which we ourselves are reading:

> Even if she should perish – and that was a real possibility – her work would survive, she thought, opening the sack and hurling bottles. But the moment

a bottle would hit the water it would be swallowed up by the sharks. The last one didn't even hit the water [...] As the shark devoured her, Skunk in a Funk realized that she was losing her life, but before she did so, she was determined to start her novel again.[88]

Writing against his imminent death, Arenas sketches this last joyous image in which writing provides an afterlife to pleasure beyond the end of history.

5

Conclusion: *One Final Gust:* Macondo and the aftermaths of modernity

No tenemos un lenguaje para los finales...
[...]
Quizá un lenguaje para los finales
exija la total abolición de los otros lenguajes,
la imperturbable síntesis
de las tierras arrasadas.
O tal vez crear un habla de intersticios,
que reúna los mínimos espacios
entreverados entre el silencio y la palabra
y las ignotas partículas sin codicia.

– Roberto Juarroz

I would like to conclude by analysing a novel that both instantiates and problematizes the teleological image of the end of progressivist history while simultaneously reimagining as nightmares the dreams upon which Latin American modernity was imagined in the nineteenth century. Talking about the authors of the Latin American Boom, Doris Sommer notes that their novels sprang from a desire to rewrite and parody the epic subtexts of Latin American development which, by the early 1960s, had 'run aground and made history stumble when it should have been going forward. Looking back at Latin American history after reaching a precipitous end, to find that end no longer meant purpose'.[1] It should be no surprise, then, that this critique of the ends of modernity is perhaps best illustrated by the concluding pages of what remains our canonical novel par excellence, a book that simultaneously marked our highest level of literary modernity as well as our cultural difference with respect to those models of Western modernity which our *letrados* had struggled to mimic for more than a century: I am speaking about Gabriel García Márquez's

Cien años de Soledad and, in particular, about the tempestuous ending which marks the final destruction of Macondo.

In that last chapter, as readers will remember, a scene of reading coincides with the catastrophic ending of the story being told. As Aureliano begins to decipher the manuscripts of the old gypsy Melquíades, he becomes enveloped by a biblical hurricane that tears asunder the world of Macondo. With the spiralling power of the hurricane gusts, the scene stages something that had remained prevalent throughout the novel: the tension between the linearity of teleological historicity and the circularity of mythical temporality. This dialectic between novelty and repetition, progress and return, history and myth reaches in those prophetic final pages its apotheosis through an apocalyptic ending that returns us readers to the very beginning of García Márquez's literary career, and to the foundation of the world of Macondo itself. In fact, the cyclonic winds that begin to tear Macondo apart uncannily echo the winds that first helped shape its universe. As readers might remember, in the prologue to his 1955 novella *La hojarasca*, where Macondo first makes an appearance within the works of the Colombian writer, its foundation is defined in relationship to the same shattering winds that will end up destroying it:

> Suddenly, as if a whirlwind had set down roots in the center of the town, the banana company arrived, pursued by a leaf storm. A whirling leaf storm, had been stirred up, formed out of the human and material dregs of other towns, the chaff of a civil war that seemed ever more remote and unlikely. The whirlwind was implacable. It contaminated everything with its swirling crowd smell, the smell of skin secretion and hidden death. In less than a year it sowed over the town the rubble of many catastrophes that had come before it, scattering its mixed cargo of rubbish in the streets.[2]

Macondo's foundation is then, from the very get go, established in relationship to both a discourse of natural catastrophe and a discourse of modernity. The whirlwind arrives alongside the banana company as the Benjaminian storm of progress that will mark its progressive yet catastrophic modernity. Foreshadowing the arrival of the banana company and its acceleration of time as it would later appear in *Cien años de soledad*, the prologue defines Macondo as a town composed out of the rubble produced by war. Macondo becomes a strange bricolage of nature and culture, whose history begins the day that this foundational leaf storm gets naturalized and the violence of its inaugural state of exception becomes second nature: 'Then the train whistled for the first time.

The leaf storm turned about and went out to greet it, and by turning it lost its drive. But it developed unity and mass; and it underwent the natural process of fermentation, becoming incorporated into the germination of the earth.'[3] From then on, its modernity will be defined by that which, following Reinhart Koselleck, we could call an ongoing crisis.[4] What remains, however, fascinating about this germinal moment is that it mimics to perfection something which I have tried to express throughout each of the preceding chapters: it sketches how at the heart of Latin America's baroque history one finds both the image of history understood as natural catastrophe and the repression of this foundational genesis. Behind the violence of this repressed founding gesture lies the tension that traverses García Márquez's work in its complex relationship to modernity, a tension which becomes explicit in the final pages of *Cien años de soledad*, as the reader witnesses how nature, under different disguises, progressively invades the realm of culture: under the image of a stranger's letter being devoured by moths, the clean whistle of the growth of weeds inside the Buendía's old house or the insects that begin to take over Macondo. The old nineteenth-century dichotomies between nature and culture, barbarism and civilization, have collapsed and history is exposed under the catastrophic rubric of natural history. Macondo, the cradle of civilization, the city built in mid-jungle, is slowly being devoured by the voracity of nature, as the potent image of the Buendía house invaded by ants eloquently suggests:

> The rest of the house was given over to the tenacious assault of destruction. The silver shop, Melquiades' room, the primitive and silent real of Santa Sofía de la Piedad remained in the depths of a domestic jungle that no one would have had the courage to penetrate. Surrounded by the voracity of nature, Aurealiano and Amaranta Úrsula continued cultivating the oregano and the begonias and defended their world with demarcations of wuicklime, building the last trenches in the age-old war between man and ant.[5]

A great reader of the nineteenth-century naturalist novel, García Márquez imagines the end of history as a monstrous invasion: that of nature upon culture, of barbarism upon civilization. The age-old battle between man and ant – as the narrator calls it – emerges forth as a symptom of history's discontent: nature erupts with the force and voracity of the Freudian return of the repressed. The novel therefore ends with a scene in which the catastrophic end of Macondo's teleological history coincides with the state of exception that gave rise to its origins.

Reading and writing the end

One must not forget, however, that the final scene of *Cien años de soledad* is indeed a scene of reading. Under the image of Aureliano Babilonia, the last living member of the condemned lineage of the Buendía family, deciphering the sense of Melquíades's script, the reader comes to understand something about the novel as a whole: the fact that it must be taken as a re-reading and rewriting of Latin American, or at least Colombian, history. What the final scene then unearths is the tension between competing models of historicity and the intuition that is precisely this tension what has led us to experience our modernity in a catastrophic manner. As Lois Parkinson Zamora has explored, the closing pages of the novel instantiate the struggle between the progressivist imaginary proper to a teleological conception of history and the circular temporality of the mythical world of Macondo. Spiralling around itself, the eschatological world of Aureliano is determined by the paradoxical coincidence of end and beginning. As the ants begin to invade the house, turning Macondo into the jungle it once was, Aureliano suddenly realizes that the terrible reality he is beginning to decipher in the manuscripts is precisely that which surrounds him. Understanding his predicament, he sees, amidst the rhye grass and the spider webs, the body of his dead son being eaten by a battalion of ants. The great nightmare of the nineteenth-century naturalist novel, the prophesied fear of his great-grandmother, has become a reality. Incest has produced a pig-tailed kid that is, in that instant, being consumed by nature. Interestingly, it is only then that the code to decrypt the manuscripts of Melquiádes is revealed to him: 'And then he saw the child. It was a dry and bloated bag of skin that all the ants in the world were dragging toward their holes along the stone path in the garden. Aurealiano could not move. Not because he was paralysed by horror but because at that prodigious instant Melquiades' final keys were revealed to him and he saw.'[6] At the sight of his pig-tailed son being devoured by ants, Aurealiano realizes he is a man living at the end of times. However, this end of history is not merely a utopic instant of absolute comprehension, but rather, as in Jorge Luis Borges's story *El aleph*, the catastrophic witnessing of a totality too vast and overwhelming to be experienced synthetically. Overwhelmed, the last member of the Buendía family realizes that he is also a victim of this catastrophe of sense:

> At that point, impatient to know his origin Aureliano skipped ahead. Then the wind began, warm, incipient, full of voices from the past, the murmurs of ancient geraniums, sighs of disenchantment that preceded the most tenacious

nostalgia. He did not notice it because at that moment he was discovering the first indications of his own being [....] He was so absorbed that he did not feel the second surge of wind either as its cyclonic strength tore the doors and windows off their hinges, pulled off the roof of the east wing, and uprooted the foundations.[7]

Under the spiralling logic of the hurricane winds, echoes of the leaf storm which gave rise to Macondo, García Márquez stages a world in which the end of history does not coincide, as Francis Fukuyama's interpretation of Hegel would have it, with the realization of the triumph of progressivist modernity and the arrival of a homogenous liberal state. Rather, what we encounter is a catastrophe that unearths the history of Macondo – and therefore, allegorically, that of Colombia and Latin America – as a history of violence, destroyed by the same progressivist logic of development that is suggested by the winds of the biblical cyclone. The end of history is seen not as the arrival of sense and the liberation from the barbarism of nature – that is to say, not as the act of revelatory uncovering suggested by the word apocalypse – but rather as the traumatic confrontation with the barbaric origins of our dreams of modernity.[8] If, as Ernst Bloch said, every epoch dreams the one to come, it could be said that the ending of *Cien años de soledad* marks a painful moment of awakening: the instant in which Latin America finally wakes up to realize its dreams of modernity were in fact nightmares.

'Every epoch dreams of itself as being annihilated by catastrophes': Adorno's reformulation of Bloch's motto, later adopted by Walter Benjamin as part of his *Arcades Project*, gains a prophetic tone within García Márquez's novel.[9] Not only, as Aureliano Babilonia soon comprehends, due to the fact that Melquíades's manuscripts already foretells the story of Macondo's catastrophic dissolution, but rather because the novel tragically presaged the political disasters that – in the form of right wing, market-espousing military dictatorships – would rock the continent in the decades to follow. Published in 1967, *Cien años de soledad* already foreshadows the historical storm which, in the name of progress and democracy, would lead to the devastating disappearance of more than 100,000 Latin Americans. The image of Aureliano Babilonia, struggling to find meaning within the ruins of Melquiades's archive, would soon become a recognizable one. Ravaged by nature and destroyed in the name of modernity, our lettered cities would soon turn into archives of ruins, among whose vestiges the writer would have to wander in search for those fragments of meaning which might help him piece together the sense of a history that had been reduced to ashes. As García Márquez himself would later explain in his 1982 novella *Crónica de una muerte anunciada*:

> Everything we know about his character has been learned from the brief, which several people helped me look for twenty years later in the Palace of Justice in Riohacha. There was no classification of files whatever and more than a century of cases were piled up on the floor of the decrepit colonial building that had been Sir Francis Drake's headquarters for two days. The ground floor would be flooded by high tides and the unbound volumes floated about the deserted offices. I myself did my searching many times with the water up to my ankles in that lagoon of lost causes, and only chance after five years of searching let me rescue some 322 pages filched from the more than 500 that the brief must have had.[10]

The archive, traditional symbol of historical memory, is here reduced to a flooded landscape, amidst which files float like forgotten remnants. *Cien años de soledad* could then be said to be a point of transition: a novel that already signals the shift that in the coming decades would replace our obsession with beginnings with a fascination towards endings and their catastrophic aftermaths. It marks a transition from the mythical foundations which, according to Roberto González Echevarría, had marked the literary preoccupations of Latin American novelists up until the boom, towards a different sort of archival fictions: ones which would question the possibility of historicity and justice after the traumatic political catastrophes that had rocked the region with the power of the worst earthquake. We must not forget that in *Myth and Archive* Melquiades's room remains the paradigm for the archive itself and that for González Echevarría this archive is always thought of in eschatological terms: 'The Archive is an image of the end of time. The Archive is apocalyptic, it is like a time capsule launched into infinity, but without hope of reaching eternity.'[11] Moreover, as the prologue to *La Hojarasca* suggests, Macondo itself is nothing but an archive of Latin American history – 'a different and more complex town, created out of the rubbish of other towns' – whose final destruction turns a foundational landscape into a Benjaminian landscape of ruins, among which the writer, reduced to a sort of bricoleur, wanders in solitude, attempting reconstruct history out of its catastrophic debris.

After Babilonia

As his name already suggests, and as the novel is quick to underline, Aureliano Babilonia is the last member in the damned lineage of the Buendía family. Locked in Melquiades's old room, surrounded by nature on all sides, he begins to decipher an archive that tells the circular story that ends when the speed of prophecy overtakes that of the present, and the destiny of the family is tragically realized. Macondo's history is that of Babylon, whose dreams of universality were reduced to a heap of rubble. Like a modern Babylon, Macondo, as Ericka Beckman has suggested in *Capital Fictions*, instantiates the violence inherent in Latin America's attempt to inscribe itself within the coordinates of globalization and its many languages: be it capital, science or information.[12]

The story of Macondo, however magical, becomes today awfully recognizable. In June 2005, a series of spontaneous explosions at Guatemala City's Mariscal Zavala military base caught the attention of the National Civic Police and as a result the police finally agreed to listen to a complaint formulated by residents of a nearby neighbourhood, who had recently protested the improper storage of explosives in a local police base. When Sergio Morales Alvarado, the country's human rights prosecutor, arrived with his team of inspectors to proceed with the removal, they unexpectedly discovered the remains of an archive that was believed to be long lost: the archive of the former National Police, whose complicity with the atrocities committed during Guatemala's civil war was such that after the war it was forced to disband. That archive, long believed to have been lost, held the records of the human rights abuses perpetuated by the State during the civil war. Interestingly, as Kristen Weld recounts in *Paper Cadavers*, when forced to describe the archives and the room they were found in, the witnesses of this seminal event can only think of it in relationship to the catastrophic image of a ruinous Babylon:

> There was an aura of decay about the massive unfinished structure, occupied only by small armies of rats and bats and reeking of mold and mildew, where detainees had once been regularly tortured to death. It lay in a scrubby field carpeted with overgrown weeds and ringed by heaps of scrapped cars. The papers it housed seemed endless, crude bundles by the millions spotted with vermin feces and cockroach carcasses, their hand-scrawled labels barely visible beneath years of dust, with puddles of cloudy water seeping up into the piles of paper and rotting them from within. The space summoned to mind images of entrapment: a concrete labyrinth, a warren of windowless cells, a zone of haunting and sepulcher. At the back of the office, humidity and neglect had conspired such that verdant plant life coiled up the walls, sprouted from within the masses of paper blanketing the earth, and hung down from the ceiling in long fronds. This last, the Project's assistant's director remembered, 'was why we gave that room the name "Babylon."'[13]

It seems almost impossible not to draw a connection between the image of this decaying room, taken over by rats and overgrown weeds, and Melquiades's room in *Cien años de soledad*. Both are ghostly spaces populated by forgotten histories, archives in ruins that open up the possibility of historical redemption. Both are, in a sense, the remainders of failed apocalypses that, however, bear inscribed upon them what Jacques Derrida has called the absolute referent of literature: 'The total destruction of the archive.'[14] And so, it would be around this archive of ruins and the models of history it proposes that the Guatemalan writer Rodrigo Rey Rosa would later write his novel *El material humano*, a book which explores the ways through which historical sense can be reconstructed out of the archival remnants left by a catastrophe too traumatic to be experienced synthetically, that is to say, in its totality.[15] One must not forget that it had been precisely around the atrocities committed during the Guatemalan civil war that Rigoberta Menchú had weaved, alongside anthropologist Elizabeth Burgos, her 1982 autobiographical testimony *Me llamo Rigoberta Menchú y así me nació la consciencia*, one of the foundational texts in what later became known as *testimonio*, the genre which briefly came to be seen as a way of bypassing the authority of the lettered city and its traditional archival fictions. However, as Roberto González Echevarría would suggest in his 1988 book *Myth and Archive*, in his discussion of Miguel Barnet's *Biografía de un cimarrón*, one of the foundational examples of testimonio, and as critics like Alberto Moreiras, Doris Sommer and Giorgio Agamben would later rephrase, despite the illusion, witnessing can't work without mediation as the voice of the witness inevitably leads back to the material foundation of the archive.

And so, upon hearing of the discovery of rat-ridden Babylon, the room which held the National Police Archives, Rey Rosa must have felt that his true place as a writer was there, alongside that archive which had been unearthed, thanks to the catastrophic power of fire. The derelict landscape of La Isla, the former detention and torture centre where the archives had been found, must have seem adequate to the story they told: surrounding the infamous warehouse, the writer found a dog pound, an abandoned hospital and a car junkyard. Around this dust and vermin-ridden labyrinth, reminiscent of the final days of Macondo, dozens of archivists moved, carefully sorting out that mass of half-rotten documents which Edilberto Cifuentes, the head of the Human Rights Ombudsman's Office Investigation Team, would later describe as 'huge volcanoes of documents'.[16] Indeed, the whole story of the discovery of Guatemala's National Police Archives was to be marked by the sign of catastrophe: having been discovered as a result of a fire explosion, the archives themselves were targeted in early 2006, when unknown individuals threw a Molotov cocktail into the warehouse, in a clear attempt to destroy evidence. As if that was not enough, one year later, the nearby residents woke up to a strange reverberation: overnight, a large block of land adjacent to the archives had been swallowed by the earth, shockingly sinking alongside it houses, business and even several residents. The decision to call the archive's room Babylon seemed to be adequate and even prophetic: the archive's existence seemed always threatened by the same catastrophic logic to which they bore witness.

As one can imagine, Rodrigo Rey Rosa's *El material humano* is then a novel about the attempt to make sense of Guatemala's traumatic recent history from within this landscape of an archive in ruins. In its pages, we find a call towards a new type of literature: one which doesn't shy away from the document, but which still finds in fiction the necessary tools for making sense of history, once the mythic foundations proposed by the *total novels* of the Latin American Boom had collapsed and the promise of *testimonio*'s transparency had proven to be nothing but a well-intentioned chimera. Composed mainly of diary jottings, literary quotes and fragments copy-pasted from the found documents, the novel mimics the structure of an archive, and in so doing reframes our sense of historicity and justice, by proposing a new mode of witnessing once the horizon of teleological history has collapsed and history risks being reduced to the silence of the unutterable. In this sense, it inscribes itself within the tradition of novels which Idelber Avelar has studied in *The Untimely Present*, a book that expounds that one of the main tasks of postdictatorial fiction was that of learning to mourn the past, which amounted to recomposing, out of the landscape of ruins and debris, an allegorical meaning:

> These images of ruins are crucial for postdictatorial memory work, for they offer anchors through which a connection with the past can be reestablished. In incessantly producing the new and discarding the old, the market also creates an array of leftovers that point towards the past, as if demanding restitution for what has been lost and forgotten. The texts I examine here insistently confront the ruins left by the dictatorship and extract from them a strong allegorical meaning.[17]

Walter Benjamin's notion of the baroque allegory, fundamental in each of the previous chapters, allows Avelar to interpret the fragmentary structures of works like Ricardo Piglia's *Respiración artificial*, Diamela Eltit's *Lumpérica* or João Gilberto Noll's *Harmada*. However, published in 1999, with the presence of the dictatorships still radiant, the book remains focused on understanding history through the lens of memory. Today, almost twenty years later, with the arrival of a new generation that didn't live through the atrocious experience of the dictatorships and the civil wars, it would seem that the work of memory explored by Avelar has given way to something else: something that, for lack of a better word, we could tentatively call, following the work of Marianne Hirsch, post-memory.[18] What comes forth in the paradigm sketched by Rey Rosa's novel is something that became already apparent in our discussion of *testimonio*: that any sort of witnessing remits us not only to the lived experience of trauma, but rather to the archival ruins or remnants that endure in the aftermath of catastrophe. As Dominic Lacapra has noted, traumatic historicity involves not so much the direct memory of trauma, but rather the catastrophic aftermath through which trauma is archived as alienated experience.[19] *El material humano* suggests that today, writers arrive always a bit late, when history has already ended, and what remains is the ruinous landscape of the lettered city. Illegitimate inheritors of Aureliano Babilonia, they attempt to reconstruct a possible sense of futurity out of the ruins left by the political catastrophes that marked Latin America's modernity.

In this sense, Rey Rosa suggests that today's archival fictions don't try to elucidate – like González Echevarría's Boom fictions – the mythic origins enclosed within the archive, but rather attempt to reconstruct historical sense as the posthumous revival of material remains. To give a voice to the remnants becomes, for what these new archival fictions, the true task of mourning, one which is not mediated by the phenomenological sphere of memory but rather by the materialism of the archive's physicality. The paradox of today's archival fictions – novels like Horacio Castellanos Moya's *Insensatez*, Rodrigo Rey Rosa's *El material humano*, Cristina Rivera Garza's *La muerte me da* or Roberto Bolaño's *2666* – lies precisely in the fact that their archives do not lead, as etymologically they should, to any origin, but rather to a catastrophic landscape that remits – in a way – to a time *after* the end of history. As Hal Foster has pointed out in relationship to the recent boom in archival art, today's archival impulse could in fact be called an *anarchival* impulse: 'In this regard archival art is as much preproduction as it is postproduction: concerned less with absolute origins than with obscure traces (perhaps anarchival impulse is the more appropriate phrase).'[20] Unlike the archival fictions of the Latin American Boom, the archive in ruins displayed here does not remit to any unifying myth, but rather to the dispersal of historical sense after the end of history. Writing from the ruins of history, each of these writers attempts to rethink what a return to history would look like after the collapse of historicity that perhaps reached its clearest expression in Francis Fukuyama's proclamation, in 1989, of the end of history. Within a world in which the possibility of human experience is questioned, these fictions focus on the postproduction of history: the attempt to make the archival material speak. Taking a new stance with regard to testimonio, they sketch what Cristina Rivera Garza, in her book *Los muertos indóciles*, has called *necroescrituras*, the posthuman conception of writing as the re-appropriation and exhumation of the voices of others:

> Far from, then, the pateralistic "giving voice" characteristic of certain imperial subjetivities or of the naive attempt to place oneself in the shoes of another, what is here sketched are a series of writing practices that bring those shoes and those others into the materiality of a text that is, in this sense, always produced relationally, that is to say, in community.[21]

Within these new *necroescrituras* which, as Rivera Garza points out, mimic 'the porous, incomplete, patchy, fragile structure of the archive', the humanist paradigm of 'let the witness speak' characteristic of *testimonio* is replaced by the subtler 'let the archive speak'.[22] As such, the archive in ruins seems to re-enter contemporary Latin American art and fiction as a *fossil* that remits us to a historicity from which we are, however, forbidden as historical subjects. And if I speak here of Latin American art and fiction, rather than only about literature, it is because I believe the same logic begins to become relevant in other mediums, such as film, photography and sculpture, from Teresa Margolles's forensic sculpture to Patricio Guzmán's *Nostalgia de la Luz*, from Marcelo Brodsky's *Los condenados de la tierra* to Albertina Carri's *Los Rubios*. In all of these *forensic fictions*, as we could call them following the works of Eyal Weizamn, the archive allegorically becomes no longer a myth of origin, but rather that which Quentin Meillassoux, in his book *After Finitude*, calls an *ancestral evidence*: a trace or fossil that remits to an event which can't be fully experienced phenomenologically.[23] As ancestral evidence the ruinous archive reminds us of those extinct or dead languages of which we have inherited their material traces but no longer hold the key to their signifying process.[24] Like the anthropologists who try to resuscitate the forgotten sounds of those dead languages, contemporary writers and artists are asked to reconstruct the historical sense of a catastrophic archive which, in the stubbornness of its materiality, points precisely towards the impossibility of a fully accountable witness.

Unearthing history

Like Aureliano Babilonia, witness of the destruction of Macondo at the hands of the very same leaf storm which marked its foundation, today we are asked to bear witness to the echoes of the foundational violence through which, in the nineteenth century, the Latin American nation-states imposed themselves as the legitimate guardians of modernity. Like the tempestuous ending of *Cien años de soledad* suggests, through that scene in which the last of the Buendía family becomes a figure akin to Benjamin's angel of history, what is disclosed by a proper catastrophic stance vis-à-vis modernity is the realization that the history of the state is that of the ongoing perpetuation of the inaugural violent state of exception declared and sustained under the pretence of progressivist modernity and its many names: liberal democracy, free market capitalism, enlightened historicity, progress or development. What the atrocities committed by the military dictatorships during the civil wars that rocked Latin America throughout the last century show, in their hypostatization of catastrophe, is the violent nature of the state as such: that which, following Walter Benjamin, one could call the mythical violence that marks both its foundation and its end.[25] It is this historical examination of the archive of our modernity that must be carried out if, as etymology suggests, the archive is both the place of memory and the place where the Greek *arkhe*, understood as 'the beginning, the first place, the government', gets embodied.[26] We need, more than ever, a revision of that founding archival violence – which Jacques Derrida has likened to the power of an earthquake – that helped establish the state's sovereignty and whose echoes still resound potently today, when the madness of the state only seems to be matched by the evidence of its failures.[27] Today, when the Latin American political landscape is sadly punctuated by the dreadful sight of *tierras arrasadas* and *fosas comunes*, by scorched lands and mass graves, a new critique of violence is needed: one which allows us to understand how state violence, understood in both its law-making and law-preserving aspects, has marked the history of our modernity as ongoing crisis. It is precisely this critique which I have attempted to sketch in *The Literature of Catastrophe: Nature, Disaster and Revolution in Latin America*, showing how only a catastrophic stance with respect to the history of Latin American modernity can help us unearth the unredeemed historical potential buried under the false progressivist tale through which the state has attempted to naturalize and therefore mask its often brutal existence.

Notes

Chapter 1

1 Piglia, Ricardo. *Artificial Respiration*. Estados Unidos: Duke University Press, 1994, 30.
2 Stavans, Ilan. 'Introduction'. In *Backlands: The Canudos Campaign*, edited by Euclides da Cunha and Elizabeth Lowe, vii–xxiii. New York: Penguin Books, 2010.
3 Da Cunha, Euclides. *Backlands: The Canudos Campaign*. Translated by Elizabeth Lowe. New York: Penguin Books, 2010, 142.
4 Andermann, Jens. *The Optic of the State: Visuality and Power in Argentina and Brazil*. Pittsburgh, PA: University of Pittsburgh Press, 2007.
5 Mitchell, W. J. Thomas. *Landscape and Power*. Chicago, IL: University of Chicago Press, 2009, 2.
6 Da Cunha, *Backlands*, 124.
7 Kane, Adrian Taylor, and Mark D. Anderson. 'National Nature and Ecologies of Abjection in Brazilian Literature at the Turn of the Twentieth Century'. Essay. In *The Natural World in Latin American Literatures: Ecocritical Essays on Twentieth Century Writings*, 208–32, 218. Jefferson, NC: McFarland & Co., 2010.
8 Da Cunha, *Backlands*, 465.
9 Da Cunha, *Backlands*, 17–18.
10 Badiou, Alain. *Being and Event*. Translated by Oliver Feltham. London: Continuum, 2006.
11 What is disclosed in catastrophe is, in a way, the non-natural side of nature itself. If, following Raymond William's definition of the term on his *Keywords*, we take nature to be 'perhaps the most complex in the language', we understand that what is highlighted by the advent of catastrophe is the folding of one of the meanings of nature against itself: in catastrophe nature ceases to be the atemporal realm of essences and becomes a historical object itself.
12 Rudwick, Martin J. S. *Bursting the Limits of Time: The Reconstruction of Geohistory in the Age of Revolution*. Chicago, IL: University of Chicago Press, 2007.
13 Da Cunha, *Backlands*, 54.
14 Badiou, *Being and Event*, 104.
15 Dabove, Juan Pablo. *Nightmares of the Lettered City: Banditry and Literature in Latin America, 1816–1929*. Pittsburgh, PA: University of Pittsburgh Press, 2007.

16. Campos Johnson, Adriana Michele. *Sentencing Canudos: Subalternity in the Backlands of Brazil*. Pittsburgh, PA: University of Pittsburgh Press, 2010.
17. Campos Johnson, *Sentencing Canudos*, 79.
18. Badiou, *Being and Event*, 25.
19. Lienhard, Martin. 'Writing and Power in the Conquest of America'. *Latin American Perspectives* 19, no. 3 (1992): 79–85.
20. Žižek, Slavoj. 'Heiner Mueller Out of Joint'. 2003. Accessed 16 January 2019. http://www.lacan.com/mueller.htm.
21. Benjamin, Walter. *Illuminations: Essays and Reflections*. Translated by Harry Zohn. Boston, MA: Mariner Books, Houghton Mifflin Harcourt, 2019, 258.
22. Da Cunha, *Backlands*, 463.
23. Da Cunha, *Backlands*, 465.
24. Benjamin, Walter. *The Arcades Project*. Edited by Rolf Tiedemann, Howard Eiland, and Kevin McLaughlin. Cambridge, MA: Belknap Press of Harvard University Press, 2002, 473.
25. Da Cunha, *Backlands*, 457.
26. Zamora, Lois Parkinson, and Alejo Carpentier. 'The Baroque and the Marvelous Real'. Essay. In *Magical Realism: Theory, History, Community*, 89–107, 105. Durham, NC: Duke University Press, 2005.
27. Gerbi, Antonello. *Nature in the New World: From Christopher Columbus to Gonzalo Fernández De Oviedo*. Pittsburgh, PA: University of Pittsburgh Press, 2010.
28. Sarmiento, Domingo Faustino. *Facundo: Civilization and Barbarism*. Translated by Kathleen Ross. Berkeley: University of California Press, 2004, 32.
29. Sarmiento, Domingo Faustino, and Ilan Stavans. *Facundo: Civilization and Barbarism*. Translated by Mary Tyler Peabody Mann. New York: Penguin Books, 1998, 75.
30. Reyes, Alfonso. *Obras Completas De Alfonso Reyes, Volume 2*. México, DF: Fondo de Cultura Económica, 1960, 34.
31. Derrida, Jacques. *Writing and Difference*. Chicago, IL: University of Chicago Press, 2017.
32. Zamora, Lois Parkinson, Monika Kaup, and Irlemar Chiampi. 'Barroco y Modernidad'. Essay. In *Baroque New Worlds: Representation, Transculturation, Counterconquest*, 500–15, 508. Durham, NC: Duke University Press, 2010.
33. Koselleck, Reinhart. *Critique and Crisis: Enlightenment and the Pathogenesis of Modern Society*. Cambridge, MA: MIT Press, 2015. Also see Man, Paul de. 'Criticism and Crisis'. Essay. In *Blindness and Insight: Essays in the Rhetoric of Contemporary Criticism*, edited by Paul de Man. London: Taylor and Francis, 2016.
34. Benjamin, *Illuminations*, 257.
35. Bolívar, Simón. *Selected Writings of Bolivar*. Edited by Vicente Lecuna. New York: Colonial Press, 1951, 628.

36 Adorno, T. W. 'The Idea of Natural History'. *Telos* 1984, no. 60 (1984): 111–24.
37 Dove, Patrick. *The Catastrophe of Modernity: Tragedy and the Nation in Latin American Literature*. Lewisburg: Bucknell University Press, 2004, 11.
38 Sommer, Doris. *Foundational Fictions: The National Romances of Latin America*. Berkeley: University of California Press, 2007. Also see Anderson, Benedict. *Imagined Communities: Reflections on the Origin and Spread of Nationalism*. London: Verso, 2016.
39 Abrams, Philip. 'Notes on the Difficulty of Studying the State (1977)'. *Twenty Years of the Journal of Historical Sociology* 1, no. 1 (1977): 11–42.
40 Alonso, Carlos J. *The Spanish American Regional Novel: Modernity and Autochthony*. Cambridge: Cambridge University Press, 2008.
41 Mitchell, *Landscape and Power*, 2.
42 Andermann, Jens. *Tierras En Trance: Arte y Naturaleza después Del Paisaje*. Santiago: Metales pesados, 2018.
43 Benjamin, Walter, and Michael W. Jennings. 'Paris, the Capital of the Nineteenth Century'. Essay. In *Selected Writings*, edited by Howard Eiland, 32–49, 45. Cambridge, MA: Belknap Press of Harvard University Press, 2006.
44 Crutzen, Paul J. 'Geology of Mankind'. *Nature* 415, no. 6867 (2002): 23.
45 Bonneuil, Christophe, and Jean-Baptiste Fressoz. *The Shock of the Anthropocene: The Earth, History, and Us*. London: Verso, 2017.
46 Bonneuil and Fressoz, *The Shock of the Anthropocene*, 199.
47 Morton, Timothy. *Dark Ecology: for a Logic of Future Coexistence*. New York: Columbia University Press, 2018.
48 Moore, Jason W. *Capitalism in the Web of Life: Ecology and the Accumulation of Capital*. New York: Verso, 2015, 250.
49 Fukuyama, Francis. 'The End of History and the Last Man'. *History and Theory* 32, no. 2 (1993): 188.
50 Žižek Slavoj. *Event*. London: Penguin, 2014, 2–3.
51 Badiou, *Being and Event*, 57.
52 Benjamin, *Illuminations*, 254.
53 Badiou, *Being and Event*, 51.
54 Moore, *Capitalism in the Web of Life*, 118.

Chapter 2

1 Voltaire. *Candide, or, Optimism*. Translated by Robert Martin Adams. New York: Norton, 1991.
2 Neiman, Susan. *Evil in Modern Thought: An Alternative History of Philosophy*. Princeton, NJ: Princeton University Press, 2015.

3   Foucault, Michel. *The Order of Things: An Archaeology of the Human Sciences*. London: Routledge, 2010, ix.
4   Humboldt, Alexander von. *Personal Narrative of a Journey to the Equinoctial Regions of the New Continent*. London: Penguin, 2006, 131.
5   Foucault, *The Order of Things*, 128.
6   Foucault, *The Order of Things*, 131.
7   Foucault, *The Order of Things*, 132.
8   Tracing its origin all the way back to Aristotle's treatise *On the Soul*, passing through Avicenna's writings, the figure of the tabula rasa had re-entered modern discussions mainly through John Locke's 1689 *An Essay Concerning Human Understanding*, where it was used to illustrate what would later become the 'nature versus nurture' debate: if the mind was like a tabula rasa, then existence had to be explained in relation to circumstance rather than essence, in relation to accidents rather than substances. With this argument Locke was, in a way, foreshadowing the empiricist critique of creationist theodicies that would eventually lead to a historiography of nature. For a condensed history of the concept, see Steven Pinker.
9   Foucault, *The Order of Things*, xxv.
10 White, Hayden. *Metahistory: The Historical Imagination in Nineteenth-Century Europe*. Baltimore: Johns Hopkins University Press, 2014.
11 Lynch, John. *The Spanish American Revolutions: 1808–1826*. New York: Norton, 1986.
12 For the paradigmatic historical reading of the *Querelle d'Amerique* and its main protagonists, see Gerbi and Cañizares-Esguerra's *How to Write the History of the New World*, a fascinating account that traces the precursors of the historical period I study. For Humboldt's precursors, see Cañizares-Esguerra's 'How Derivative was Humboldt'?
13 Humboldt, *Personal Narrative of a Journey*, 142.
14 Hamacher, Werner. 'The Quaking of Presentation'. Essay. In *Premises: Essays on Philosophy and Literature from Kant to Celan*, 261–93, 270. Stanford, CA: Stanford University Press, 1999.
15 In *Paradigms for a Metaphorology*, Hans Blumenberg explores the connection between the discursive layer of metaphor and the material practices of the underlying culture, as well as the processes through which a metaphor comes to establish a paradigm of knowledge. This notion of a paradigm of knowledge, similar to that of Thomas Kuhn, suggests that what is at stake here is something like Michel Foucault's notion of a discursive formation: the relationship between the language field and political actions.
16 For a historiographical analysis of the figure of the historical sublime, please refer to Amy Elias's *Sublime Desire: History and Post-1960s Fiction* or to Hayden White's *The Content of Form*.

17 Pratt, Mary Louise. 'Humboldt y La Reinvencion De America'. *Nuevo Texto Crítico* 1, no. 1 (1988): 35–53.
18 Dolomieu, *L'Étude de la géologie* (1797), 256.
19 Cañizares-Esguerra Jorge. *How to Write the History of the New World: Histories, Epistemologies, and Identities in the Eighteenth-Century Atlantic World*. Stanford, CA: Stanford University Press, 2004.
20 My translation from the original, as it appears in Díaz José Domingo. *Recuerdos Sobre La rebelión De Caracas*. Caracas: Academia Nacional de la Historia, 1961, 20.

> En aquel momento me hallaba solo en el medio de la plaza y de las ruinas; oí los alaridos de los que morían dentro del templo; subí por ellas y entré al reciento.... En lo más elevado encontré a don Simón Bolívar que en mangas de camisa trepaba por ellas paras hacer el mismo examen. En su semblante estaba pintado el sumo terror, o la suma desesperación. Me vio y me dirigió estas impías y extravagantes palabras: "Si se opone la naturaleza, lucharemos contra ella y haremos que nos obedezca".

21 Badiou, Alain. *The Century*. Translated by Alberto Toscano. Cambridge: Polity, 2008, 15.
22 Bolívar Simón, and Gerardo Rivas Moreno. *Simón Bolívar: Obras Completas*. Bucaramanga: Fundación para la Investigación y la Cultura, 2009, 211.
23 Bolivar, Simón. *El Libertador: Writings of Simon Bolivar*. Translated by David Bushnell and Fred Fornoff. Oxford: Oxford University Press, USA, 2003, 74.
24 Bolivar, *El Libertador: Writings of Simon Bolivar*, 7.
25 Zea, Leopoldo. *Simón Bolívar: integración En La Libertad*. México, DF: Edicol, 1980, 68.
26 Bolivar, *El Libertador: Writings of Simon Bolivar*, 31.
27 Humboldt, Alexander Von, Ottmar Ette, and Vera M. Kutzinski. 'The Art of Science'. Essay. In *Views of the Cordilleras and Monuments of the Indigenous Peoples of the Americas*, xv–xxxv, xxi. Chicago: University of Chicago Press, 2013.
28 Humboldt, *Views of the Cordilleras and Monuments of the Indigenous Peoples of the Americas*, 34.
29 Shaw, Philip. *The Sublime*. Florence: Taylor and Francis, 2017.
30 See White, Hayden. 'The Politics of Historical Interpretation'. Essay. In *The Content of the Form: Narrative Discourse and Historical Representation*, 58–82. Baltimore: Johns Hopkins University Press, 1990 and also Huet, Marie-Helene. 'The Revolutionary Sublime'. *Eighteenth-Century Studies* 28, no. 1 (1994): 51–81.
31 Burke, Edmund. *A Philosophical Enquiry into the Origin of Our Ideas of the Sublime and Beautiful*. Sydney, New South Wales: Wentworth Press, 2016.
32 White, 'The Politics of Historical Interpretation', 129.
33 Humboldt, *Personal Narrative of a Journey*, 53.

34 Pratt, Mary Louise. *Imperial Eyes: Travel Writing and Transculturation*. London: Routledge, Taylor & Francis, 2017, 118.
35 Kant, Immanuel. *Critique of the Power of Judgment*. Cambridge: Cambridge University Press, 2009, 120.
36 Schiller, Friedrich. 'On the Sublime'. Champollion Deciphered Rosetta Stone, 1801. Accessed 2 July 2016. https://archive.schillerinstitute.com/transl/trans_on_sublime.html.
37 Schiller, 'On the Sublime'.
38 P'att, *Imperial Eyes*, 120.
39 Ankersmit, Franklin Rudolf. *Sublime Historical Experience*. Stanford, CA: Stanford University Press, 2005.
40 Bolívar and Rivas Moreno, *Obras Completas*, 211.
41 Humboldt, *Personal Narrative of a Journey*, 142.
42 For two interesting readings of the role of neoclassical rhetoric within Bolívar's speeches and writings, see Antonio Cussen's *Bello and Bolívar: Poetry and Politics in the Spanish American Revolution* and Rafael Rojas's *Las repúblicas del aire*. Both agree that at the very centre of the revolutionary enterprise, there existed a tension between a neoclassical conservative discourse and more radical romantic approach.
43 O'Leary, Daniel Florencio. *The 'Detached Recollections' of General D.F. O'Leary*. London: R. A. Humphreys, 1969, 67.
44 My translation as it appears in Lozano Y Lozano, Fabio. *El maestro de la libertad*. Paris: Librería P. Ollendorff, 1913, 85.

> La civilización que ha soplado del Oriente, exclama Bolívar, ha mostrado aquí todas sus fases, ha hecho ver todos sus elementos; más en cuanto a resolver el gran problema del hombre en libertad, parece que el asunto ha sido desconocido, y que el despejo de esa misteriosa incógnita no ha de verificarse sino en el Nuevo Mundo.

45 Bolivar, *El Libertador: Writings of Simon Bolivar*, 18.
46 Zea, Leopoldo. *Discurso desde la marginación y la barbarie*. México, DF: Fondo de Cultura Económico, 1990.
47 My translation as it appears in Bolívar and Rivas Moreno, *Obras Completas*, 313.

> Echando la vista por otra parte, observe usted estos trastornos de las cosas humanas: en todo tiempo las obras de los hombres han sido frágiles, más en el día son como los embriones nonatos que perecen antes de desenvolver sus facultades, por todas partes me asaltan los espantosos ruidos de las caídas, mi época es de catástrofes: todo nace y muere a mi vista como si fuese relámpago, todo no hace más que pasar, ¡y necio de mí si me lisonjease quedar de pie

firme en medio de tales convulsiones, en medio de tantas ruinas, en medio del trastorno moral del universo!

48 Castillo-Durante, Daniel. *Latin American Postmodernisms*. Edited by Richard A. Young. Amsterdam: Rodopi, 1997. Print. 53–62.
49 Rojas, Rafael. *Las repúblicas De Aire: utopía y Desencanto En La revolución De Hispanoamérica*. Madrid: Santillana Ediciones Generales, 2009.
50 My translation as it appears in Bolívar and Rivas Moreno, *Obras Completas*, 246.
51 Bolivar, *El Libertador: Writings of Simon Bolivar*, 25.
52 Adelman, Jeremy. *Sovereignty and Revolution in the Iberian Atlantic*. Princeton, NJ: Princeton University Press, 2006, 323.
53 Agamben, Giorgio. *Sovereign Power and Bare Life*. Stanford, CA: Stanford University Press, 1998, 15.
54 Bolivar, *El Libertador: Writings of Simon Bolivar*, 26.
55 My translation, as it appears in Bolívar and Rivas Moreno, *Obras Completas*, 313.
56 Derrida, Jacques. *Archive Fever: A Freudian Impression*. Chicago, IL: University of Chicago Press, 2017, 17.
57 Aira, César. *An Episode in the Life of a Landscape Painter*. Translated by Chris Andrews. New York: New Directions, 2006, 5.
58 Sarmiento, Domingo Faustino. *Facundo: Civilization and Barbarism*. Edited by Ilan Stavans. New York: Penguin Books, 1998.
59 Aira, *An Episode in the Life of a Landscape Painter*, 5.
60 Aira, *An Episode in the Life of a Landscape Painter*, 5–6.
61 Borges, Jorge Luis. *The Aleph*. Translated by Andrew Hurley. New York: Penguin Books, 2004, 137.
62 Aira, *An Episode in the Life of a Landscape Painter*, 30.
63 Aira, *An Episode in the Life of a Landscape Painter*, 27.
64 Aira, *An Episode in the Life of a Landscape Painter*, 3.
65 Dabove, *Nightmares of the Lettered City: Banditry and Literature in Latin America, 1816–1929*.
66 Aira, *An Episode in the Life of a Landscape Painter*, 25.
67 Benjamin, *Illuminations*, 254.
68 Aira, *An Episode in the Life of a Landscape Painter*, 54.
69 Koselleck, *Critique and Crisis*, 15.
70 Benjamin, Walter. 'Surrealism'. In *Walter Benjamin: Selected Writings Volume 2*, edited by Rodney Livingstone, Michael William Jennings, and Howard Eiland. Cambridge, MA: Harvard University Press, 2005.
71 Badiou, Alain. *Logic of Worlds: Being and Event*. Translated by Alberto Toscano. London: Bloomsbury, 2013.
72 Aira, *An Episode in the Life of a Landscape Painter*, 2.

73 Aira, *An Episode in the Life of a Landscape Painter*, 37.
74 Aira, *An Episode in the Life of a Landscape Painter*, 42.
75 Cadava, Eduardo. *Words of Light Theses on the Photography of History*. Princeton, NJ: Princeton University Press, 1998, 61.
76 Aira, *An Episode in the Life of a Landscape Painter*, 32.

Chapter 3

1 Lowry, Malcolm. *Under the Volcano*. London: Penguin in Association with J. Cape, 2000, 242.
2 Lowry, *Under the Volcano*, 243.
3 Lowry, *Under the Volcano*, 243.
4 Hegel, G. W. F. *Phenomenology of Spirit*. Translated by A. V. Miller. Oxford: Oxford University Press, 2013, 19.
5 Bosteels, Bruno. *Marx and Freud in Latin America: Politics, Psychoanalysis, and Religion in Times of Terror*. New York: Verso, 2012, 160.
6 Rudwick, *Bursting the Limits of Time*, 363.
7 As Mark Anderson has explained in Anderson, Mark. 'The Grounds of Crisis and the Geopolitics of Depth'. Essay. In *Ecological Crisis and Cultural Representation in Latin America*, edited by Mark Anderson and Zelia Bora, 99–122. Lanham, MD: Lexington Books, 2018: The term deep time was coined by Scottish geologist James Hutton in the eighteenth century to refer to geological time; it has become a key term in ecocritical circles in recent years to counter the velocity that predominates in modern notions of time, in which events that happened only a year or two ago abruptly become ancient history.
8 Foucault, *The Order of Things*.
9 My translation, as it appears in Heredia, José María. *Antología herediana*. La Habana: El Siglo xx, 1939, 104–05.

> Después de siglos y siglos han aparecidos esos huesos, para indicárnoslo, como el desnudo mástil de un navío que arrastrado a las playas por las ondas anuncia vagamente un ignorado naufragio. Y nosotros, nosotros también, sufriremos igual suerte el día que se abra una página de cólera en el libro eterno de los destinos, y los seres que nos suceden buscarán tal vez noticias nuestras tan vanamente como queremos nosotros penetrar en las tinieblas insondables que nos separan de la época en que existió sobre la tierra ese gigantesco cadáver.

10 Rojas, *Las repúblicas De Aire: utopía y Desencanto En La revolución De Hispanoamérica*.
11 Bolívar, *Selected Writings of Bolivar*, 125.

12 In a gesture that became characteristic of many romantic poets, Heredia worked on this poem throughout the years, only producing the 'final' poem as a sequence of fragments. The original fragments date from his 1820 trip and were entitled 'Fragmentos descriptivos de un poema mexicano'. As Emilio Carilla's genetic study of the composition has shown, later revisions date from 1825. The final edition, published under the title of 'En el teocalli de Cholula', dates from 1832. It is this edition that we presently use.

13 Horowitz, Gabriel. 'The Natural History of Latin American Independence'. *CR: The New Centennial Review* 16, no. 3 (2016): 211–32, 223.

14 Heredia, José María, and Daniel Charles Thomas. 'On the Teocalli of Cholula'. On the Teocalli of Cholula (Heredia) – Poem, Last modified 2001. Accessed 15 September 2017. http://www.gastown.com/xanadu/cholu01.htm.

15 Horowitz, 'The Natural History of Latin American Independence', 217.

16 Heredia and Thomas. 'On the Teocalli of Cholula'.

17 Freud, Sigmund. 'The General Meaning of Symptoms'. Essay. In *A General Introduction to Psychoanalysis*, 151–60. Lexington: Renaissance Classics, 2012.

18 Heredia and Thomas. 'On the Teocalli of Cholula'.

19 As Rafael Rojas has explored in his book *Las repúblicas del aire* the Mexico to which Heredia arrives is a post-revolutionary anarchic Mexico. Although the 'Grito de Dolores', Mexico's cry of Independence dates from 1810, the war would extend up to 27 September 1821 when the Creoles, led by Agustín de Iturbide, agreed to sign the Treaty of Córdoba. As such, Heredia's reflections on war, violence and melancholic serenity must be read within the atmosphere of violence and anarchy that prevailed both in his native Cuba and in Mexico during the second decade of the twentieth century.

20 Cancellier, Antonella. 'Estética Romántica De La Arqueología: La Poética De Las Ruinas En José María Heredia'. *Anales De Literatura Española Anales De Literatura Española*, no. 18 (2005): 79–87.

21 My translation, from Heredia, José María. *Antología Herediana. Selección de las mejores poesías líricas, obras dramáticas, cartas, discursos y artículos varios de José María Heredia Y Heredia*. Brasil: A. Muñiz y Hnos, 1939, 76.

22 As Reinhart Koselleck has explored in his book *Critique and Crisis* there is a direct relationship between the rise of modernity, the emergence of the modern state and secrecy. As Koselleck explores in relationship to the rise of free masonry, this triple link lies at the very heart of that strange phenomenon which saw, in the late eighteenth century, a rise in critical philosophies of history. It must be highlighted that José María Heredia formed part of the masonic lodge 'Los Caballeros Racionales'. A whole theory of history is disclosed by a modern stance regarding the secret.

23 Hegel, Georg Wilhelm Friedrich. *Aesthetics: Lectures on Fine Art*. Translated by Thomas Malcolm Knox. Oxford: Clarendon Press, 2010, 356.

24 Hegel, *Aesthetics*, 357.
25 Heredia and Thomas. 'On the Teocalli of Cholula'.
26 Bosteels, *Marx and Freud in Latin America*, 5.
27 Paz, Octavio. *The Labyrinth of Solitude; and, the Other Mexico; Return to the Labyrinth of Solitude; Mexico and the United States; The Philanthropic Ogre*. New York: Grove Press, 2001, 287.
28 For a recent study of Freud's relationship to Mexico, see Rubén Gallo's *Freud's México: Into the Wilds of Psychoanalysis* in which the author explores the ways Freud's theories influenced the way Mexican modernists conceived of themselves and their modernizing task. Of particular importance for us are Gallo's reflections concerning the similitude and difference between Freud's concepts of melancholia and malaise, on the one hand, and Octavio Paz's notion of solitude, on the other.
29 Freud, Sigmund. *Five Lectures on Psychoanalysis*. London: Read Books, 2013, 45.
30 Freud, *Five Lectures on Psychoanalysis*, 47.
31 Abraham, Nicolas, and Maria Torok. *The Shell and the Kernel: Renewals of Psychoanalysis*. Translated by Nicholas T. Rand. Chicago: University of Chicago Press, 1994.
32 Derrida, Jacques. *Specters of Marx: The State of the Debt, the Work of Mourning, and the New International*. New York: Routledge, 2011, 10.
33 Bhabha, Homi K. *The Location of Culture*. London: Routledge, 2010, 254.
34 Bhabha, *The Location of Culture*, 252.
35 Gramsci, Antonio, and David Forgacs. *The Gramsci Reader: Selected Writings, 1916–1935*. New York: New York University Press, 2000, 156.
36 Demarest, Arthur A. *Ancient Maya: The Rise and Fall of a Rainforest Civilization*. Cambridge: Cambridge University Press, 2011.
37 Historians are still unclear as to the origins of the myth regarding the flight and eventual return of Quetzcoatl. As Susan D. Gillespie expounds in her 1989 book *The Aztec Kings*, it is believed that the myth regarding Quetzcoatl's return *as* Hernán Cortés was in fact a Spanish construction made to pacify Carlos V's anxieties. However, rather than refuting my argument the ambiguity regarding the myth's origin reaffirms its importance. The widespread belief in the myth within the mestizo culture that emerged and within the Mesoamerican imaginary points to its imaginative potential as a hermeneutic tool. Namely, what interests me is not the veracity of the myth, nor its origin, but rather its function as historical catalyser within the social imaginary.
38 Bhabha, *The Location of Culture*, 252.
39 Bhabha, *The Location of Culture*, 204.
40 My translation. Quoted in Rojas, Rafael. *Las repúblicas de aire: utopía y desencanto en la revolución de hispanoamérica*. Mexico, DF: Taurus, 2009, 76.
41 Le Plongeon, Augustus. *Sacred Mysteries among the Mayas and the Quiches*. New York: Cosimo, 2007, 41.

42 See Bueno, Christina. *The Pursuit of Ruins: Archaeology, History, and the Making of Modern Mexico*. New York: University of New Mexico Press, 2016 and Castro-Klarén Sara, and John Charles Chasteen. *Beyond Imagined Communities: Reading and Writing the Nation in Nineteenth-Century Latin America*. Washington: Woodrow Wilson Center Press, 2004.
43 Koselleck, *Critique and Crisis*, 85.
44 Desmond, Lawrence Gustave. *Yucatán through Her Eyes: Alice Dixon Le Plongeon, Writer & Expeditionary Photographer*. Albuquerque: University of New Mexico Press, 2009, 125.
45 Benjamin, Walter. *The Origin of German Tragic Drama*. London: Verso, 2009, 75.
46 On the topic of translation and universality, several books are of importance: George Steiner's 1975 classic *After Babel*, Etienne Balibar's essay 'Ambiguous universality' and Alain Badiou's *Saint Paul: The Foundation of Universalism*.
47 Desmond, *Yucatán through Her Eyes: Alice Dixon Le Plongeon, Writer & Expeditionary Photographer*, 153.
48 For a more comprehensive treatment of the topic of dispersal, reproduction and itineracy in its relationship to the photographic archive, the reader is referred to the essays compiled in Eduardo Cadava and Gabriela Nouzeilles's *The Itinerant Languages of Photography*. As Nouzeilles points out in her essay 'The Archival Paradox': 'As Marcel Duchamp so wonderfully expressed in his conceptual work *Boîte-en-valise* (1935–1941) – the portable authorial museum consisting of scaled-down reproductions of his works, all neatly kept in a suitcase – the content of the archive is always on the move. And because it is itinerant, because it moves, there is always the chance that it will be unsettled, undermined, sabotaged, erased and even smashed' (41).
49 Benn Michael, Walter. 'Photography and Fossils'. Essay. In *Photography Theory*, 431–47. New York: Routledge, 2007.
50 Rosenthal, Lecia. *Mourning Modernism: Literature, Catastrophe, and the Politics of Consolation*. New York: Fordham University Press, 2011, 4.
51 Holloway, John. *Crack Capitalism*. London: Sage, 2012, 25.
52 Dixon, Alice. 'Yucatán since the Conquest'. *Magazine of American History*, 1893.
53 My translation. From Orozco, José Clemente. *Autobiografía*. Mexico: Ediciones Era, 1970, 56.

Nos hablaba con mucho fuego de la Capilla Sixtina y de Leonardo. ¡Las grandes pinturas murales! Los inmensos frescos renacentistas, algo increíble y tan misterioso como las pirámides faraónicas [...] En esas veladas de jóvenes aprendices de pintura apareció el primer brote revolucionario en el campo de las artes de México. En aquellos talleres nocturnos donde oíamos la entusiasta voz del Doctor Atl, el agitador, empezamos a sospechar que toda aquella situación colonial era solamente un truco de comerciantes internacionales.

54 Interestingly it would seem as if it had been Murillo who has been forgotten by art historians. Whereas Orozco, Siqueiros and Rivera share the glory of Mexican modernism, Murillo remains an esoteric figure, a singular individual whose eccentricity sometimes seems to overshadow his towering importance.

55 My translation. From Dr Atl. *Las sinfonías Del Popocatépetl*. Mexico: Verdehalago, 1999, 15.

56 Dr Atl's friendship with José Vasconcelos seems to have been problematic one, starting from their joint efforts as part of Alvaro Obregón's government, leading to Atl's fight with Obregón and his rough discrepancies with Vasconcelos who, as an insult, he would later call 'Pepito' Vasconcelos.

57 My translation. From Dr Atl, *Las sinfonías Del Popocatépetl*, 107.

> Pero las fuerzas del pasado acechaban, y arteramente se arrojaron en avalancha contra la Civilización, paralizando de un golpe la marcha del progreso, destruyendo las vidas, aniquilando las voluntades y cubriendo la ruta luminosa con inconmensurables errores y con millones de cadáveres. A mi me tocaba luchar en la palestra donde se habían librado durante siglos cruentas luchas entre hombres bárbaros semidesnudos y hombres más bárbaros aún vestidos de hierro y de zayal.

58 My translation. From Dr Atl, *Las sinfonías Del Popocatépetl*, 39.

> Sobre las ruinas y sobre los sepulcros florecen las plantas y viven los animals – sobre la tumba augusta, mausoleo de la energía terrestre, vibran las sinfonías de la energía terrestre, vibran las sinfonías vivificantes de la naturaleza.

59 My translation. From Dr Atl, *Las sinfonías Del Popocatépetl*, 115–16.

> La montaña ha revivido. Millones de años durmió en el silencio de la muerte, millones de años el viento la azotó, millones de años las fuerzas de la naturaleza trataron de destruirla, cerraron su boca, carcomieron su vertebras, sacudieron su masa formidable, y desgarraron sus labios en otros tiempos vibrantes de elocuencia fulminantes... Nada es viejo ni nada ha muerto: en el término de la destrucción está la vida.

60 My translation. From Dr Atl. *Cómo Nace y Crece Un volcán: El Parícutin*. Ciudad de Mexico: El Colegio Nacional, 2017, 25.

61 My translation. From Dr Atl, *Cómo Nace y Crece Un volcán: El Parícutin*, 45.

62 My translation. From Dr Atl, *Cómo Nace y Crece Un volcán: El Parícutin*, 41.

63 Following Giorgio Agamben's discussion of the state of exception and Alain Badiou's theory of the event as the emergence of the exceptional, it seems that the constellation of our present-day political theory calls for a theory of emergency both as a political and as a historical category. Namely: what does it mean for

something to be in a state of emergency, to be emerging? How does emergency as a category work within the framework of representation to which we are accustomed? How to think the violence implicit in the concept of emergency? It seems that every philosophy of history is a philosophy of emergency and exceptionality.

64 My translation. From Dr Atl, *Cómo Nace y Crece Un volcán: El Parícutin*, 37.
65 My translation. From Sáenz Olga. *El símbolo y La acción: Vida y Obra De Gerardo Murillo, Dr. Atl*. Mexico: Colegio Nacional, 2012, 79.

Solo hay un medio para crear una nueva civilización: construir una Ciudad hoc-foce de la cultura universal, para reconcentrar en ella la potencia mental del hombre y dirigirla no hacia el bienestar general, sino hacia conquista del Universo, meta inmediata del progreso humano.

66 From Fray Bartolomé de las Casas's *Brevísima Historia de la Destrucción de las Indias* to Gabriel García Márquez's *Cien Años de Soledad*, it would seem that a dialectic between utopia and catastrophe guides Latin American history. For a book on a similar topic, the reader is referred to Susan Buck-Morss's 2002 book *Dreamworld and Catastrophe*, where she analyses these dialectics in relationship to the works of Walter Benjamin.
67 My translation. From Sáenz Olga, *El símbolo y La acción: Vida y Obra De Gerardo Murillo, Dr. Atl*, 85.
68 Horkheimer, Max, and Theodor W. Adorno. *Dialectic of Enlightenment*. London: Verso, 1997.
69 Mraz, John. *Looking for Mexico: Modern Visual Culture and National Identity*. Durham, NC: Duke University Press, 2009.
70 Salazkina, Masha. *In Excess: Sergei Eisenstein's Mexico*. Chicago, IL: University of Chicago Press, 2009.
71 Lowry, *Under the Volcano*, 283.
72 Lowry, *Under the Volcano*, 89.
73 Lowry, *Under the Volcano*.
74 Lowry, *Under the Volcano*, 60.
75 Lowry, *Under the Volcano*, 88.
76 Gabara, Esther. *Errant Modernism: The Ethos of Photography in Mexico and Brazil*. Durham, NC: Duke University Press, 2008.
77 Lowry, *Under the Volcano*, 175.
78 Andermann, *Tierras En Trance: Arte y Naturaleza después Del Paisaje*, 10.
79 Lowry, *Under the Volcano*, 398.
80 Paz, Octavio. *The Labyrinth of Solitude and Other Writings*. New York: Grove Press, 2001, 288.

81 Paz, *The Labyrinth of Solitude and Other Writings*, 293.
82 Paz, *The Labyrinth of Solitude and Other Writings*, 321.
83 Bosteels, *Marx and Freud in Latin America*, 184.
84 Lowry, *Under the Volcano*, 85.
85 Bosteels, *Marx and Freud in Latin America*, 184.
86 Lowry, *Under the Volcano*, 72.
87 Lowry, *Under the Volcano*, 198.
88 Lowry, *Under the Volcano*, 300.
89 Lowry, *Under the Volcano*, 125.
90 Lowry, *Under the Volcano*, 46.
91 Lowry, *Under the Volcano*, 235.
92 Lowry, *Under the Volcano*, 297.
93 Lowry, *Under the Volcano*, 175.
94 Henry James on Letter to Howard Sturgis on 5 August 1914.
95 Lowry, Malcolm, and Sherrill Grace. *Sursum Corda!: The Collected Letters of Malcolm Lowry*. Toronto: University of Toronto Press, 1997, 335.
96 Lowry, *Under the Volcano*, 124.
97 Lowry, *Under the Volcano*, 45.
98 Vasconcelos José. *The Cosmic Race*. Translated by Jaén Didier Tisdel and Joseba Gabilondo. Baltimore, MD: Johns Hopkins University Press, 1997, 7.
99 Lowry, *Under the Volcano*, 283.
100 Lowry, *Under the Volcano*, 311.
101 Lowry, *Under the Volcano*, 213.
102 Lowry, *Under the Volcano*, 214.
103 Bonfil, Batalla Guillermo, and Philip Adams Dennis. *México profundo: Reclaiming a Civilization*. Austin: University of Texas Press, 2007, 12.
104 Taussig, Michael T. *Defacement: Public Secrecy and the Labor of the Negative*. Stanford, CA: Stanford University Press, 1999, 2.

Chapter 4

1 Hobbes, Thomas. *Leviathan*. Harmondsworth: Penguin, 1985.
2 Mitropoulos, Angela. *Contract & Contagion: From Biopolitics to Oikonomia*. Brooklyn, NY: Minor Compositions, 2013, 67.
3 Gilbert, Nicolas Pierre. *Histoire Médicale De L'armée Française à Saint-Domingue, En L'an Dix; Ou, Mémoire Sur La Fièvre Jaune, Avec Un Aperçu De La Topographie Medicale De Cette Colonie*. Paris: Gabon, 1803.
4 Gilbert, *Mémoire Sur La Fièvre Jaune*, 66.

5   McNeill, John Robert. *Mosquito Empires: Ecology and War in the Greater Caribbean, 1620–1914*. New York: Cambridge University Press, 2010, 5.
6   Esposito, Roberto. *Immunitas: The Protection and Negation of Life*. Cambridge, UK: Blackwell, 2011, 114.
7   Ellenberger, Henri F. *The Discovery of the Unconscious: The History and Evolution of Dynamic Psychiatry*. New York: Basic, 1970, 73.
8   Delbourgo, James, and Nicholas Dew, eds. *Science and Empire in the Atlantic World*. New York: Routledge, 2008, 73.
9   Regourd, François. 'Mesmerism in Saint Domingue'. In *Colonialism and Science: Saint Domingue in the Old Regime*, edited by James E. McClellan, 121, 311–33. Baltimore: Johns Hopkins University Press, 1992.
10 Gilroy, Paul. *The Black Atlantic: Modernity and Double Consciousness*. London: Verso, 1993.
11 Artaud, Antonin. *The Theater and Its Double*. New York: Grove, 1958, 45.
12 Esposito, *Immunitas*, 15.
13 The prologue of *El Reino de este mundo* marks the first appearance and theorization of what is perhaps the most famous aesthetic concept within Latin American literature: lo *real maravilloso*. Interestingly, little if any attention has been paid to the politics of witnessing that are there disclosed under the rubric of the category itself. As Carpentier suggests in regard to Mackandal's flight, the real maravilloso is a category that posits the event as such a question regarding the politics of witness, interpellation and faith: Who sees what? Who is radicalized by what? To some extent, what Carpentier discusses in relationship to Mackandal has the structure of the radical event as discussed by Badiou.
14 Carpentier, Alejo. *The Kingdom of This World*. Translated by Harriet De Onís. New York: Farrar, Straus and Giroux, 2006, 45–46.
15 See Taussig, Michael T. *Shamanism, Colonialism and the Wild Man: A Study in Terror and Healing*. Chicago, IL: University of Chicago Press, 2012, Kohn, Eduardo. *How Forests Think: Toward an Anthropology beyond the Human*. Berkeley, London: University of California Press, 2015, and Agamben, Giorgio. *The Open: Man and Animal*. Stanford, CA: Stanford University Press, 2012.
16 Deleuze, Gilles, and Félix Guattari. *A Thousand Plateaus: Capitalism and Schizophrenia*. Translated by Brian Massumi. London: Bloomsbury Academic, 2017, 286.
17 Deleuze, Gilles, and Félix Guattari. *Kafka: Toward a Minor Literature*. Minneapolis, MI: University of Minnesota Press, 2012, 22.
18 For a more informed discussion of Finlay's discovery as well as its place within the political ecology of Cuban history, please see 'chapter four: The Hunt for the Mosquito' in Espinosa, Mariola. *Epidemic Invasions: Yellow Fever and the Limits of Cuban Independence, 1878–1930*. Chicago, IL: The University of Chicago Press, 2009.
19 McNeill, *Mosquito Empires*, 33.

20. Benítez Rojo, Antonio. *The Repeating Island: The Caribbean and the Postmodern Perspective*. Durham, NC: Duke University Press, 2006.
21. McCook, Stuart George. *States of Nature: Science, Agriculture, and Environment in the Spanish Caribbean, 1760–1940*. Austin: University of Texas, 2002, 33.
22. McNeill, J. R. 'Ecology, Epidemics and Empires: Environmental Change and the Geopolitics of Tropical America, 1600–1825'. *Environment and History* 5, no. 2 (1999): 175–84.
23. Moore, Jason W. 'Ecology, Capital, and the Nature of Our Times: Accumulation & Crisis in the Capitalist World-Ecology'. *Journal of World-Systems Research* 17, no. 1 (2011): 107–46, 110.
24. As James E. McClellan III discusses in his book on the topic, mesmerism was not the only pseudo-scientific theory to arrive to Saint Domingue. Rather to the country, the island quickly became a perfect environment for the proliferation and mutation of scientific discourses coming from Europe, prominent among them, the theory of electricity.
25. For a broader and more informed discussion of Snow's discovery as well as of the emergence of medical cartography, please see Tom Koch's fascinating book *Cartographies of Disease: Maps, Mapping and Medicine*.
26. Darnton, Robert. *Mesmerism and the End of the Enlightenment in France*. Cambridge, MA: Harvard University Press, 1968, 3.
27. Besides the apparent relationship with the medieval humorism and its theory of disease, one can easily detect the relationship of mesmerism to modern scientific discourse regarding action-at-a-distance like electricity and magnetism. The possibility of thinking the medium of contagion as such would be crucial for modern science and would in turn prove to be a crucial metaphor for the social sciences.
28. Darnton, *Mesmerism and the End of the Enlightenment in France*, 8.
29. Darnton, *Mesmerism and the End of the Enlightenment in France*, 178.
30. Deleuze and Guattari, *A Thousand Plateaus: Capitalism and Schizophrenia*, 27.
31. Delbourgo and Dew, *Science and Empire in the Atlantic World*, 321.
32. Regourd, 'Mesmerism in Saint Domingue', 121, 311–33.
33. Darnton, *Mesmerism and the End of the Enlightenment in France*, 274.
34. Weaver, Karol K. *Medical Revolutionaries: The Enslaved Healers of Eighteenth-Century Saint Domingue*. Urbana: University of Illinois, 2006, 108.
35. The concept of desire-events I borrow from Tony D. Sampson's usage of the term in his book *Virality: Contagion Theory in the Age of Networks*. There, departing from Gabriel Tarde's differential microsociology and its adaptation by Deleuze and Guattari, Sampson builds a theory of the relationship between the viral proliferation of desire and a theory of the event.
36. Guattari, Félix. *The Three Ecologies*. London: Bloomsbury, 2014, 74.
37. Guattari, *The Three Ecologies*, 74.

38 Hardt, Michael, and Antonio Negri. *Empire*. Cambridge, MA: Harvard University Press, 2000, 61.
39 Esposito, *Immunitas*, 31.
40 Gilbert, Nicolas Pierre. *Histoire Médicale De L'Armée Française, a Saint-Domingue, En L'An Dix, Ou Mémoire Sur La Fièvre Jaune*. Paris: Forgotten Books, 2017, 5–6.
41 Carpentier, Alejo. *The Kingdom of This World*. Translated by Pablo Medina. New York: Farrar, Straus and Giroux, 2017, 75.
42 Foucault, Michel. *Discipline and Punish: The Birth of the Prison*. New York: Vintage, 2009, 197.
43 Foucault, *Discipline and Punish*, 198.
44 Foucault, *Discipline and Punish*, 201.
45 Foucault, *Discipline and Punish*, 197.
46 Esposito, *Immunitas*, 9.
47 Esposito, *Immunitas*, 9.
48 Zola, Émile. *The Experimental Novel, and Other Essays*. Translated by Belle M. Sherman. United States: Sagwan Press, 2015, 20.
49 Feliú Matilla, Fernando. 'Del Microscopio Al Automóvil: Hacia Una Redefinición De La Novela Naturalista En Puerto Rico'. *Revista Nuestra América* 8, no. 120 (2010): 225–43.
50 My translation. From Feliú Matilla, 'Del Microscopio Al Automóvil: Hacia Una Redefinición De La Novela Naturalista En Puerto Rico', 229.

'La'novela naturalista extirpa los cánceres sociales, ocultos en su mayor parte tras la pulcra vestimenta de la humanidad'.

51 Zeno Gandía, Manuel. *The Pond (La Charca)*. Translated by Kal Wagenheim. Princeton, NJ: M. Wiener, 1999, 52.

Sí, aquello era una tumba de vivos. El glóbulo rojo, combatido por la sangre blanca, había huido para siempre de aquella gran masa de pálidos. Era una muchedumbre de contornos inciertos, borrosos, indecisos... Un haz de retorcidos sarmientos en que vicios y virtudes se enredaban, se enmarañaban de tal suerte, que siguiendo el sarmiento de una noble calidad se llegaba al vicio, y sacudiendo el de un defecto se llegaba a la virtud. ¡Ah! ¿cómo definirlos?

52 Nouzeilles, Gabriela. 'La Esfinge Del Monstruo'. *Latin American Literary Review* 25, no. 50 (1997): 89–107.
53 Nouzeilles, Gabriela. *Ficciones Somáticas: Naturalismo, Nacionalismo Y Políticas Médicas Del Cuerpo (Argentina 1880–1910)*. Rosario: Viterbo, 2000.
54 Bersani, Leo. *A Future for Astyanax: Character and Desire in Literature*. Boston, MA: Little, Brown, 1976.

55 Quote from Salvador Brau's *Las Clases Jornaleras,* in Brau, Salvador. *Disquisiciones Sociológicas Y Otros Ensayos: Salvador Brau.* Puerto Rico: Universidad De Puerto Rico, 1956, 182: 'Hay en ese carácter, por plumas tan eminentes descrito, un germen potente capaz de adquirir productivo desarrollo: si ese desarrollo no se ha adquirido, fuerza es que causas, visibles u ocultas, lo hayan cohibido e esterilizado. A semejanza de O'Reylly y del Padre Iñigo, síguese hoy atribuyendo, por algunos, a las influencias del clima, las condiciones del carácter de nuestro pueblo. Convendremos en que el sol ardoroso de los trópicos enerva y modifica la vida animal; pero si O'Reylly y el padre Iñigo pudieran levantarse de sus tumbas, para comparar esta sociedad puertorriqueña del siglo XIX, con aquella que ellos conocieron y estudiaron tan a fondo' (182).

56 Bataille, Georges, and Robert Hurley. *The Accursed Share: An Essay on General Economy.* New York: Zone, 1988.

57 Zeno Gandía, *The Pond (La Charca),* 51.

58 Zeno Gandía, *The Pond (La Charca),* 51.

¡Cómo! ¿Era aquello un conjunto social? ¿Estaban aquellas clases reguladas por las leyes generales de la moral, de la justicia y del deber? ¿Las gentes que veía agrupadas en las estribaciones del monte, eran piara, eran rebaños? […] No, no era el espíritu… El contaminado, el raquítico, el deformado era el cuerpo.

59 See Bon, Gustave Le. *The Crowd: A Study of the Popular Mind.* Singapore: Origami Books, 2018.

60 My translation. From Zeno Gandía, Manuel. *Higiene De La Infancia Al Alcance De Las Madres De Familia.* New York: Andesite Press, 2017, 15.

61 Zeno Gandía, *The Pond (La Charca),* 190.

62 My translation. From Zeno Gandía, Manuel. *Garduña.* San Juan, Puerto Rico: La Editorial de la Universidad de Puerto Rico, 2010, 17.

63 My translation. From Zeno Gandía, *Garduña,* 16.

64 My translation. From Zeno Gandía, *Garduña,* 19.

65 Negri, Antonio, and Timothy S. Murphy. *Subversive Spinoza (Un)Contemporary Variations.* Manchester: Manchester University Press, 2008, 31.

66 My translation. From Zeno Gandía, *Garduña,* 207.

67 My translation. From Zeno Gandía, *Garduña,* 212.

68 Zeno Gandía, *The Pond (La Charca),* 144.

69 Ashford, Bailey K. *Uncinariasis (Hookworm Disease) in Porto Rico: A Medical and Economic Problem (Classic Reprint).* Washington, DC: Forgotten Books, 2017.

70 Ashford, *Uncinarisis (Hookworm Disease) in Porto Rico,* 5.

71 Ashford, *Uncinarisis (Hookworm Disease) in Porto Rico,* 12.

72 Clark, Truman R. *Puerto Rico and the United States, 1917–1933.* Pittsburgh: University of Pittsburgh Press, 2009, 151–54.

73 I take this quote from Jorge Olivares's *Becoming Reinaldo Arenas: Family, Sexuality and the Cuban Revolution.*
74 Arenas, Reinaldo. *The Color of Summer, or, the New Garden of Earthly Delights.* Translated by Andrew Hurley. New York: Penguin Books, 2001, v.
75 Arenas, *The Color of Summer, or, the New Garden of Earthly Delights,* 125.
76 For an interesting book on AIDS as discourse, its relationship to circulation and globalization, see Lina Meruane's *Viral Voyages.*
77 Arenas, *The Color of Summer, or, the New Garden of Earthly Delights,* 75.
78 The category of the neo-baroque finds perhaps its best theorization in Severo Sarduy's writings, and in particular, through his essay 'Barroco y NeoBarroco'. There he defines the neo-baroque as reflecting 'the disharmony, the rupture of homogeneity, the lack that constitutes our epistemic foundation. Neobaroque of disequilibrium, structural reflection of a desire that cannot attain its object' (289).
79 Sontag, Susan. *Illness as Metaphor and AIDS and Its Metaphors.* New York: Picador, 1990.
80 Arenas, *The Color of Summer, or, the New Garden of Earthly Delights,* 408.
81 Arenas, *The Color of Summer, or, the New Garden of Earthly Delights,* 164.
82 Arenas, *The Color of Summer, or, the New Garden of Earthly Delights,* 109.

> Ara, are, IRA, oro, uri…
>
> Con un aro y dos cadenas ara Arenas entre las hienas, horadando los eriales en aras de más aromas y orando a Ares por más oro porque todo su tesoro (incluyendo los aretes que usaba en sus aréitos) los heredó un buga moro luego de hacerle maromas en él área de un urinario de Roma. Mas no es Arenas sino Hera quien con su ira oye sus lloros. Y Arenas, arañando lomas, con su aro y sus cadenas, en el infierno carena teniendo por toda era (¡ella que era la que era!) un gran orinal de harina oreado con sus orinas.
>
> (Para Reinaldo Arenas)

83 Arenas, *The Color of Summer, or, the New Garden of Earthly Delights,* 446.

> Vamos pues marcialmente hacia un mar maciliento, donde una marmórea marmota murmura miríada de maltratos: mas se va, finalmente, al confín de todas las pifias, al gran prostíbulo sumergido donde aún farfulla un fonógrafo su fofa filantropía y una mefítica sifilítica, afónica y antifotogénica nos ofrece piafando la ofensa de su furiosa fisionomía.
>
> (A todos nosotros)

84 Arenas, *The Color of Summer, or, the New Garden of Earthly Delights,* 125.
85 Also look at Düttmann, Alexander García. *At Odds with AIDS: Thinking and Talking about a Virus.* Stanford, CA: Stanford University Press, 1996. Avital Ronell, in her

essay 'Queens of the Night', has also explored the catastrophic undertones of the discourse surrounding AIDS in its biopolitical relationship to a technology of the internal rumour. Also worth quoting is Susan Sontag's now-famous book on the topic *Illness as Metaphor* where, exploring the semantic network of disease, she points out: 'What make the viral assault [AIDS] so terrifying is that contamination, and therefore vulnerability, is understood as permanent. Even if someone infected were never to develop any symptoms the viral enemy would be forever within' (106).

86 Arenas, *The Color of Summer, or, the New Garden of Earthly Delights*, 172.
87 Arenas, *The Color of Summer, or, the New Garden of Earthly Delights*, 449.
88 Arenas, *The Color of Summer, or, the New Garden of Earthly Delights*, 454.

Chapter 5

1 Sommer, *Foundational Fictions*, 2.
2 García Márquez, Gabriel. *Leaf Storm*. London: Penguin Books, 2014, 1.
3 García Márquez, *Leaf Storm*, 3.
4 Koselleck, *Critique and Crisis*.
5 García Márquez, Gabriel. *One Hundred Years of Solitude*. Translated by Gregory Rabassa. London: Penguin Books, 2014, 414.
6 García Márquez, *One Hundred Years of Solitude*, 414.
7 García Márquez, *One Hundred Years of Solitude*, 417.
8 Derrida, Jacques. 'No Apocalypse, Not Now (Full Speed Ahead, Seven Missiles, Seven Missives)'. Translated by Catherine Porter and Philip Lewis. *Diacritics* 14, no. 2 (1984): 20–33.
9 Benjamin, Walter. *Walter Benjamin: Selected Writings 1935–1938*. Edited by Howard Eiland and Michael W. Jennings. Cambridge, MA: Harvard University Press, 2006, 58.
10 García Márquez, Gabriel. *Chronicle of a Death Foretold*. Translated by Gregory Rabassa. London: Viking, 2014, 75.
11 Echevarría Roberto González. *Myth and Archive: A Theory of Latin American Narrative*. Cambridge: Cambridge University Press, 1990, 18.
12 Beckman, Ericka. *Capital Fictions: The Literature of Latin America's Export Age*. Minneapolis, MI: University of Minnesota Press, 2013, 15.
13 Weld, Kirsten. *Paper Cadavers: The Archives of Dictatorship in Guatemala*. London: Duke University Press, 2015, 29.
14 Derrida, 'No Apocalypse', 28.
15 Rosa, Rodrigo Rey. *El Material Humano*. Madrid: Alfaguara, 2017.
16 Weld, *Paper Cadavers*, 33.

17 Avelar, Idelber. *The Untimely Present: Postdictatorial Latin American Fiction and the Task of Mourning*. Durham, NC: Duke University Press, 1999, 2.
18 Hirsch, Marianne. *The Generation of Postmemory: Writing and Visual Culture after the Holocaust*. New York: Columbia University Press, 2012.
19 LaCapra, Dominick. *Writing History, Writing Trauma: With a New Preface*. Baltimore, MD: Johns Hopkins University Press, 2014.
20 Foster, Hal. 'An Archival Impulse'. *October* 110 (2004): 3–22.
21 My translation. From Rivera Garza, Cristina. *Los Muertos indóciles: Necroescrituras y desapropiación*. México, DF: Tusquets Editores México, 2013, 23.
22 Rivera Garza, *Los Muertos indóciles: Necroescrituras y desapropiación*, 45.
23 Keenan, Thomas, and Eyal Weizman. *Mengele's Skull: The Advent of a Forensic Aesthetics*. Berlin: Sternberg Press, 2012.
24 Meillassoux, Quentin. *After Finitude: An Essay on the Necessity of Contingency*. Translated by Ray Brassier. London: Bloomsbury, 2017.
25 Benjamin, Walter, Marcus Bullock, and Michael W. Jennings. 'Critique of Violence'. Essay. In *Walter Benjamin: Selected Writings*, 236–52. Cambridge, MA: Belknap Press of Harvard University Press, 1996.
26 Taylor, Diana. *The Archive and the Repertoire: Performing Cultural Memory in the Americas*. Durham, NC: Duke University Press, 2007, 24.
27 Derrida, *Archive Fever: A Freudian Impression*, 17.

Index

Note: Locators with letter 'n' refer to notes.

Abraham, Nicolas 71–2, 82
Abrams, Phillip 15
Acción Revolucionaria Mexicanista 95
addiction 57, 58, 98, 100, 109–10
Adelman, Jeremy 45–6
Adorno, Theodor 1, 14, 95, 163
Aedes aegypti 123, 126
aesthetics 12, 36, 38, 49, 51, 67, 90, 95, 131, 185 n.13
After Babel (Steiner) 181 n.46
After Finitude (Meillassoux) 169
aftermaths 9, 14, 20, 61, 63, 76, 79, 86, 96, 97, 101, 110, 111, 143, 159–70
Agamben, Giorgio 46, 113, 121, 166, 182 n.63
'Age of Imperial Revolutions, An' (Adelman) 45–6
Age of Revolutions 7–8, 14, 27
AIDS 114, 149–58, 190 n.85
Aiken, Conrad 104, 107
Aira, Cesar 48–56
A la Gran Pirámide de Egipto (Heredia) 74
Aldrovandi, Ulisse 26
allegory 12, 14, 41, 43, 46, 79, 82–8, 98, 133, 151–6, 163, 167, 169
Alonso, Carlos 15–16, 140
Al Popocatepl (Heredia) 74
anaemia 139–42, 147–8
anarchy 14, 35, 44, 63, 68, 85, 88–9, 90, 100, 168, 179 n.19
Ancient Maya: The Rise and Fall of a Rainforest Civilization (Demarest) 73
Anderman, Jens 3, 16, 100
Anderson, Benedict 15, 45
Anderson, Mark 4
Ángel, Manuel Uribe 41
Angel of History 43, 44
Angostura Congress 43, 44

animism 131, 132
Ankersmit, Frank 36, 40
anthrax vaccine 136
Anthropocene 1, 2, 17–19, 21
Antonio Vicente Mendes Maciel. *See* Antônio Conselheiro
Arcades Project (Benjamin) 55, 163
archaeological symbol 60, 70, 71, 74, 76–8, 80–3, 85, 102
Archive Fever (Derrida) 48
archives 25, 26, 28–9, 31, 39, 45–51, 53, 55, 84, 163–70, 181 n.48
Arenas, Reinaldo 114, 149–58, 189 nn.82–3
Aristotle 79
art, idea of 50, 55–6, 59, 67, 84, 168, 169
Artaud, Antonin 97, 120
Ashford, Bailey K. 146, 147
assemblage 16, 19, 122, 124, 131–4, 149, 150, 154
Assis, Machado de 5
astonishment 37
Atl, Dr (Gerardo Murillo) 20, 60, 88–95, 98, 100, 102, 107–9, 182 n.54, 182 n.56
Atlantis theme 77–88, 91, 94, 106–8
Autobiografía (Orozco) 89
Avelar, Idelber 167, 168

Badiou, Alain 5, 6, 7, 19, 20, 21, 29, 33, 48, 54
Balibar, Etienne 181 n.46
barbarism 4, 7–8, 10–13, 15, 42, 49, 50, 63, 64, 91, 113, 161, 163
Barnet, Miguel 166
baroque 10–13, 14, 82, 153–6, 161, 167, 189 n.78
'Baroque and the Marvellous Real' (Carpentier) 10
Barroco y Modernidad (Chiampi) 12

Batalla, Guillermo Bonfil 61, 76, 101, 110–11
Baumgarten 36
Beckman, Ericka 165
Bello, Andrés 11, 64
Benítez Rojo, Antonio 123
Benjamin, Walter 7–9, 13–14, 20, 42–4, 46, 48, 53–5, 67, 82–3, 85, 88, 92, 95, 111, 132, 160, 163, 164, 167, 170
Bentham, Jeremy 134–5
Bergasse, Nicolas 126
Bersani, Leo 140, 153
Bhabha, Homi 72, 74, 75
Biografía de un cimarrón (Barnet) 166
biopolitics 20–1, 116, 119, 120, 128–9, 131–5, 139, 144, 145, 190 n.85
Black Death 135, 152
Bloch, Ernst 163
Blumenberg, Hans 29, 174 n.15
Boccaccio 135
body politic 21, 116, 120, 138–40
Bolaño, Roberto 72, 168
Bolívar, Simón 13–14, 20–1, 24, 28, 31–6, 39, 40–9, 57, 63, 176 n.42
Bonaparte, Pauline 133
Bonnefuil, Christophe 17
Bonpland 79
Boom fictions 97, 123, 159, 164, 167, 168
Borges, Jorge Luis 51, 94, 162
Bosch, Hieronymus 152, 153, 157
Bosteels, Bruno 59, 69, 102, 103
Brasseur de Bourbourg, Charles Etienne 77, 79
Brau, Salvador 140, 147
Bravo, Manuel Álvarez 96–8, 110
Brehme, Hugo 96, 98, 110
Brodsky, Marcelo 169
Buck-Morss, Susan 183 n.66
Buenos, Christina 79
Buffon, Comte de 26, 28
Burgos, Elizabeth 166
Burke, Edmund 36–7
Burnett, Whit 107
Bursting the Limits of Time (Rudwick) 27
Byron, Lord 36

Cadava, Eduardo 55, 181 n.48
'Cançao de piratas (de Assis) 6

Candide, ou L'Optimisme (Voltaire) 23, 26, 30, 38–40
Canellier, Antonella 66
Cañizares-Esguerra, Jorge 32, 80
Canterbury Tales (Chaucer) 135
Canudos War 2–4, 9
Capital Fictions (Beckman) 165
capitalism 14, 18, 37, 43, 87, 123–4, 170
Capitolocene 18
Caracas earthquake (Earthquake of Maundy Thursday; 1812) 24, 28, 32–5, 43, 44
Cárdenas, Lázaro 95, 108
Carpentier, Alejo 10–12, 120–2, 130, 133, 185 n.13
Carranza, Venustiano 90
Carri, Albertina 169
Carta de Jamaica (Bolívar) 40–1
Cartagena Manifesto (Bolívar) 24, 31–6
Casas, Bartolomé de las 87–8, 183 n.66
Caste War (Augustus and Alice) 7, 77, 79, 81, 86, 87
Castillo-Durante, Daniel 43
Castro, Fidel 150, 154
Castro-Klaren, Sara 79
catastrophe
  definition 43
  etymology 18–19
  history as 46, 60, 62
  and reconstruction 42–3
Catastrophe of the Nation, The (Dove) 15
catastrophism 19, 32, 61, 85–6
'chain of being' 24–9, 61, 126, 127
Charnay, Claude-Joseph Désiré 79
Chaucer 135
Che Guevara 38
Chiampi, Irlemar 12
Cien años de Soledad (García Márquez) 159–70, 183 n.66
civilization, origin of 77–9, 83, 85, 86, 90, 91, 94, 99, 100, 108, 111
Cocorobó Dam 1–2, 5, 13, 21
colonialism 18, 41–2, 49, 63–5, 68, 72–3, 76, 89, 93, 111, 118, 121–2, 128, 130, 132, 146–8, 164
Colonialism and Science: Saint Domingue in the Old Regime (McClellan) 118
Columbian exchange 119, 123

Como Nace y Crece un Volcán (Dr Atl) 92, 93
Confucius 91
Conquest of America 18, 47
Conquistas del Desierto 7
Conselheiro, Antônio 2–3, 5–6
conservatism 6, 32, 75, 102–3
Constitution 35, 42, 44, 47, 115
contagion 113–24, 131, 132, 133, 136, 137, 139, 141, 142, 186 n.27
Contract and Contagion (Mitropoulos) 113
Cosas (González García) 138
Crack Capitalism (Holloway) 87
Crítica de la Pirámide (Paz) 61, 71, 76, 98, 101
Critique and Crisis (Koselleck) 80, 179 n.22
Critique of Judgment (Kant) 37
Crónica de una muerte anunciada (García Márquez) 163–4
Crónicas de un Mundo Enfermo (Zeno Gandía) 138–9
Crónicas de un Pueblo Enfermo (Zeno Gandía) 139, 140, 143
Crónicas para un Mundo Enfermo (Zeno Gandía) 134–7, 141
Crosby, Alfred 123
crowd 114, 121, 128, 130, 132, 141, 153, 154, 156–8
Crutzen, Paul 17
Cruz, Sor Juana Inés de la 64, 67
cryptonymy 71, 72
Cullen, Henry 41
Cuvier, George 5, 19, 61–2, 85–6
cybernetics 22

Dabove, Juan Pablo 52
da Cunha, Euclides 3–10, 12
Dance Macabre 135
Dante 99–100
Darío, Rubén 61, 90
Darnton, Robert 118, 126, 127
Darwin, Charles 62, 91
Darwinism 144
Day of the Dead 97
de Andrade Guimarães, Arthur Oscar 3, 8

death 8, 58–9, 64, 67, 72, 81–2, 84, 87, 98, 99, 109, 150
Death and the Idea of México (Lomnitz) 59
Decameron (Boccaccio) 135
de Castro, Eduardo Viveiros 16
Declaración de la Selva Lacandona (Zapatista) 76
deep time 62, 65, 111, 178 n.7
Defacement (Taussig) 59
Deleuze, Gilles 21, 122, 128, 149, 154
del Toro, Fernando 41
de Man, Paul 12
Demarest, Arthur 73
Derrida, Jacques 12, 48, 67, 72, 121, 166, 170
Descola, Philipe 16
Description topographique (Saint-Méry) 130
desire 39, 45, 52, 67, 68–9, 75, 80, 139–40, 149, 151, 153, 186 n.35
desiring machine 128, 149, 150, 153–6
Desmond, Lawrence 83–4
despotism 49
determinism 4, 145, 146
Dialectic of the Enlightenment 89, 95
Díaz, José Domingo 33, 44
Díaz, Porfirio 79, 97
différance 12
Discovery of the Unconscious, The (Ellenberger) 117
Discurso de Angostura (Bolívar) 44–7
Discurso desde la Marginación y la Barbarie (Zea) 42
Dixon, Alice 77, 81–4, 87–8, 92, 98, 107
Dixon, Henry 77
Dove, Patrick 15
Dream of Atlantis, A (Dixon, Alice) 83–8
drought 1–2, 5–7

'Earthquake in Chile, The' (Von Kleist) 29–30
Earthquake of Maundy Thursday (1812). *See* Caracas earthquake
earthquakes 18, 23–47
El aleph (Borges) 162–3
El Color del Verano (Arenas) 114, 149, 156–8
El Hacedor (Borges) 51

Ellenberger, Henri F. 117, 129
El Libertador (Lynch) 34, 41, 42, 44
El material humano (Rey Rosa) 166, 167, 168
El Mensajero (Aira) 49
El reino de este mundo (Carpentier) 12, 120, 133, 185 n.13
El siglo de las luces (Carpentier) 12
El Símbolo y la Acción (Sáenz) 90
Eltit, Diamela 167
Ema la cautiva (Aira) 49
Empire (Negri and Hardt) 132
En el teocali de Cholula (Heredia) 63–8, 72, 76
Enlightenment 12, 13, 24, 36–8, 40–3, 76, 80, 88, 89, 95, 113, 118–20, 124
En una Tempestad (Heredia) 13, 65
'En una tempestad' (Heredia) 13, 65
environmental determinism 4
epidemics 18, 20, 21, 77, 113–48
Esposito, Roberto 116, 120, 131, 132, 136, 137
Essay Concerning Human Understanding, An (Locke) 174 n.8
Estado de São Paulo 4
Ette, Ottmar 36, 38
Evil in Modern Thought (Neiman) 23
evolutionary theory 62
exile 62, 71, 74, 78, 83–5
Experimental Novel, The (Zola) 137
exploitation 17, 18, 123–4
Extimate Revolt: Mesmerism, Haiti and the Origin of Pyschoanalysis (Gorelick) 118

Facundo (Sarmiento) 11, 50
fascism 88, 90, 95, 101
favelas 9
Ferri, Enrico 90
Ficciones somáticas (Nouzeilles) 139
Finlay, Carlos J. 122–3, 185 n.18
First World 43
Five Lectures in Psychoanalysis (Freud) 69
fossils 3–5, 25, 32, 61–2, 85–6, 111, 169
Foster, Hal 168
Foucault, Michael 24, 26, 27, 62, 73, 134–7, 174 n.15
Foundational Fictions (Sommer) 15, 45, 145

founding fathers 47, 63, 79
fragmentation 40
Frankfurt school 95
Free Masonry 79–81, 179 n.22
Free Trade Commerce Agreement 76, 111
French Revolution 32, 36, 85
Fressoz, Jean-Baptiste 17
Freud, Sigmund 20, 48–9, 65, 68–71, 75, 87, 109–10, 128, 161, 180 n.28
Freud's México (Gallo) 69
Fukuyama, Francis 18, 163, 169
futurism 90, 95

Gabara, Esther 99
Gallo, Rubén 69, 180 n.28
García Márquez, Gabriel 11, 159–70
Garden of Earthly Delights, The (Bosch) 152, 157
Garduña (Zeno Gandía) 140, 143–6
Gerbi, Antonello 11
German Idealism 36
germ theory of disease 124, 125, 136
Gilbert, Nicolas-Pierre 115–17, 133–4
Gillespie, Susan D. 180 n.37
Gilroy, Paul 118
Glissant, Édouard 12
globalization 123, 165, 189 n.76
Goethe 10–12, 88
Gómez de Avellaneda, Gertrudis 150
González Echevarría, Roberto 164, 166, 168
González García, Matías 138
Gorelick, Nathan 118
Gramsci, Antonio 73
Great Fire of London (1666) 70
Guattari, Felix 21, 122, 128, 131, 154
Guzmán, Patricio 169

Hahnemann 136
Haitian Revolution 20, 67, 114–20, 122, 126–33, 137
Hamacher, Werner 29, 30
Hardt, Michael 132
Harmada (Noll) 167
hauntology 72
Heart for the Gods of México, A (Aiken) 104
Hegel 19, 28, 36, 59, 67–8, 102, 129, 163

Hegel, Haiti and Universal History (Morr) 80
Herder, Johann Gottfried von 88
Heredia, José María 11, 13, 16, 20, 21, 60, 61–8, 70–8, 88, 92, 95–8, 102, 107, 110, 179 n.12, 179 n.19, 179 n.22
Heredia, Jose María de (cousin) 62
Higiene de la Infancia al Alcance de las Madres de Familia (Zeno Gandía) 142
Hinnant, Charles 36
Hirsch, Marianne 168
Histoire médicale de l'armée française à Saint-Domingue (Gilbert) 115
Historia de la Destrucción de las Indias (Casas) 87–8
historical sciences 62
historical sublime 12, 21, 31, 36–40, 42, 127, 131, 169, 174 n.16
history
  art and 55
  concept of 14, 44, 46
  end of 2, 6, 10, 18, 158, 161–3, 168–9
  modern historicism 19–22
  narratives 45–6
  natural/naturalization of 25–31, 45, 48
  non-narrative 45
Hobbes, Thomas 113
Holocene 17
homeopathy 133, 135–8, 140
Horowitz, Gabriel 63, 64, 76
horse theme 104–6, 110, 143
How Forests Think (Kohn) 121
How to Write the History of the New World? (Cañizares-Esguerra) 32, 80
Huet, Marie-Hélène 36
Humboldt, Alexander Von 11, 13, 16, 20, 24–40, 42–3, 47–51, 55, 63, 79
Hundred Years of Solitude, A (Márquez) 11
hurricanes 13, 18, 35, 38, 44, 106, 111, 160, 163
Hutton, James 62, 65, 178 n.7
hysteria 70

'Idea of Natural History, The' (Adorno) 14
imagery 14, 21, 122, 135, 142, 149, 152
Imagined Communities (Anderson, Benedict) 45
immune system 114, 116, 134–43, 146, 148, 150, 156
Immunitas (Esposito) 116, 132
Imperial Eyes (Pratt) 22, 39
in-betweenness 100, 109
Inferno (Dante) 99–100
Insensatez (Moya) 168
Interpretation of Dreams, The (Freud) 69
interregnum 73
Introduction to Hermann (Abraham) 71
invisibility 111, 121
Ixtacihuatl 109

James, Henry 107
Jefferson, Thomas 28
Jenner, Edward 136
jíbaros (working classes) 142, 147
Johnson, Adriana Campos 6
Joyce, James 60
Juárez, Benito 98
Juncos, Manuel Fernández 138, 147

Kafka, Franz 122
Kant, Immanuel 19, 23, 30, 36–8
Kepler, Johannes 91
Kohn, Eduardo 121
Koselleck, Reinhart 12, 24, 54, 80, 161
Kutzinski, Vera M. 36

Lacan, Jacques 18, 20
Lacapra, Dominic 168
La carta de Jamaica (Bolívar) 40
La Charca (Zeno Gandía) 139, 140–3, 146–7
'La Esfinge del Monstruo' (Nouzeilles) 139
La Gran Marcha de la Humanidad (Siquiero) 72
La muerte me da (Rivera Garza) 168
landscape, concept of 16
landscape painting, 'other side' of 49–56
La Psychologie des Foules (Le Bon) 141
La Raza Cósmica (Vasconcelos) 91, 108
Las Multitudes Argentinas (Mejías) 141
laughter 149
laziness 146–8
Le Blond, Jean Baptiste 125
Le Bon, Gustave 141

Leclerc, Charles Victoire Emmanuel 115–17, 119, 131, 133
L'Ecorce et le Nouyau (Abraham) 71
Lectures on Aesthetics (Hegel) 67
Leibniz, Gottfried Wilhelm 23
Le Plongeon, Augustus 60, 74–5, 77–88, 92, 98, 102, 107
Levinson, Brett 52
liberty 41, 44
Lienhard, Martin 7
Lima, Lezama 12
Linnaeus, Carolus 25, 26, 28
Lisbon Earthquake (1755) 23, 30, 37, 40, 78, 81
literary activism 150
Locke, John 34, 174 n.8
Lomnitz, Claudio 59
Longinus, Cassius 36
Los condenados de la tierra (Brodsky) 169
Los muertos indóciles (Rivera Garza) 169
Los Rubios (Carri) 169
L'Ouverture, Toussaint 115, 117
Lowry, Malcolm 57, 60–1, 72, 96–111
Lugones, Leopoldo 60, 88, 90
Luhmann, Niklas 136
Lumpérica (Eltit) 167
Lynch, John 28, 33–4, 41

Mackandal, François 13, 20, 21, 117, 121, 122, 130, 185 n.13
Maladie du deuil et fantasme du cadavre exquis (Torok) 71
Mantilla, Fernando Feliú 138
Manual de Fotografía (Le Plongeon) 84
Marcos, Subcomandante 38, 61, 71
Margolles, Teresa 169
Martí, José 63, 64, 151
Marx, Karl 20
Marx and Freud in Latin America (Bosteels) 69
Marxism 21, 95
Maximilian Von Habsburg 98–100, 102
Mayanism 60
McClellan, James E. 118
McCook, Stuart 119, 123, 124
McNeill, J. R. 116, 119, 123
Medical Revolutionaries (Weaver) 118
Meillassoux, Quentin 169

Mejías, J. M. Ramos 141
melancholia 12, 13, 21, 60, 63, 68, 70–6, 98, 99, 102, 179 n.19, 180 n.28
Mémoire sur la fièvre jaune (Gilbert) 115–16, 133
memory 1–2, 5–6, 8, 21, 28, 59, 69, 91–2, 113, 130, 152, 164, 167, 168, 170
Menchú, Rigoberta 166
Mesmer, Franz Anton 117–18, 126–7
mesmerism 114–20, 126–33
Mesmerism and the Ends of the Enlightenment (Darnton) 118
Mesmerism in Saint Domingue (Regourd) 118
Metahistory (White) 28
metamorphosis 55, 121–2, 130–2
metaphors 11, 26, 29–30, 39–40, 44–5, 66, 102, 111, 114, 116, 122, 131, 139, 150, 174 n.15, 186 n.27
Metropolitan Museum 89
Mexican Revolution 60, 76, 88–90, 92, 93, 96–7
Mexican War of Independence 60, 76, 86
Mexico City earthquake (1985) 61, 76, 101, 110, 111
México Profundo (Batalla) 61, 75, 76, 101, 111
miasma theory of disease 125
Michaels, Walter Benn 85
Michelangelo 90
Michelet, Jules 17, 19
Millet, Jeanne-Eulailie 117, 128, 132
Mitchell, W.J.T. 3, 49
Mitropoulos, Angela 113
modernity, definitions of 24, 54
modernization 3, 9, 21, 22, 89, 111
Monument to the Great Fire of London, The (Freud) 69–70
Moore, Jason 18, 123–4
Morr, Susan Buck 80
Morton, Timothy 18
Mosquito Empires (McNeill) 119, 123
mosquitoes 16, 20, 120–6, 130–1
mourning and melancholia 12, 68–9, 74
Mourning and Melancholia (Freud) 70, 71
Mourning Modernism (Rosenthal) 86–7
Moya, Horacio Castellanos 168
muralism 60, 76, 89–90, 98

Murillo, Gerardo. *See* Atl, Dr
mysticism 89, 90, 91, 92, 93
myth/mythology 2–3, 10, 31, 73, 78, 82, 86, 88, 91, 94–5, 102, 103, 106–7, 130, 160, 162, 164–70, 180 n.37

Napoleon 16, 98, 115, 126, 133
'Nation in Ruins, The' (Castro-Klaren) 79
natural history 20, 25, 26–7, 29, 31, 45, 60–2, 79, 125–7, 161
naturalism 138, 143–6
naturalization 15, 26–7, 48, 61, 64, 80, 103, 111
nature-culture relationship 1–19, 62, 66, 96, 160–1
necroescrituras 169
Negri, Antonio 132, 145
Neiman, Susan 23
neo-baroque 153–6, 189 n.78
neoclassism 41, 62, 66, 71, 75, 176 n.42
neurotic symptom 69–70, 130
New World 18, 27, 28, 32–8, 41, 74, 77–80, 93–4, 106–7, 115, 118–19
Nietzsche, Friedrich 88, 89, 92, 94, 95
Noll, João Gilberto 167
Nostalgia de la Luz (Guzmán) 169
'Notes on the Difficulty of Studying the State' (Abrams) 15
Nouzeilles, Gabriela 139–41, 181 n.48

Obregón, Alvaro 90–1, 182 n.56
Observations sur la fièvre jaune (Le Blond) 125
Oda al Niágara (Heredia) 60, 61–6
O'Leary, Daniel 41
Olinka 94–5
On the Soul (Aristotle) 174 n.8
'On the Sublime' (Schiller) 36, 38, 43
optical unconscious 54
Order of Things, The (Foucault) 24, 26, 27, 62
Orozco, José Clemente 89–90, 182 n.54
Os sertões: campanha de Canudos (da Cunha) 3, 4, 7–10

Páez, José Antonio 14, 40
panopticism 134–5, 137
Paper Cadavers (Weld) 165

paradigm of knowledge 26, 37, 174 n.15
Paradigms for a Metaphorology (Blumenberg) 174 n.15
Pasteur, Louis 136
Paula Santander, Francisco de 34, 42, 47
Paz, Octavio 61, 69, 71, 76, 80, 98, 101–3, 180 n.28
Pedro Páramo (Rulfo) 72
Perlongher, Néstor 12
Personal Narrative of Travels to the Equinoctial Regions of America (Humboldt) 27–8
Peter the Great 124
Philosophical Enquiry into the Origin of Our Ideas of the Sublime and the Beautiful, A (Burke) 37
photography 22, 48, 50, 53–6, 60, 77, 79, 84–6, 89, 96, 98, 109, 110, 137, 155, 169, 181 n.48
'Photography and Fossils' (Michaels) 85
Piglia, Ricardo 1, 167
Piñera, Virgilio 157
Pit and the Pyramid, The (Derrida) 67
Placeres de la melancolía (Heredia) 66
Plague and the Theater, The (Artaud) 120
Plato 78
political event 5, 7, 19–21, 24, 26, 29, 48, 50, 103, 120
Popocatepetl 57–8, 89, 91, 94, 96, 97, 98, 106, 109, 110
positivism 4, 7–10, 32, 69, 76, 94, 119, 135, 136
post-memory 168
Pratt, Mary Louise 22, 30, 37, 39, 63, 76
Primer Sueño (Cruz) 64, 67–75
progressivism 2–11, 13–15, 17, 18, 20, 37, 43, 53, 57–66, 68–72, 74, 76, 81–2, 86–8, 91–5, 98–9, 102, 108–11, 124, 136, 152, 159–63, 170
psychoanalysis 17, 20, 21, 27, 48–9, 54, 69, 71–2, 75, 102, 118, 128
Puerto Rico Anemia Commission 147–8
Pulido, Dionisio 92
Pursuit of Ruins, The (Buenos) 79
Puységur, Antonine-Hyacinth de 127
pyramids 16, 58–81, 88–90, 93–8, 101–3, 110

'Quaking of Presentation, The' (Hamacher) 29
Queen Móo and the Egyptian Sphinx (Le Plongeon) 83, 85
Queen Móo's Talisman (Dixon, Alice) 83, 85

rabies vaccine 136
Ranke, Leopold von 19
Raphael 90
realism 138, 140, 154
redemption 14, 47, 59–60, 75–6
Reed, Walter 120
Regourd, François 118
'Reinvention of America, The' (Pratt) 30
repetition 52, 55–6, 87, 93, 98–100, 104–5, 160
representation 7–8, 16, 20, 24–31, 35, 37, 39, 42, 44–5, 48–54, 76, 82, 96, 124–6, 130, 137, 152, 183 n.63
Respiración artificial (Piglia) 1, 167
Reyes, Alfonso 12
Rey Rosa, Rodrigo 166–8
Rivera, Diego 89–90, 97–8, 168, 169, 182 n.54
Rivera Garza, Cristina 168, 169
Roads, Cornelius 148
Rockefeller Foundation 148
Rodriguez, Simón 41
Rojas, Rafael 44, 176 n.42
Romanticism 36–8, 63, 65, 66, 71
Rome, ruins of 40–4, 46–7, 75, 90
Rosenthal, Lecia 86–7
Rousseau, Jean Jacques 23
Rozitchner, León 69
Rudwick, Martin 5, 27, 31, 61
Rugendas, Johann Moritz 48–56
ruins, discourse of 8, 35, 39–43, 46–7, 60, 62–4, 66, 71, 75, 77, 79, 163–4, 166–7
Rulfo, Juan 72

Sacred Mysteries among the Mayas and the Quiches (Le Plongeon) 78–9, 81, 107
Sáenz, Olga 90
Saint Domingue 25, 115–20, 124, 127, 129, 133

Saint-Méry, Médéric Moreau de 130
Sampson, Tony D. 186 n.35
Sandino 38
Santander, Francisco de Paula 34, 42, 47
Santiago de Chile 29
Sanz del Rí, Alberto Regúlez y 138
Sarduy, Severo 12, 153, 189 n.78
Sarmiento, Doming 11–12, 49–51
Schiller, Friedrich 36, 38, 40, 88
Schmitt, Carl 46
Second World War 13, 95, 97, 108
secrecy 8, 16, 44, 53, 58–61, 66–9, 76–82, 86–8, 98, 101–9, 111, 118, 143–4, 160, 179 n.22
sertanejos 5–7
Shaw, Phillip 36
Shock of the Anthropocene, The (Bonnefuil and Fressoz) 17
Silva a la agricultura de la zona tórrida (Bello) 11, 64
Sinarquistas, the 95, 101, 104, 105, 110
Siquiero, David Alvaro 72, 90
slavery 47, 57, 115, 119, 128
    abolition of 140
smallpox vaccine 136
Snow, John 125
Soho cholera outbreak 124–5
solitude 13, 101, 164, 180 n.28
Sommer, Doris 15, 45, 139–40, 159, 166
sovereignty 6, 13, 20, 45–7, 113–48, 150, 170
Spanish American Revolutions, The (Lynch) 28
Spanish American wars of independence 24, 146
Spanish Empire 41–2, 138, 147
spectrality 48, 54–5, 58–61, 65–9, 72–5, 86, 89, 98–9, 101–3
Spinoza, Baruch 145
spiritism 77, 91
state, emergence of the 43–7, 49
state of exception 15, 46–7, 135–6, 160, 161, 170, 182 n.63
Steiner, George 181 n.46
Stengers, Isabelle 122
subjectivity 13, 16, 19–22, 54, 66, 103, 106, 110, 114–19, 125, 126–34, 130–2

sublime, the 3, 11, 12, 16, 30, 35, 36–43, 47–50, 54, 63, 66, 68, 74–5, 93, 96, 174 n.16
symbolism 5, 16, 38, 49–50, 53, 69–85, 89, 91, 94–9, 102, 104, 109, 111, 164
symptom, the 3, 13, 17–18, 24, 26, 27, 32, 54, 65, 69–76, 80, 83, 89, 102, 109–10, 115–16, 126–7, 133–4, 161, 190 n.85

Taine, Hippolyte 4
Talbot, Henry Fox 84
Tarde, Gabriel 21, 186 n.35
Taussig, Michael 59, 76, 80, 111, 121
telegraphy 22, 57, 96, 99, 104, 107–8
temporality
    and meaning 28
theodicy 23–4, 27, 31, 33–4, 39, 174 n.8
'Thesis on the Philosophy of History' (Benjamin) 8, 13, 43
Third World 18, 43
Thousand Plateaus, A (Guattari and Deleuze) 122, 128
Three Ecologies, The (Guattari) 131
time lag 72–3, 76
time of catastrophe 54
Tlatelolco Massacre 59, 61, 71, 76, 101
Torok, Maria 71–2, 75, 82
Toste, Cayetano Coll y 147
tragedy 30, 58–9, 75–6, 100–1, 103, 105–6
translation 71, 79–84, 102, 138
Trauerspiel (Benjamin) 43
trauma 8, 40, 48, 68–9, 71–2, 81, 103, 163–4, 166–168
Trembley, Jean 128
trope 5, 19, 28, 29, 48, 62, 152
tsunami 18
2666 (Bolaño) 72, 166

Ulloa, Antonio de 28
'Un Centro Internacional de la Cultura' (Dr Atl) 94
Unciniariasis (Hookworm Disease) in Porto Rico (Ashford) 147
Under the Volcano (Lowry) 57–61, 72, 96–111
Un episodio en la vida del pintor viajero (Aira) 49–56
Un Grito en la Atlántida (Atl) 91, 108

unity 25, 27, 35, 38–40, 42–3, 46–7, 51, 78, 122, 128, 130, 143–4, 149, 153, 161
universal history 24, 39, 80–3, 86, 88, 91, 107–8
Untimely Present, The (Avelar) 167
utopia 7, 8, 40, 43, 92, 94, 103, 134

vaccines 136, 138
Valle Atiles, Francisco del 147
Vasconcelos, José 91, 97, 108, 182 n.56
Views of the Cordilleras and Monuments of the Indigenous Peoples of the Americas (Humboldt) 36
Vigil, Arturo Díaz 98
violence 3–4, 8–9, 14–15, 20–1, 27, 46, 48, 51–3, 57–60, 64, 68, 72, 74, 76, 81, 89, 92, 95–8, 102, 110, 136–7, 160–1, 163, 165, 170, 179 n.19, 183 n.63
'Visión de Anáhuac' (Reyes) 12
volcanoes 11, 14, 16, 18, 20–1, 37–8, 57–111, 166
Voltaire 23
Von Kleist, Heinrich 29
voodoo 118, 121, 129, 130, 133

War of the Triple Alliance 7
Weaver, Karol M. 118, 130
Weizamn, Eyal 169
Weld, Kristen 165
White, Hayden 28, 29, 36, 37, 121, 139, 140, 142
William, Raymond 171 n.11
Wilson, Jason 27
Words of Light (Cadava) 55
Wordsworth, Williams 36
world history 36, 38, 100

Yáñez, Agustín 94
yellow fever 77, 114–23, 128, 131, 133
Yucatán Through her Eyes (Desmond) 83–4

Zamora, Louis Parkinson 162
Zapatistas 76, 86, 87, 111
Zea, Leopoldo 35, 42
Zeno Gandía, Manuel 114, 134–44, 147
Zizek, Slavoj 7, 19
Zola, Emile 137, 138

www.ingramcontent.com/pod-product-compliance
Lightning Source LLC
Chambersburg PA
CBHW070637300426
44111CB00013B/2138